André Malraux

The Indochina Adventure

André Malraux

The Indochina Adventure

WALTER G. LANGLOIS

FREDERICK A. PRAEGER, *Publishers*
New York · Washington · London

FREDERICK A. PRAEGER, PUBLISHERS

111 Fourth Avenue, New York, N.Y. 10003, U.S.A.
77–79 Charlotte Street, London, W.1, England

Published in the United States of America in 1966
by Frederick A. Praeger, Inc., Publishers

Library of Congress Catalog Card Number: 65–24947

Printed in the United States of America

TO

HENRI M. PEYRE

Preface

Malraux's two-year sojourn in Indochina (1923–24) was a critical time for him, as a man and as a writer. The youth who had been known in France as the author of literary fantasies returned from the Far East a deeply committed social reformer. His first three novels, his various speeches and newspaper articles, and his feverish political activity during the 1930's are eloquent indications of how deeply he had been marked by his colonial adventure. Although it is nearly impossible to reach a full understanding of Malraux without a knowledge of this crucial two-year period in his life, scholars have not examined it in any detail.

Malraux really had two adventures in Indochina. The first was his trial on the charge of having taken pieces of sculpture from a ruined temple in the jungles of Cambodia; the second was his involvement in the Annamite nationalist movement and his editorship of a political newspaper supporting its program. Both have long been surrounded by a mass of legend and contradictory information. Malraux is rumored to have been an art thief, a Communist organizer, an unprincipled plunderer of religious shrines, an anti-French revolutionary, and a political agitator in the pay of the Chinese Bolsheviks. The subject of all these calumnies has never seen fit to set the record straight, and literary historians have had great difficulty in separating fact from fiction.

Fortunately, there are a number of primary printed sources available. While most of the accounts of Malraux's trial published in the Paris press were deliberate distortions, the newspapers in Indochina presented fairly accurate and detailed reports of the proceedings. From them and from information generously supplied by two eyewitnesses, it has been possible to shed some light on the infamous "Angkor affair." As for the more complex and delicate matter of Malraux's political activities in the colony, much will always remain obscure. Scholars have long known that in 1925 Malraux edited a short-lived Saigon newspaper called *Indochine*; during a year of research in Indochina in 1956–57, I discovered that this publication subsequently reappeared under the title *Indochine Enchaînée*. These two periodicals, totaling about 800 pages, are very revealing of political and social conditions in the colony, but they are important to the literary historian primarily because of thirty major articles by Malraux. These articles not only give invaluable details about his deepening social concern; in style and content they bridge the gap between his light cubist "poems in prose" and the passionately committed novels of his mature period. Without these texts, it would be difficult to understand how the elegant dilettante of the early 1920's could have become the fervent anti-fascist of the 1930's. (The complex problem of Malraux's post-1930 political beliefs is clearly beyond the scope of the present book, but it is the subject of a second volume now in preparation.)

It is hoped that the information presented in this study will lay to rest the conflicting rumors about Malraux's conduct in the Far East. The facts indicate that the Angkor affair was simply an incident of youthful exuberance and poor judgment—an incident deliberately exaggerated by local authorities for personal and political reasons. Malraux's really important adventure in Indochina was his spirited campaign to defend the oppressed Indochinese. A courageous, idealistic, and talented young writer, he threw himself with abandon into the fight against an all-powerful Colonial Administration that was robbing the natives of their fundamental rights. At the age of twenty-four, Malraux had already begun the crusade that was to lead him to the heights of *Man's Fate* and *Man's Hope*.

I would be ungrateful indeed if I did not acknowledge my debt to a number of persons who were directly helpful to me in preparing this book: to Professor W. M. Frohock, whose provocative work *André Malraux and the Tragic Imagination* originally gave me the idea for this study and who personally offered me information and encouragement on several occasions; to Rawson L. Wood, whose affectionate interest and advice were largely responsible for the successful completion of the project; to my former departmental chairman, the Reverend J. D. Gauthier, S. J., who was kind enough to comment on several of the chapters and to permit me to offer a graduate course on Malraux; to Mme. Guy Lebreton, and to the reference librarians at Harvard University and at the Bibliothèque Nationale, who were especially cooperative and patient in obtaining needed microfilm; to Malraux's friends René-Louis Doyon and Georges Gabory, for their help; and to M. Raymond Roche, a retired colonial magistrate who prepared a substantial dossier of information for me. My debt to M. and Mme. Louis Chevasson is enormous. They gave me stimulus, information, and—most important of all—friendship at a critical moment in this undertaking; I shall never forget their kindness. Malraux himself on several occasions took time from his heavy ministerial duties to reply to my letters, and I am most grateful to him for this thoughtfulness, as well as for his generosity in permitting me to quote extensively from his articles in the Indochinese newspapers. (I deeply regret that it was not possible to present these texts in the original French. All translations are mine, unless otherwise indicated.)

My deepest debt, however, is to the two persons without whom the book would not have been written at all: to my wife, who has been a patient and understanding companion throughout this whole project, accepting cheerfully the considerable burdens it placed on her and making invaluable suggestions for stylistic improvements; and to my teacher, Henri M. Peyre, who—like Malraux—personifies the most exciting and appealing of all adventures, that of the spirit.

W.G.L.

Fall, 1964

Contents

André Malraux

The Indochina Adventure

I

In Search of Banteay Srei

In early autumn, 1924, *The New York Times* published an article that was a masterpiece of misinformation. Though virtually every fact in it is incorrect, it recounts a major part of the legend of Malraux's first adventure in Indochina.

FRENCH SLEUTH TRAILS MAN TO ANNAM JUNGLE, DROPS HIS DISGUISE AND ARRESTS ROBBER OF PARIS MUSEUMS AND NATIVE TEMPLES.

PARIS, August 25 (Associated Press Correspondence).

This is the story of a Paris detective who traveled half way around the world for his quarry, and finally, in the dense jungle of Annam, threw aside his disguise and arrested his man, who is now doing three years in jail.

An antiquary named Malraux was under the observance of the Paris police, suspected of being responsible for thefts from French museums. It was thought he had designs on collections of antiques in one of the French provinces, and as a matter of routine a detective was assigned to trail Malraux and a companion, wherever they might go.

The pair went to a seaport and there took passage on a steamer for Saigon, French Indo-China, and the detective went along on the same vessel. He did not even have time to buy a change of clothing, but made friends among the crew and borrowed what he needed.

At Saigon Malraux and his friend posed as rich travelers, anxious to see the country, while the detective kept in the background. He had, however, made known his mission to the local French authorities, and when Malraux asked for guides to the remote dis-

3

tricts of Annam, the detective was among the natives assigned, but cleverly disguised.

The party scoured the region of Angkor, rich in holy relics and fine specimens of old Chinese art, and Malraux and his companion bought freely. Also they did not hesitate, conditions being favorable, to rob Annamite temples of particularly fine specimens.

The border of Siam was not far away, and the collectors, having decided to leave the country by that route, called up the native guides and dismissed them.

Then the Paris detective had his day. The humble disguise was cast aside, the French policeman stepped out, and Malraux and his friend were placed under arrest.[1]

Similar startling accounts of the arrest and trial of a young French writer had appeared some three weeks earlier in several Paris newspapers. *The Times* had alluded to these stories on August 3 in a brief report from a French source.[2] The item alleged that one Georges Malraux, an "art agent" for a New York antique dealer, had been apprehended "collecting with hammer and chisel on the walls of the ruins at Angkor" in Cambodia, French Indochina; after a trial at the Cambodian capital, Pnom Penh, Malraux and his assistant, Louis Chevasson, had been sentenced to prison for theft. The AP dispatch of August 25 published by *The Times* simply added details that had been revealed in the intervening French accounts.

The *"affaire d'Angkor"* caused quite a stir in Parisian literary circles. Most columnists were quick to condemn the audacity of the young man, and his side of the story was never really presented. Later literary historians usually have restricted themselves to a very brief mention of the incident. Some undoubtedly have been reluctant to bring up a youthful "indiscretion" that might embarrass one of France's greatest writers, while others probably considered it a very minor experience in the development of the author of *Man's Fate*. However, as we shall see, the facts not only exonerate Malraux, but also make it very clear that this experience with the injustices of the Colonial Administration of Indochina was a turning point in his life.

Pascal Pia, writing of his long-time friend Malraux, has said: "A love of art and a taste for travel tormented him from his youth. Even before he went to the Far East, Marco Polo, Rubruquis, and Plano Carpini fed his dreams. As we left the Bibliothèque Nationale, we would question each other, half seriously, half in jest,

about the identity of Prester John. What had he been, a prince or
a devil? The great Khan or the Negus? Suppose we were to go out
there to see for ourselves." [3] To be sure, Malraux and Pia were
not alone in their fascination with the Orient. Interest in the Far
East had grown rapidly in France during the decade following
World War I.[4] Young people avidly read not only the exciting accounts of adventurers who had visited these far-off lands, but also
scholarly translations of Oriental literary works and learned articles
about Asian art and archaeology.

The foremost French society in this field was the Ecole Française
d'Extrême-Orient (EFEO), which had been created late in 1898
to undertake "the archaeological and philological exploration
of the Indochinese peninsula." [5] Although it operated on a very
limited budget, the organization had made a fairly comprehensive
inventory of the archaeological remains of French-controlled
Indochina, especially those in the Angkor region of the protectorate Kingdom of Cambodia. The various capitals of the ancient Khmer empire had been located in this area, which was very
rich in temple ruins. The scholarly members of the School were
responsible for detailed studies of these ruins, but a number of
interested amateurs—doctors, soldiers, civil servants assigned to
Indochina—had been of invaluable assistance in locating and
making preliminary surveys of previously undiscovered sites in the
jungle.

The School regularly published news of archaeological activities
and discoveries in its *Bulletin,* which had been suspended during
the war. The first postwar issues presented a number of monographs that had been completed several years earlier. One of these
caught the eye of young Malraux as he pored over books on Oriental archaeology in the Bibliothèque Nationale. It was a lengthy
study by Henri Parmentier, chief of the Archaeological Section of
the School. In this essay, entitled "The Art of Indravarman,"
Parmentier maintained that there was a previously unrecognized
period of Khmer art, a very distinctive phase that separated the early
brick temples of the seventh and eighth centuries from the classical art of Angkor Wat, which came some 500 years later. He
named it after King Indravarman I, in whose reign it had reached
its peak. His discussion centered on twelve groups of ruins that ex-
hibited the characteristics of this transitional style, including "the
pretty, newly discovered sandstone temple that the natives call
Banteay Srei." [6]

Banteay Srei had been found accidentally early in 1914 by a
Lieutenant Marek of the Colonial Geological Service,[7] who had
immediately reported his discovery to the authorities. The School
had dispatched a young architect, Georges Demasur, to study and
photograph the site, but unfortunately the war and Demasur's un-
timely death had interrupted the project. Parmentier himself completed the preliminary survey in 1916, and this material—including
four pages of photographs and three of drawings—formed a large
part of his monograph on the art of Indravarman. The Banteay
Srei temple complex was not very extensive compared with others
in the nearby Angkor area; its importance lay in the quality of its
sculptured decoration. The central sanctuary and its two flanking
towers were the most elaborately ornamented parts of the complex, but each of the minor outbuildings and gates possessed at
least a carved pediment. According to Parmentier, all of this
sculpture had been done with particular care and was noteworthy
both in subject matter and in style.

The photographs that accompanied his article bore out this
judgment. However, they showed most of the site to be little more
than a mound of rubble. The collapse of the buildings had been
due partly to the disintegration of wooden timbers and the friable
types of stone occasionally used in Khmer structures, but mostly to
the damage done by huge trees whose great roots sometimes held
the edifices together crazily in a gigantic mesh but more often
pried the stones apart so that they tumbled down. Yet, here and
there, through the curtain of vegetation that draped the few remaining upright walls, one could glimpse the vestiges of a rich
decoration of carving. In spite of Parmentier's favorable comments, the *Bulletin* gave no indication that the School had any
plans to restore the site or even to investigate it further.

Malraux had been an enthusiastic student of Asian art for several years,[8] and he was increasingly fascinated with what he was
able to learn about Banteay Srei. He carefully read the laws regarding archaeological sites in Indochina published in the *Bulletin* and
in other official organs, and he became convinced that this temple
was—legally speaking—abandoned property. Sometime in the
summer or early autumn of 1923, he made a momentous decision:
he would undertake an archaeological expedition to Cambodia. He
went to the Colonial Office and requested the necessary authorization, which was granted. News of the project traveled quickly
among his friends. Early in October, Max Jacob, the poet to whom

Malraux had dedicated his first book, *Paper Moons* (*Lunes en papier*), commented: "A mission for Malraux! . . . Well, he'll find himself in the Orient. He'll become an Orientalist and end up in the Collège de France, like Claudel. He's cut out to be an academic." [9] Jacob was not far wrong. His young protégé did, indeed, "find himself" in Indochina.

Why did Malraux undertake such a mission? This was one of the first questions that the poet Valéry asked him on his return,[10] and it has been asked many times since, but Malraux has never been able to give a satisfactory answer. His motivation may have been at least partly financial. To be sure, he was not poor; he was an editor at a small but successful publishing firm, and he had recently married into a wealthy family. He was on good terms with his father and apparently received an allowance from him. However, he was a highly intelligent and sensitive young man, and he had the rather special, and expensive, tastes of an aesthete. He was somewhat of a dandy and liked to appear at the theater and in Parisian night spots in very elegant attire. The house in the fashionable Auteuil section of Paris that he and his wife shared with her family was decorated with original works by artists such as Galanis, Derain, Picasso, and Braque which he had bought at auctions, and with art objects from Africa and Asia. Moreover, it was well known to his literary friends that he was interested in high finance and had invested in the Paris stock exchange between his visits to the nearby Bibliothèque Nationale.[11] Although he was competent in the market, he may have suffered some financial losses in the spring of 1923 that he wished to recoup in Indochina.[12]

A student and collector of Asian art, Malraux must have been a familiar figure at auction houses and in the shops of dealers in Oriental antiquities. A shrewd businessman as well as a connoisseur, he was fully aware that a postwar vogue was constantly driving up the prices of such objects. Numerous sources in the Far East— usually enterprising dealers or individuals in the foreign services of the various colonial administrations—continued to send to European markets artifacts that had been "discovered" in the jungle or procured from natives living near important archaeological sites.[13] Authorities in Indochina, after repeated proddings from the EFEO, had made intermittent and halfhearted attempts to curb this traffic. However, most provincial officials—like the French Commissioner at Siem Reap in Malraux's novel *The Royal Way*

—were pragmatists, not aesthetes. They were too preoccupied with the thriving commerce in rubber, timber, and rice to bother much with the traffic in old stones. Any European who wished to acquire a few "souvenirs" during his excursions into the jungle could usually count on the local French official to look the other way, especially after a gift of cash. Even if the official was honest, the various regulatory decrees issued by the Colonial Administration were so vague, obscure, and even contradictory that they were exceedingly difficult to apply.

In the early 1920's, several particularly flagrant expropriations of Cambodian antiquities forced the Governor General of Indochina to take corrective action. He appointed a special commission to study the situation and to make recommendations for a new and more coherent body of regulations to preserve the historical and archaeological remains of the peninsula. The new commission and the Governor General's plans for reforms were announced in a decree, dated August 21, 1923, but not actually published in the EFEO *Bulletin* until the end of the year.[14] It is possible that Malraux learned of these moves and realized that if he was to act it must be quickly, before it became impossible for anyone except a member of the EFEO to remove any archaeological remains whatsoever from the peninsula. Although he probably planned to sell part of whatever he found in order to defray the expenses of the expedition, his greatest concern was to obtain some outstanding objects for his own artistic studies. He has specifically stated that he intended eventually to present any superior pieces he might find to the School's rival in Paris, the Musée Guimet, whose remarkable collection of Asian materials had been built up by just such gifts from dedicated private collectors, archaeologists, and retired colonial civil servants.[15]

Someone among Malraux's friends—an art dealer with international connections—learned that he was going to Indochina and asked him to negotiate the purchase, on commission, of an important collection of Asian art. The prospective buyer was an American connoisseur; the owner was a sixty-year-old Siamese prince and scholar named Damrong, a former member of the King's Cabinet and a long-time collaborator of the EFEO.[16] Malraux accepted the assignment. He subsequently disclosed that he had been authorized to pay as much as $50,000 for the collection. Garbled rumors of this arrangement were doubtless responsible for the newspaper accusations that he had gone to Cambodia as the agent of an American antique dealer. Malraux planned to arrange for this purchase in Thailand *after* he had seen his own sculptures safely shipped off to France, but his arrest and trial postponed the transaction.[17]

The unfavorable contemporary newspaper accounts of the "Angkor affair" implied that money had been the primary motivation—perhaps the only one—behind the expedition into the jungles of Cambodia. In reality, this was the least important of the many reasons that led Malraux into this much publicized adventure. For example, on an aesthetic level, he has long maintained that a deep knowledge of other cultures, especially those outside the Greco-Roman tradition, is an essential prerequisite for a greater appreciation of Western civilization. He stated this succinctly in his very first essay on art, the 1922 preface to an exhibition of paintings by his Greek friend Galanis: "We can feel only by comparison. . . . The Greek genius will be better understood through the contrast of a Greek statue with an Egyptian or Asian statue than by the examination of a hundred Greek statues." [18] He hoped that his first-hand contact with the non-Western cultures of the Indochina peninsula would sharpen his artistic awareness and awaken in him a new sense of identity, both as a Westerner and as an individual. As one of his characters, writing to a friend of another race, puts it: "How can I see myself, except by looking at you?" [19]

Also, as Malraux made clear at the time of his trial, he was planning to write a detailed comparison of Khmer and Siamese art based on his discoveries in the jungle.[20] Not only would the study reveal new aspects of the cultural complex of Indochina but his reactions to these ancient artifacts would stimulate new insights into the civilization that had resurrected them—his own.[21] Perhaps he also hoped that such a provocative study would win him a certain fame in his chosen field of art and archaeology, just as his controversial essay on cubist poetry had done several years earlier in the field of literature.

If for Malraux the Indochina expedition was to a large extent the trial of his aesthetic credo, it was, on another level, the trial of his manhood. More than an adventure, it was to be an exercise of the will in which he could test his resources and feel out the contours, the limitations, of himself as a person. His background, like that of the characters in his book *The Temptation of the West*, had been exclusively bookish, and he was eager to change it into something more intimate, more active, more "alive," through his experiences in Asia. As he told an interviewer later, such an undertaking was first of all a personal confrontation with extreme physical discomfort and danger, with "ants that are mashed beneath your hand, insects, reptiles, repulsive dangers at each step you take in the bush." [22] To overcome such obstacles required the fullest exercise of the will—the choice, repeated thousands of times, to push on toward the goal. Each of these tiny decisions was significant because, in his eyes, "after each act, whatever its importance, a life still hidden proposes its innumerable ramifications. Life is a series of possibilities." [23] In Asia Malraux hoped to glimpse new possibilities for his own life.

Even more important, an experience entailing such decisions represented in a very real sense the conquest of death. In this kind of intense personal struggle within oneself—this "combat" with mortality, as Malraux has called it—a human being becomes heroic, able to "possess more than himself, to escape from the lowly life of men" that he sees each day.[24] To an intellectual like Malraux, whose experiences and trials had been purely bookish or imaginary, this mission to Indochina seemed to offer a superb opportunity to test himself in the crucible of reality, to free himself at last from a "life given over to hopes and dreams." [25] For, as he wrote in the epigram that opens his *Temptation,* "He who long gazes on dreams becomes like his shadow." [26] His friend Marcel Arland understood all this better than anyone else among his associates. He wrote a moving tribute in which he pointed out that "at an age when some waste themselves in gestures and words, and seek easy notoriety in petty scandals," Malraux had come to realize that "literature could not satisfy him." [27] It was this above all that drove him into the jungles of Indochina.

Many obscure points surround the granting of official permission for Malraux's archaeological expedition. It seems highly unlikely that he revealed to the Colonial Office his plan to go to Banteay Srei; any such interest in the ruin would have called attention to the fact that for one reason or another the appropriate authorities in Indochina had not yet officially listed it as a "classified" monument; that is, one which had been taken under the direct control and protection of the state. This classifying would have had important legal consequences, but as Malraux later pointed out, until it had actually been done the temple remains were no more than abandoned rubble in the jungle to be had for the taking. "Others could have gone before me and taken the sculptures that I brought back . . . if they had wanted to strike out into the bush." [28] In any case, his project was approved by the authorities. According to some sources, this was due to the support of certain powerful friends in Paris,[29] but it might also be surmised that young Malraux's verbal prowess was enough to inspire the confidence of any government bureaucrat.

It was apparently not too difficult to obtain a "warrant" for archaeological exploration. Actually, it amounted to little more than official permission to go to the colony for that particular purpose. The only concrete assistance that the government gave such an enterprise was to issue a "certificate of requisition." This authorized the French representative of the Colonial Administration in the area to recruit local farmers and their wagons to transport the expedition's baggage into the bush. No other help of any sort was given to Malraux. The document he obtained from the Colonial Office was very specific: "It is clearly understood that *all* the expenses necessary for this mission, without exception, are to be paid by M. Malraux." [30]

This arrangement was quite satisfactory to Malraux. Since he was paying his own expenses, he was "in no way an appointed official, held to certain obligations." [31] However, in return for this permission and as a condition of its being validated, the young explorer was obliged to agree to furnish the authorities in Indochina with details of his plans immediately upon his arrival. These authorities included the representatives of the Colonial Administration and, more important, the Hanoi Director of the Ecole Française d'Extrême-Orient, who controlled all archaeological activities in the colony.

Late in October or early in November, Malraux went to Marseilles and embarked with his wife, Clara, on a ship of the Compagnie des Messageries Maritimes. His friend and associate in the venture, Louis Chevasson, followed on the next sailing, a fortnight later. Ships such as the *Porthos* and the *Chambord* linked France to her Far Eastern empire with regular biweekly sailings. Details of the three-and-a-half-week itinerary have been recorded by many writers who made the trip, including Clara Malraux.[32] Moreover, numerous passages of highly colored prose in Malraux's own books clearly reflect his intensely romantic reaction to certain scenes and events of the long voyage. As always, his mind quickly transformed these lyric emotions into abstractions.

As the ship moved down through the Tyrrhenian Sea off the coast of Italy, then past Sicily—a Greek colony in ancient times—and Crete, cradle of the Minoan culture, Malraux was already being stimulated to work out many of the ideas that he subsequently incorporated into *The Temptation of the West* and "Concerning a European Youth." Italy recalled the Latin-Christian tradition that had molded Western man into "a race burdened with a heavy crown of power and suffering," a civilization highly conscious of the "individual existence" of each human being. It was to this part of the Mediterranean, to pagan Greece and to Christian Rome, that "the greatest minds of that race come to seek out . . . a clear image of what they are." [33] It was here that Europeans found their Reality, the basic frame of reference of their cultural past within which they could comprehend life, the world, and themselves. The impact of this part of the voyage was heightened by his anticipation of the entirely different culture to which he was going.

After crossing the remaining strip of the Mediterranean, the ships of the Messageries stood off the great harbor of Port Said. There the statue of Ferdinand de Lesseps proudly pointed to the entrance to the Suez Canal. To Malraux, the canal seemed a particularly fitting monument to the energy, power, and ability to dominate nature that were fundamental characteristics of Occidental civilization. The vast expanse of the international port facilities, together with the Western city that circled it, was eloquent testimony to the aggressive materialism of the "whites." [34] It was primarily a desire for profit that had driven large numbers of Europeans beyond the rim of their Greco-Roman world into the wide reaches of Asia, and the economic prosperity of all Europe had soon become closely linked with the successful exploitation of the various colonial empires.

As the ship slowly moved through the canal, it seemed to Malraux that the West he knew was reduced to a narrow band on each side of the channel and to the ship itself, a great floating island, towering grotesquely above banks of empty sand. Reality suddenly was closely restricted, centered, and magnified by this isolating passage through a burning waste. At last he was drawing near those "fabulous realms" where his imagination, nurtured by an extensive knowledge of archaeology, had long wandered. Looking out over the vast desert sands, he envisioned a fantastic "caravan of peoples and kingdoms slowly taking shape." To the west was Egypt. An alien land, it was still within the realm of European civilization because of its links with Greece, Rome, and early Christianity. To the east, however, lay mystery—the endless plains of Asia. Close by was Arabia, with its misty legends of the lost capital of the Queen of Sheba, and Persia, with its tombs and the dying beauties of Isphahan. Beyond lay the "sterile plains of Samarkand," and the broad steppes of Mongolia, over which Tamerlane, bearing "lofty banners . . . emblazoned with very ancient signs" had led his marauding hordes. On the distant horizon, among the wild grasses, lines of whitened bones marked the passage of the armies of countless forgotten conquerors. Here, perhaps, lay the fabled empire of Prester John. In the far distance, at the very limit of the continent, was wondrous Cathay, that "noble old blind man, crowned with black poppies." [35] As Malraux stood on the deck of the steamer, he became almost intoxicated with this new "fairyland," so unlike and yet in a way so closely related to the cubist fantasies he had recorded in *Paper Moons* and *The Fabulous Realm*.

When the ship reached the end of the canal, at the upper tip of the Red Sea, swarms of natives swept out from the shore on a myriad of strange craft, offering the passengers bizarre fruits on exotic trays. Under the piercing gaze of these Asians, Malraux experienced another new sensation—a sense of alienation, of separation. Reality was represented by these agitated hawkers; *he* was now the foreigner, the outsider. He also became aware of a certain loss of personal identity. To the dark-skinned men in the harbor, every European was part of a faceless mass referred to as the "whites." In an effort to regain his individuality, an essential element of the personality in the Western view, Malraux looked into himself with new acuity. He began to realize that in this new cultural context, he *was* what he *did*: he existed as he acted in response to the dictates of his will. In a sense, this rather Nietzschean affirmation was a testimony to the essentially Western character of his personality. His meditations on the whole problem form a large part of *The Temptation of the West*.

Malraux's first direct contact with the Orient came when the ship docked for a day or two at Djibouti, seat of the Colonial Administration of French Somaliland. The native section of the city, a stinking sore of human misery, surrounded a small, affluent European quarter. The "whites" not only reaped enormous profits from the commercial exploitation of the area, but also siphoned off huge sums from the public treasury. The whole situation was so flagrantly corrupt that shocked visitors often spoke of protesting directly to Paris.[36] Nothing ever came of such protests—if, indeed, they were ever actually made. Malraux, who had never been interested in politics, was very disturbed by the economic and social injustices he saw as he stood on the threshold of France's colonial empire. Clearly, the vast majority of French *colons*, or settlers, did not regard liberty, equality, and fraternity as exportable items.

Psychologically, Djibouti made an even deeper impression on him, a shock that was subsequently mirrored in the pages of *Temptation* and *The Royal Way*.[37] This thoroughly Eastern city afforded the European traveler a point outside his own civilization and race from which he could gain new insights into the real nature of Western society and culture. Against a background of different values, the qualities that his civilization had always encouraged—aggressiveness, acquisitiveness, sensuality, physical strength—stood revealed as brutality, greed, lust, and the oppression of the weak by the strong. Through the crowded and dirty streets of this city on the coast of a wild continent moved the shadows of concupiscence and perversion of every kind. No longer fettered by the conventions of Western society, grotesque figures emerged from the darkness of the European psyche. Beneath insect-covered kerosene lamps, strange erotic dramas were acted out by vibrant young Negresses and outcast European adventurers. To a young, sensitive, and rather idealistic Frenchman like Malraux, Djibouti must have been a painful revelation of a new and ugly face of the Occident.

After passing through the Bab-el-Mandeb, the Gates of Death, at the end of the Red Sea, the ship entered the Indian Ocean, heading for Colombo, Ceylon. For a week, in the middle of an empty sea, the vessel became a world unto itself. The passengers grouped themselves into a social hierarchy that was no longer that of metropolitan France but a prefiguration of colonial society. Here Malraux had his first contact with the rigidity, shortsightedness, and selfishness of the colonial mentality, against which he was to struggle so energetically during his two years in Indochina.[38]

At the summit of the social ladder were the high officials sent by the metropolitan government to be the top administrators of France's overseas possessions. Unfortunately, these important and sensitive appointments were frequently made as the result of political intrigue rather than in recognition of ability. Men who were supposedly the embodiment of the political ideals of liberty and justice for which France stood often turned out to be little more than selfish authoritarians. Despite their loud pronouncements on the *duties* of colonialism, many of them seemed primarily concerned with its personal prerogatives. In the very worst tradition of the old French absolutist ideal, these bourgeois saw Indochina as a vast feudal state and themselves as its lords.

Beneath these high-ranking figures was an army of civil servants of all grades. Most of them faithfully mirrored the attitudes of those at the top. Usually only half-educated, these ultraconservative subordinates were little concerned with the "civilizing mission" of France in the Far East. They were sailing for Indochina because for them, especially in the years 1924–25, it was El Dorado. Thanks to an extremely favorable exchange rate and an economy geared to the profit of the French masters, a not too scrupulous civil servant—even a minor one—could send large sums of money back to France and still lead a life of luxury in Indochina. An insignificant functionary from a Paris bureau arrived in the colonies to find himself suddenly transformed into a prince with power, servants, and the finest house in the village. Small wonder that he became zealous in defending the *status quo*.

There were other people aboard who were not part of the Administration but were closely linked to it. At the top were the big businessmen—ruthless directors of mines in Tonkin; energetic pioneers who had carved vast rubber plantations out of the jungle and reclaimed swamps and brush for rice fields; "operators" who had encouraged the opium trade or acquired control over liquor, gambling, and brothels. Allied with the big businessmen were the directors of banks and other semi-official enterprises, such as the government-subsidized hotel chains. Although a few of these men were genuinely interested in the welfare of the colony and its native peoples, most of them were concerned only with amassing a personal fortune in the shortest possible time.

Further down the hierarchy were officers and soldiers of the French Colonial Army and specialists attached to nonadministrative services of the colonial government. At the very bottom were members of the paramilitary political police, the Sûreté, which apparently had a sizable proportion of sadistic undesirables. These "colonials" were welded together not only by a common attitude toward the colonies and the native people, but even more by a wholehearted commitment to preserve the *status quo* and keep the piasters flowing. One can well imagine the reactions of twenty-two-year-old Malraux, confined aboard ship for more than three weeks with these people, many of whom were traitors to the ideals upon which republican France had been built.

To be sure, there were some congenial passengers, but most of them belonged to the "out group." This usually included the Annamites and Franco-Annamite half-castes; a scattering of businessmen of other nationalities, mainly Chinese or Hindu Indians; some of the more liberal and humanitarian French doctors, teachers, and missionaries; and a number of what were darkly referred to as "adventurers." These might include a highly educated Annamite with liberal political ideas returning to his homeland after a long exile, the half-caste son of a French father who preferred the company of Asians to that of Europeans and who made himself the defender of the rights of Annamites, a Russian gun dealer or a mercenary soldier of fortune in the employ of a native prince—or even an "amateur" archaeologist who presumed to explore independently, though with official permission, the domains of the EFEO. Anyone who did not fit conveniently into the official hierarchy or whose ideas were not shared by the conservative majority was regarded as a suspicious character—at best an annoyance, at worst a revolutionary or Bolshevik. Outspoken, brilliant, liberal, and haughty, Malraux must have made many enemies and few friends during the long journey across the Indian Ocean.

Early one morning in late October, after brief stops at Colombo and Singapore, the ship at last stood off the coast of French Indochina. This peninsular colony was larger in area than any nation in Europe and was a quarter greater than France itself. Here lived a community of nearly 20 million souls whose destiny—economic and political—was entirely in the hands of a tiny minority of foreigners with virtually unlimited authority. The French conquerors had divided the area into five parts: the landlocked protectorate Kingdom of Laos in the northwest, the protectorate Kingdom of Cambodia in the southwest, the directly administered protectorate province of Tonkin in the north, the protectorate empire of Annam in the central coastal region, and the colony of Cochinchina in the south.[39]

The largest city of Indochina was Saigon, the capital of Cochinchina and a great port and market place in the delta of the Mekong. This rambling waterway begins in the wilds of Tibet and winds some 2,600 miles through the peninsula before emptying into the China Sea. The Mekong linked together such scattered administrative centers and capitals as Luang Prabang, Vientiane, and Pnom Penh. Moreover, its extensive system of tributaries and canals gave the French a great natural artery for transporting products from rich areas of the interior to the coast, whence they could be exported. As the central rice market and port for southern Indochina, Saigon was one of the most affluent cities in the French colonial empire.

Malraux and his wife did not disembark at Saigon but remained aboard until the ship docked at Haiphong, the port serving Hanoi, the capital of Tonkin and the second largest city in Indochina. Hanoi was the administrative center for the entire peninsula. Here were located the offices and residence of the Governor General of Indochina, and the headquarters of the organizations under his jurisdiction, including the EFEO. Malraux was obliged to visit the School immediately for validation of the certificate of requisition that had been granted him by the Colonial Office. Although word of his impending arrival had been received from Paris, he was not greeted very warmly. The authorities of the School, jealous of their prerogatives and distrustful of anyone lacking their academic and philological training, were displeased that a Paris Ministry had seen fit to authorize a rank "amateur" to undertake an archaeological exploration, even though it was entirely at his own expense. Malraux, well aware of their attitude, was prepared to encounter difficulties.

The head of the School, Louis Finot, had left for Siam shortly before Malraux's arrival, and Leonard Aurousseau had been named Acting Director.[40] Like Ramèges, who received the archaeologist-adventurer Vannec in *The Royal Way*, Aurousseau was primarily a linguistic specialist. A permanent member of the School at Hanoi, where he was professor of Chinese, he was known for his work on the history of South China and Annam. As an archaeologist formed in the disciplines of philology and history, he must have had considerable misgivings about Malraux's lack of traditional academic training and serious reservations concerning his "artistic" approach to the study of ancient civilizations. However, the young man was on a mission authorized by Paris, and so Aurousseau received him politely.

Malraux apparently had represented his project to the Colonial Office as—at least in part—an attempt to relocate the main Khmer road linking the capital at Angkor with the northern provinces of

the empire in the area of present-day Laos. Southern sections of
this extensive network of ancient highways were well known and
had even been utilized by French engineers in their own road-
building projects, but little exploration had been done north of
Angkor. The region was wild, covered with "brush forest" or
dense tropical jungle, and was inhabited by native tribes that had
not yet accepted the French conquest. The Administration considered this "zone of dissidence" very dangerous for Europeans.

Aurousseau warned that two scholars from the School had already been killed there, but Malraux refused to be dissuaded from
his project. He spoke of his firm intention of making an artistic
study of the temple remains he hoped to discover along the ancient highway. The Acting Director pointed out that according to
a new policy recently adopted by the government at the suggestion
of the School authorities, any objects found in the jungle must be
left *in situ*. A detailed report was then to be filed with the School,
whose Archaeological Service would decide what should be done
with them. Malraux protested that individuals on previous mis-
sions authorized by Paris had been permitted to take back at least
some of their discoveries for museums in France. After all, the
School was not the only French group interested in the art history
of the Far East, and it had no authority to declare Indochina its
private preserve. He proceeded to outline his theories on the relationship between Khmer and Siamese art, insisting that his discoveries along the Royal Highway across the Empire would enable
him to shed new light on the subject.

Aurousseau countered by explaining that a new directive from
the Governor General's office would soon clarify the rather vague
administrative decree of 1908 that gave the School exclusive rights
in Indochina.[41] In any case, he continued, in order to have his
certificate of requisition validated, Malraux must sign a "written
agreement to permit the EFEO to benefit from the results of the
research that he came . . . to undertake at his own expense in the
land of the Khmers." [42] Thus, no matter what the new directive
would say, the School could claim part of the credit for any discoveries made, since under the agreement it would become—
nominally at least—the sponsor of the expedition. Malraux signed.
Later, at the time of his trial, he stated (probably not without
irony) that his expedition into the jungles of Cambodia was one
"to which the School deigned to grant its distinguished patronage,
at the time of my visit to Hanoi." [43]

Malraux's rather chilly reception was partly due to the personal animosity of the Acting Director. Even more important, however, was Aurousseau's feeling that the prestige of his School was at stake. He was less interested in protecting the sites against "looting" than in making sure that all looting was done for the benefit of the EFEO. Malraux was well aware of this. His character Vannec's thoughts on leaving the interview with Ramèges (in *The Royal Way*) certainly echo his own reflections at a similar moment:

> It's in his own interest to try and get out of me whatever I can bring him, since it's obvious that none of his present assistants will risk their skins out there. He's acting like an administrator who is building up an inventory. . . . In thirty years, will his Institute still be here, and the French still in Indochina? He is probably even thinking that if his two expedition leaders died, it was so that their colleagues might carry on their work, although neither one of them died for his Institute. . . . If in fighting for himself, he is also defending a collectivity, he will become nasty; if he thinks he's fighting for his dead, he will become rabid: I've got to try and figure out what he's going to dream up.[44]

In his wildest imaginings, Malraux could not have foreseen what was going to be dreamt up around his mission to Cambodia.

After obtaining Aurousseau's validation, Malraux and his wife left for Saigon. They probably traveled overland along the coastal Mandarin Road and made a brief visit to Hué. This old city, the capital of the Annamite Empire, contained the Imperial Palace and a number of other important historical buildings that Malraux was eager to see. On reaching Saigon, he found his friend Chevasson, newly arrived from France, waiting for him.[45] The two men, accompanied by Clara, left almost immediately for Pnom Penh, capital of Cambodia. Chevasson remained there a few days, but Malraux and his wife caught a riverboat for Siem Reap, the provincial town a few miles from the Angkor ruins. The rainy season had ended some weeks earlier, and the flood that yearly fertilized the great Cambodian plain had begun to recede. As a motorboat brought them to shore, carefully weaving through the forest of tree trunks that emerged from the muddy water, Malraux observed that they were circled with rings of dried mud marking the retreat of the inundation. The jungle trails north of Angkor would almost certainly be passable. On landing, he hired a car and proceeded to the local "bungalow," the generic name given to the modest hostelries for Europeans maintained in many provincial centers of the colony. Angkor was the main tourist attraction of Cambodia, and a small but comfortable bungalow for Siem Reap had been built about five miles from the town, almost directly across from the stone mortuary temple of Angkor Wat, the most imposing structure remaining from the days of the ancient Khmer kings. Here Malraux and his wife took a room and began making final preparations for his expedition into the bush.

His first act was to call upon the local representative of the French Administration, a minor official named Crémazy. From Hanoi, the School had already sent him word of Malraux's anticipated arrival and had made clear just what assistance was authorized for him. A scene in *The Royal Way* suggests that Crémazy had also been instructed to give Malraux several documents that apparently amplified the administrative decision requiring all archaeological discoveries to be left *in situ*. Malraux was convinced that any such restriction could be applied only to *classified* ruins, that is, to those which had been formally placed under the protection of the state by the action of a competent authority. Moreover, he suspected that the School was aware that it had been remiss in its duty to protect desirable monuments in this way; the head of its Archaeological Service had recently begun to visit a number of neglected sites to prepare a list for the Governor General's office.[46] Since Banteay Srei had not yet been classified, Malraux decided not to abandon his plan to visit the temple ruin there.

In accordance with his instructions from Hanoi, Crémazy undertook to requisition the Cambodian guides and drivers required for the purported search for the lost Royal Highway. This recruiting took several days. Malraux and his wife, together with the newly arrived Chevasson, took the opportunity to visit the Khmer ruins of the Angkor area. According to Chinese records, this ancient civilization of Hindu origin had been present on the peninsula early in the Christian era.[47] By about the seventh century, a number of minor Indian princedoms had been welded into one large state which, during the next 200 years, gradually extended its hegemony over most of the Indonesian archipelago. Before this great empire collapsed late in the fourteenth century, from internal strains and the constant pressure of the invading Siamese, its rulers erected numerous stone temples on the peninsula, mostly in the immediate area of Angkor, the site of the successive royal capitals. By the time the Europeans came in the latter part of the nineteenth century, most of these temples had been completely forgotten and lay buried under the extravagant vegetation of the tropical jungle. By 1923, the archaeologists of the EFEO had gradually rediscovered and cleared most of the edifices in the Angkor area, making a minimum of restorative repairs. To facilitate visits, the major sites had been linked together with a road. Travelers usually stayed at the bungalow across from Angkor Wat and spent several days making the rounds of the temple remains by automobile, ricksha, horse, or even elephant.

Malraux naturally stopped at the principal monuments on this "circuit," as it was called, including the Bayon Temple; the Royal Square, with the Terrace of the Leper King and the remains of the Imperial Palace compound; the vast Srah Srang, or Royal Pool; the uncleared sanctuary of Ta Prohm; and of course, Angkor Wat.[48] Moreover, from his extensive studies of the *Bulletin* and similar publications, he knew about a number of rarely visited sites outside the main circuit. Apparently, he went to see several of these, notably one known to the natives as Banteay Srei, located a short distance southeast of the Roluos group and about twelve miles from Angkor Wat. As sometimes happened in rural Cambodia, a modern Buddhist pagoda had been built over part of the ruins of the ancient Khmer temple, and little of archaeological interest remained. Of course, this was not the Banteay Srei from which he was planning to obtain his sculptures.[49]

Crémazy at last sent word that everything was ready. He had obtained a Cambodian guide and boss for the drivers of the half-dozen ox carts required to transport baggage, and horses had been acquired for the three Europeans. Malraux had hired a guide of his own, together with several Annamites to act as personal servants. All together, the little caravan that set out in the crisp coolness of an early morning in December included fewer than twenty people.[50]

Leaving the circuit road near the northeast corner of the Angkor area, the party crossed a ridge which marked the outer dike of one of the immense water reservoirs of the ancient Khmer capital and plunged into the jungle. The two-wheeled Cambodian carts moved slowly over the faint local trails. There were some muddy stretches, not yet dried out after the heavy monsoon rains; in other places, the cart wheels sank deep into soft sand. But the teams of wide-horned water buffalo were astonishingly powerful, and progress was steady. The route Malraux had planned led almost due north, paralleling the Siem Reap River. However, the meanderings of the native paths forced him to cover nearly forty miles in order to reach a site only about half that distance from the bungalow.

The area was sparsely inhabited, and the jungle was very dense in spots. In *The Royal Way*, Malraux vividly describes the exaggerated effects that the damp heat and the profuse vegetation and insect life had on his taut nerves during these hours.[51] It was probably no later than the second day that the party finally crossed the river—only a small stream at that point—and approached the temple of Banteay Srei. It was little more than a mound of stone buried in a tangle of undergrowth, just as Marek and Parmentier had described it. After making their way into the inner courtyard, choked with rubble and the sprawling roots of great trees, Malraux and his party stood before three truncated stone towers scarcely twice the height of a man. This was all that remained of the central sanctuary and its two flanking structures.

Malraux carefully examined a number of stones that had fallen from various parts of the buildings, and saw that their sculptured surfaces had been seriously eroded by weather and vegetation. The only sculptures of artistic value were on the stones that still remained in place in the walls. The central sanctuary was rather inaccessible because it was surrounded by debris fallen from the side towers. Fortunately, the outer walls of these towers faced the open courtyard and were relatively free. Malraux noted that the cornerstones of the south tower contained several of the finest Khmer figures he had ever seen. Carved in high relief and standing within deep niches were a series of nearly life-size devatas, or guardian goddesses, richly adorned and beautiful. They occupied the surfaces of three superposed blocks and were in excellent condition.[52]

To obtain these prizes, Malraux and Chevasson proceeded exactly as described in *The Royal Way*.[53] Wherever possible, they pried the stones loose. They used stone saws and chisels on those that remained stubbornly wedged in the walls of the tower. Since the carved blocks formed the corners of the building, they bore carvings of goddesses on *two* sides. Exercising great care, Malraux

succeeded in removing six of these stones, together with "several
figured roof ornaments from the upper stories." [54] Then the Cambodian drivers helped load the great blocks into the baggage carts
for the trip back to Siem Reap. The whole adventure had taken
less than a week. [55]

When Malraux and his caravan drew up in front of the bungalow, they were met by the manager, M. Debyser. It was obvious
that the water buffaloes were hauling more than the personal effects
of the party, and Debyser forthwith informed Crémazy that the
expedition had brought back nearly a ton of material from the
short excursion into the jungle. This information was then telegraphed to the High Commissioner in the Cambodian capital,
who was shortly afterward alerted that the Malraux couple and
Chevasson had boarded a riverboat for Pnom Penh. Stored in the
hold as part of their luggage were a number of crates, addressed to
a firm in Saigon.

Hurriedly the Commissioner dispatched the director of the local
archaeological museum, M. Groslier, a member of the EFEO and
a specialist in Khmer art, to intercept the vessel at Kompong
Chnang, a port about sixty miles above Pnom Penh on the river
leading from the great Tonlé Sap Lake. After ascertaining that the
crates were indeed in the hold, Groslier so informed the Commissioner, who thereupon ordered a local judge to issue seizure
warrants. When the boat docked at Pnom Penh late in the evening of December 24, it was immediately boarded by the police. A
local reporter described the scene in vivid prose:

> On December 24, 1923, toward midnight, at the very hour when
> the bells of the churches of Pnom Penh were calling the faithful
> to celebrate the anniversary of the birth of Christ, two inspectors
> from the Sûreté boarded the steamer of the River Transports Com-
> pany arriving from Siem Reap, and after indicating to two passen-
> gers, MM. Malraux and Chevasson, that they had been ordered to
> search their baggage, had the latter opened and found . . . some
> pieces of statuary from the Angkor ruins.
> The search then being extended to some crates addressed to the
> firm of Berthet and Charrière, in Saigon . . . brought about the
> discovery of seven stone blocks, one representing two gods and the
> six others some Buddhist angels.
> These pieces were immediately impounded and then taken to the
> Albert Sarraut Museum, where M. Groslier quickly identified them
> and established that they were part of the bas-reliefs of the temple

of Banteay Srei, a tiny structure but one full of rare and very valuable sculptures.[56]

Malraux had accomplished part of his Indochina mission. He had found and brought out of the jungle the sculpture he wanted. He would, however, pay dearly for this brief success.

II

The Angkor Affair

Malraux and Chevasson were arrested but not actually incarcerated. They were simply "requested to keep themselves available to the court until further notice." [1] Malraux took a room with his wife at the Grand Hotel, the center of social life in the capital, and rumors of his adventure were soon rampant amidst the tightly knit little colony of Europeans. However, not a word about the matter appeared in print until January 5, 1924, when the weekly Cambodian newspaper *L'Echo du Cambodge* broke the story under the headline "Pillage of the Angkor Ruins." The editor felt it necessary to explain his previous silence, evidently ordered by the French High Commissioner for Cambodia:

> From the very first, widespread rumor propagated a story so fantastic that it was difficult to lend credence to such hearsay. Our duty as informant compelled us to be prudent; that is why we did not consider ourselves obliged to acquaint our readers with it. . . . Today, certain information from an authoritative source permits us to give some precise details about this act of pillage, which bespeaks an unbelievable audacity on the part of its authors and special knowledge of the value of the sculptures that were stolen.

The important role attributed to the Administration elsewhere in the story left little doubt as to the identity of the source. The article, an essentially accurate account of what had happened, was a far cry from the fantasies that subsequently appeared in newspapers in Paris and New York.

The Cambodian editor expressed the hope that "a severe example" would be made of the two young men—a significant indication of how the colonial authorities already intended to treat the case. This note was sounded even more vigorously three days later in Saigon in another government-backed newspaper, the daily *Impartial*. On January 8, under the inflammatory heading "Vandals and Pillagers of Ruins," its editor, Henry Chavigny, cited verbatim several paragraphs from the Cambodian article and echoed the hope that the authorities would pursue the matter energetically.[2] Such severe morality from a man who had been revealed in court as a philanderer, extortionist, and malingerer must have surprised knowledgeable readers in Saigon. To arouse public opinion further, the *Impartial* article related details of an incident in which an ancient statue of the god Ganesh, uncovered during repairs to a provincial road near Saigon, had been stolen while on display in a local schoolhouse. Chavigny blamed this theft on the flourishing illicit traffic in antiquities: "Such a statue has considerable archaeological value, and we would not be surprised if we were told that a foreign country more concerned than our own about ancient history and epigraphy would be capable of paying a very high price for such a work." Chavigny insinuated that Malraux and Chevasson had been exclusively motivated by a similar financial consideration and suggested more effective means of protecting the archaeological remains of the area. These included the establishment of a government department responsible for the care of Indochinese antiquities, and the exhaustive listing of all historical sites so that they could be classified officially and caretakers assigned to them.

No other articles on the Malraux-Chevasson case appeared in any Indochinese papers until it came to trial six months later. This silence was due, as one correspondent openly admitted, to the "very great discretion of the magistrate responsible for the preliminary inquiry, M. Bartet."[3] In French legal practice, when a criminal charge has been made against a suspect, the local public prosecutor appoints an Examining Magistrate for the case. This judge compiles a dossier of depositions and other relevant material that enables him to make a preliminary decision as to whether the evidence warrants taking the case to court. Although he consults police reports and takes affidavits from prisoners, he does not take part in the investigation. To avoid abuses, French law expressly prohibits him from sitting on the bench in any case that he has prepared. Judge Bartet, appointed to inquire into the Malraux-

Chevasson case immediately after the young men were apprehended, was exemplary in carrying out his duties. Later, in one of his few direct references to the trial, Malraux praised the judge for being "absolutely fair." [4]

From the beginning, Bartet was under heavy pressure from Hanoi to imprison the two young men. Crémazy, in an obvious attempt to curry favor, had telegraphed to M. Habert, Director of Justice for Indochina, a greatly exaggerated account of the incident, a report which eventually found its way to the Colonial Office in Paris. Bartet steadfastly refused to comply, on the grounds that incarceration was entirely out of proportion for the offense. Instead, he dispatched Henri Parmentier to Banteay Srei. The archaeologist had already made a preliminary survey of the site immediately after the sculptures had been seized, but now the judge wanted a detailed report of the damage done by Malraux and the importance of the theft.[5] Parmentier arrived at the ruin on January 17, accompanied by a young scholar, Victor Goloubew, acting as his assistant and photographer. Several days later they were joined by Louis Finot, the director of the EFEO, who had recently returned from Siam. After examining the partly cleared area, Finot agreed that Banteay Srei was indeed a remarkable specimen of Khmer art, though badly deteriorated, and he ordered the principal structures to be completely uncovered. As the *Bulletin* of the School later noted, this work, which took until February 14, revealed a whole new series of inscriptions and some "very remarkable sculpture . . . which adds interesting new facts to our knowledge of Khmer art." [6] Thus, the temple that Malraux had chosen turned out to be much more remarkable than Parmentier's earlier survey had indicated. Was this simply luck, or did it indicate Malraux's superior artistic insight? Parmentier seemed to believe the latter, because subsequently in open court he referred to the accused as "amateur archaeologists of very great worth."

Bartet's next step in preparing the trial dossier was to request information on Malraux and Chevasson from police files in Paris. He quickly learned that the two young men had no criminal record. However—probably at the suggestion of the Colonial Office, which had transmitted Bartet's request—a special detail of the Paris police was assigned to make a more thorough investigation into their backgrounds.[7] Little of interest was discovered about Chevasson; the police reports described him as a "modest bookstore clerk" who was "industrious, sober, thrifty." [8] The re-

port on Malraux was more extensive. Much of the information collected about him was biographical and therefore pertinent to the
judicial inquiry. However, also included among the documents
were many so-called *political* items, some so secret that they had to
be written in code.[9] Such material was clearly irrelevant in a criminal proceeding, but legal niceties were not always observed in the
courts of the French colonies.

The Paris police report revealed that Georges-André Malraux
was born on the Rue Damrémont, in the Montmartre section of
Paris, on November 3, 1901. His father, Fernand-Georges Malraux, was a businessman who speculated extensively on the stock
market. Sometime before World War I, Malraux's parents had
separated, and while attending the Lycée Condorcet in Paris, the
young man had lived with his grandmother at 16 Rue de la Gare,
in the Parisian suburb of Bondy, a mile or two north of the capital.
Malraux never took much interest in his lycée studies.[10] As one of
his friends put it, he was too enterprising a youth to be comfortable in any traditional academic routine; he wanted to seek his fortune energetically in the world.[11]

According to the police investigations, about a year after the war
nineteen-year-old Malraux, gifted with a quick mind and an extraordinary memory, began to frequent the quays and secondhand
bookshops of Paris, seeking unrecognized bibliophilic treasures.
He soon became well known to a number of rare-book dealers,
who relied heavily on such young *chineurs*, or searchers, in meeting the orders of their wealthy collector clients. One dealer for
whom he worked, René-Louis Doyon, founded a review early in
1920, and to it Malraux contributed his first literary article, a study
of cubist poetry. For Doyon, who was also starting a publishing
business, he then prepared two volumes of the "unpublished" writings of the poet Jules Laforgue.[12] When Simon Kra, another bookdealer friend, decided to launch a publishing house with his son
Lucien early in 1920, Malraux joined the enterprise as director of
its demi-luxe publications. The resulting Editions du Sagittaire,
aimed at the growing middle-class bibliophile market, were a
tribute to both his artistic taste and his business acumen.[13]

The police also reported that Malraux was a frequent companion of the bohemians of Montmartre and Montparnasse. He
could be seen at dinners and art exhibits arranged by little avant-
garde reviews, at Max Jacob's soirees in a restaurant near Sacré
Coeur, and at the fashionable Boeuf sur le Toit. He was a faithful

visitor to the studios of certain painters, especially that of D. Galanis, and on occasion he attended the Sunday-afternoon teas of the German expatriate D.-H. Kahnweiler, the foremost dealer, patron, and friend of the cubist painters. At one of these literary-artistic gatherings he met Clara Goldschmidt, the daughter of a wealthy German-Jewish family, who subsequently became his wife.[14]

If the conservative investigators were suspicious of Malraux's bohemian friends and tastes and of his marriage into a German-Jewish family, they were positively alarmed at his literary activities. He had written an incomprehensible book, a long fantasy called *Paper Moons*, which had been illustrated by the cubist artist Fernand Léger and published by Kahnweiler as part of his series of luxury volumes.[15] An equally imaginative literary effort, called "Written for a Trunked Idol" ("Ecrit pour une idole à trompe"), though not formally published, had been circulated among his friends in mimeographed form.[16] In addition, Malraux had written for a number of the little literary magazines that proliferated in the early 1920's. In the eyes of the police, this was tantamount to subversive political agitation because, as a contemporary conservative put it, "the so-called 'avant-garde' reviews, sprung up since the war, are almost all based on the triple formula: cubism, dadaism, and Bolshevism." [17] Among those to which Malraux contributed were *La Connaissance*, published by the crusty iconoclast René-Louis Doyon; *Signaux de France et de Belgique* and *Le Disque vert*, both edited by several writers closely associated with cubism; *Dés*, a short-lived magazine that was an offshoot of the dadaist publication *Aventure*; and the *Nouvelle Revue Française*, founded by a confessed homosexual, André Gide.

Malraux's most sustained—and suspicious—collaboration was with *Action*, a review that had long been under official surveillance. Indeed, its very first issue had been seized by the police because of a "subversive" article in praise of the infamous murderer Landru, which had been written by Malraux's close friend Georges Gabory.[18] The magazine, lavishly illustrated with cubist woodcuts and photographs of primitive African masks, regularly carried advertisements for other avant-garde reviews and publishers. Among the latter was one Jacques Povolozky, an importer and specialist in Russian books, who for a time was also the general distributor for *Action*. Certain of the police investigators who prepared Malraux's dossier saw this as proof that the magazine was tainted with anarchic Russian Bolshevism. Their conclusion was strengthened by the fact that its editors had once shared the address and telephone number of a certain "School of Marxist Socialism." As an advertisement in the first issue indicated, this school not only gave instruction in Marxism, but also encouraged "the search for new values in the doctrines of the Communists, Bolshevists, maximalists, etc." [19]

Malraux became a regular, albeit modest, collaborator in this review, beginning with the third issue (April, 1920), and was briefly a co-editor. In spite of a prepublication commitment to a broad artistic and political reform program, the magazine was concerned almost exclusively with art and literature, not politics. Malraux's contributions, entirely literary, included critical articles on Lautréamont and Gide, reviews of two books by André Salmon and one by Breton, and three groups of his own cubist-inspired "poems in prose." [20]

Such, in essence, was the documentation on Malraux collected by the French police and turned over to the Colonial Office in Paris. This Office made a careful selection of the strictly judicial material and then forwarded it to Bartet in Pnom Penh, to be included in his report and—if the case went to trial—to be made available to both prosecution and defense. Had this judicial dossier been the only file sent from Paris, Malraux's trial would surely have taken a very different direction. Indeed, as Bartet's information grew, he apparently became more and more skeptical about the legal basis for the case and increasingly disposed to issue an order of dismissal. When his attitude became known, the Administration replaced him with another Examining Magistrate. When the second judge also proved to be uncooperative, the colonial authorities appointed a more tractable individual recently arrived from Pondicherry. The desired indictment was shortly forthcoming. [21]

In France, such intervention by the Administration in the functioning of the judiciary would have been unthinkable. But as a number of contemporary writers reveal, the carrying out of justice in the French colonies had become a parody of orthodox legal practice. [22] Indochina, like most of the colonial empire, was governed primarily by direct administrative decrees, rather than through legislation by the Chamber of Deputies. These decrees were issued by the Colonial Office, which also appointed the Examining Magistrates and the Colonial Judges. A judge's term ran for three years, but he could be transferred at any time, without explanation, by the Colonial Office. Traditional French judicial safeguards were further weakened because in the colonies only *one* trial judge was usually required instead of the three customary in France itself. As might be expected under the circumstances, the colonial judiciary had become increasingly sensitive to the wishes of the local civil Administration. Political considerations were frequently introduced into criminal trials, and in many instances the courts actually aided an ultra-conservative bureaucracy in maintaining an illegal, repressive domination over the peoples under its jurisdiction.

The basic technique for political intervention in a criminal trial, as Malraux later described it with some acrimony, was to prepare *two* dossiers—"one administrative, the other judicial. If need be —where I am involved, for example—the administrative investigation is at the same time a political one. The administrative dossier, or the impression conveyed by it, or the impression 'that should be conveyed by it' is communicated to the judges but carefully kept away from the defense." [23] He was here evidently alluding to the fact that only the judicial material that the Colonial Office had forwarded to Bartet for the legal dossier had been made available to Malraux's lawyers. A second dossier, prepared by the Colonial Office from the pseudo-political material furnished by the Paris police, had also been sent to Pnom Penh. This file was revealed only to the public prosecutor and the trial judge. Such duplicity was later justified on the ground that state secrets were involved!

Objectively, it is difficult to see how anything in Malraux's early career could have been considered politically dangerous. It was true that he was not a conservative petit bourgeois; that he moved in a rather arty group of writers and artists; that he sometimes dressed extravagantly; and that he had written for several avant-garde reviews. In addition, he had married into a German-Jewish family and counted among his friends a number of Jews, including several of German descent—Kra, Kahnweiler, and Léon Pierre-Quint. In a country that had been torn by the Dreyfus case only twenty years before and that had just ended a long and bitter war with Germany, these facts were sure to seem incriminating, at least to some people. They help to explain the vehemence with which the young man was attacked, both in France and in Indochina, at the time of his trial.

After six months of preparation, the trial of Malraux and

Chevasson was finally held on Wednesday and Thursday, July 16–17, 1924, in Pnom Penh. The case had aroused extraordinary interest among the Europeans there, and the courtroom was filled by 7:30 A.M., half an hour before the session was to begin. A large bloc of seats had been roped off for special guests, and this "reserved gallery where the elegant dresses of the ladies mingled with the spotless white suits of the elect" gave the courtroom the appearance of a theater. According to a reporter who covered the event, it was primarily Malraux's personality that had unexpectedly "attracted to the temple of Themis a crowd as numerous as it was elegant." [24] During the long months before the trial, his intellectual brilliance—as well as his sharp tongue—had made him a well-known figure in the French community of the Cambodian capital. Also, there was considerable interest in seeing how Judge Jodin would conduct himself. He had come from India the previous year and was somewhat of a social outcast. His very appearance was disconcerting because his habitual attire—complete with pith helmet and dark glasses—was so extreme as to be a caricature of colonial dress. Moreover, his marital situation was highly irregular. Rumored to be divorced, he had arrived in Pnom Penh with an attractive woman companion whom he presented as his daughter's governess. His manner was distant, haughty, austere; he had "a harsh disposition," according to a contemporary. He also gave the distinct impression of being resentful that the Colonial Office had ignored his superior intellectual abilities and had not advanced him rapidly in his judicial career. It was anticipated that a sharp clash of personalities might develop between this judge and young Malraux.[25]

The first morning of the hearing was given over to the interrogation of the two accused. They were officially charged with having broken parts of the temple of Banteay Srei and of having taken sections of a bas-relief from the site. Present in the courtroom were M. Giordani, the public prosecutor of Pnom Penh; MM. de Parcevaux and Dufond, lawyers for Malraux and Chevasson, respectively; and a legal representative of the Administration, M. Faurie. It was noted that this last official "followed the proceedings for the purpose of intervening as a civil authority if he judged it necessary," [26] but such intervention was not required. Clara Malraux was not in court because some days earlier she had gone to Saigon and boarded a ship for the long voyage back to France. She wanted to be in Paris so that if the judgment went against her husband she would be able to get help from his literary friends there.

Malraux and Chevasson had secretly agreed that it would be best for their defense if one of them took full blame; the other, if acquitted, could immediately return to Paris to prepare an appeal to a higher French court.[27] Since Malraux was better known and had more contacts in Paris, Chevasson had insisted on assuming the entire responsibility for the theft and had affirmed his guilt from the very beginning of the inquiry. At the trial, during the judge's interrogation, he repeated his confession, "admitting the alleged acts and accusing himself of being solely responsible for them." [28] His lawyer could offer little defense for him in the face of these admissions.

For Malraux, the situation was quite different. During much of the proceedings, he acted as his own lawyer. The correspondent for *L'Impartial* described him as "a tall youth, thin, pale, with a beardless face illuminated by two extremely intense eyes. He is very eloquent and defends himself with a keenness that reveals in him unquestionable qualities of energy and tenacity." When interrogated by the presiding judge, he was able to uphold "his position with surprising vigor, refuting all the charges in the indictment." A major contention of the prosecution was that the accused was a mere adventurer, not the scholarly explorer he pretended to be. To prove that he was educated, Malraux replied at length to a variety of questions, going so far as to recite from the *Aeneid* to show that he knew Latin.[29] It was evident that he had an extensive background in many areas, including art. His discussion of ancient Khmer sculpture was so knowledgeable that, as the *Echo du Cambodge* reporter put it, those in the courtroom felt that they had been permitted to "listen to a full-fledged course in archaeology." Although he had never studied the subject formally, Malraux was clearly a gifted archaeologist and an outstanding connoisseur. The principal sculpture he had taken from Banteay Srei, then on display at the Pnom Penh Museum, was being hailed as "one of the most beautiful specimens of Khmer sculpture" ever found.[30]

Although Malraux impressed many in the courtroom with his intellectual gifts, his brilliant and energetic defense was his undoing. After such a demonstration, it was almost impossible to believe that—as Chevasson maintained—he had had no part in the theft. Moreover, his haughty manner and air of superiority obviously irritated Jodin; the judge's questions showed that he was little disposed to admit of any extenuating circumstances or to be lenient with the accused. By the time the court recessed for the midday meal, the two young men were painfully aware that their plan to obtain freedom for at least one of them was not succeeding and that they would probably both be found guilty.

The long afternoon session was given over to the testimony of witnesses. Debyser, the first of these, simply gave a brief narration of the activities of Malraux and Chevasson during the time they were lodged at his bungalow. However, the second witness, Crémazy, recently promoted to a responsible position at Administration headquarters in Pnom Penh, added a significant new dimension to the proceeding. On several points his testimony differed from the account that had been published six months earlier, at the time of the arrests.

According to Crémazy, about a month after Malraux's arrival in Indochina on a mission approved by the Colonial Office, that Office, "belatedly but better informed," had sent to the Governor General and to the Director of the School a "coded telegram" warning them that the young man was "a person to be watched." Crémazy testified that, as the government representative at Siem Reap, he had received this information, which came just before Malraux and Chevasson arrived. He had immediately ordered the pair to be closely watched. From the very beginning, all their actions "were faithfully reported each day by policemen of whom Malraux and Chevasson had absolutely no suspicion." He stated that he had alerted Parmentier, but that the latter had refused to take the matter at all seriously. When the Malraux expedition returned from the jungle, Crémazy immediately sent word to the authorities in Pnom Penh; later, he informed them that the crates had been loaded onto the riverboat for shipment to Saigon.[31]

Malraux and his lawyer vigorously protested that much of this testimony was unsupported by any documents in the trial dossier. In cross-questioning Crémazy, they demanded to know just what "information" furnished to the Colonial Office had cast suspicion on Malraux, and when. Why was he "to be watched," and what was the precise text of the mysterious coded telegram? Had the government delegate at Siem Reap become suspicious of the young archaeologist the moment he arrived, or only when Debyser had reported the extra baggage with which Malraux had returned from the jungle? Were there any reasons that might have led this government witness to alter his presentation of the facts?

To all these questions, Crémazy made vague and evasive replies, alleging that he could not give more precise information because it would involve confidential government matters. The defense heatedly declared that a trial for the theft of archaeological remains could hardly be connected with state secrets, but its protests were to no avail. Crémazy's damaging and uncorroborated testimony stood. As Malraux later wrote bitterly, he was convicted on the basis of "coded items slipped into the dossier but not translated, and labeled 'Not to be communicated to the defense because of their confidential political character.' " [32]

Parmentier was the day's third witness. As head of the Archaeological Service, he was open to criticism for his failure to include Banteay Srei in the list of monuments to be classified, and he was not eager to paint an alluring picture of the site. As he described it, the temple was little more than a pile of stone rubble lost in the jungle. Still, as a responsible scholar, he was obliged to expand on what he had suggested in his 1919 essay: that the quality of its sculptured decoration was indeed remarkable; that he regretted the School had not cleared the site sooner. Questioned as to the damage done by Malraux and Chevasson in obtaining their carvings, he noted that they had apparently been obliged to break into the corner walls of a tower. He hastened to add, however, that the sculptured surfaces had been removed with very great care "by means of picks and stone saws," a task that must have taken several days. He concluded his testimony with words of praise for the flair shown by the two young amateurs.[33]

The remainder of the session was devoted to corroborative testimony by the police inspector who had directed the search on board the river steamer at Pnom Penh, and to statements by the fourteen Annamites and Cambodians who had been the servants and drivers for the expedition.[34] These simple men apparently were reluctant to say what the prosecution required of them, and Malraux later sarcastically suggested that their statements were a tribute to the Sûreté's skill in "the art of making silent farmers speak." [35] Their testimony simply confirmed the government's version of the theft in the jungle.

Malraux was frustrated and angry when court finally recessed for the day. He had been fortunate in having an honest Examining

Magistrate to prepare most of the case, and he had probably nurtured the hope that he would receive at least the semblance of a fair hearing. He had been wrong. Crémazy and the secret dossier had been a severe blow, but even more ominous was the attitude of the presiding judge. As Malraux described him, he was much more concerned with several "attractive ladies who had been given 'good seats' " than with the defense presentation; he turned "from time to time to smile at them with a knowing air." [36] However, he did seem to have respect for Malraux's lawyer because "he incessantly prevented him from speaking." Malraux later lashed out with bitter sarcasm at Jodin's strange view of this fundamental element of the legal process: "In itself, the defense is a harmful institution. Deplorably, it stands in opposition to the Administration which, as everyone well knows, is the very foundation of the State. It dares to try and make the acts of the accused understood, a thing which—if laws were well made—would suffice to send lawyers to prison." [37] Jodin's unfavorable attitude toward Malraux and Chevasson may have been due to his sincere conviction as to their guilt, compounded by a personality clash. But he was certainly not unaware of the Administration's interest in the case. He may have been hoping that his conduct would gain him favor with his superiors.

The closing arguments of both prosecution and defense were heard during the second morning of the trial, on Thursday, July 17. Chevasson's attorney respectfully asked the court to take into consideration the sober and blameless life that his client had previously led, but Malraux's lawyer took a very different tack. He maintained that no crime had been committed because the ruined Banteay Srei had never been officially classified as an "historic monument" by the colonial government. Even if it had been, the classification would be invalid because the temple was not under the jurisdiction of that authority. Although he developed these points at length with appropriate legal documentation, Judge Jodin refused to entertain an argument that would tend to raise jurisdictional questions. Nor would he take into account any mitigating circumstances. On the following Monday morning, July 21, he handed down the severe sentences requested by the public prosecutor: for Malraux, three years in prison and a five-year prohibition of residence in Indochina; for Chevasson, eighteen months in prison. Both young men were ruled ineligible for a suspended sentence, and they had to relinquish all claims on the sculpture in favor of the government.[38]

This severity was legally unjustified because it did not take into account a number of extenuating circumstances—the age of the accused, the modest proportions of the "crime," the reluctance of two examining magistrates to turn in an indictment, the secret nature of the administrative dossier, and most important of all, the uncertain legal status of the temple. As the defense lawyer had argued, in point of law the ruin was apparently still unclassified and was perhaps not even within the jurisdiction of the colonial authorities to classify. Malraux and Chevasson may well have believed in good faith that the site was abandoned, a *res derelicta.* Both the prosecution and defense attorneys wished to clarify this legal point—for totally different reasons, of course—and they both immediately petitioned for a hearing before the Court of Appeals in Saigon. A date in September was set.[39]

During the weeks before the appeal hearing, a furor over the case arose in France. Although a brief reference to a nameless poet's "lively adventures" in Indochina had appeared in the Parisian literary paper *Comoedia* on July 17, 1924—the day the summations were being made in Pnom Penh [40]—the story did not really break in the metropolis until more than two weeks later. On Saturday, August 2, several evening papers carried a brief notice that André Malraux had been sentenced to three years in prison for theft. This news, cabled from Hanoi by the Governor General of Indochina, had evidently been released through the Colonial Office in Paris. The next day, four Parisian newspapers— *Comoedia, L'Eclair, Le Journal,* and *Le Matin*—published follow-up stories. The shortest of these, a single paragraph on an inside page of *Comoedia,* gave no information about the trial except Malraux's sentence. The rest of the item vaunted his creative talents, noting among other things that his prose writings "had a poetic cast" reminiscent of the style of Lautréamont. The editor summed up the feelings of most literary personalities in Paris when he concluded sadly: "Those of our colleagues who knew this young man, a devotee of art in its most original expressions, can only regret this 'adventure' which, alas, is not just an episode in an adventure novel but a very unhappy reality." [41]

The front-page *Eclair* story [42] likewise praised Malraux's remarkable gifts and noted that he was well known in intellectual circles as "the third member (Radiguet and Georges Gabary [*sic*] being the two others) of a youthful trio of astonishing literary precocity." The rest of the brief article was more revealing because it purported to be a factual summary of his crime. These details—later amplified in *The New York Times*—differ considerably from what was disclosed at the trial:

> A few months ago, the police were informed that a certain individual calling himself a man of letters, André Malraux, had entered into relations with an American antiquary and another from Cologne for the purpose of carrying out some thefts from the temples in the Angkor area. This individual left for Indochina with one Louis Chevasson. Upon arriving in Saigon, they were pointed out as suspicious persons to be put under surveillance, which did not prevent them from slipping off to the area of the temples and stealing a certain number of bas-reliefs and statuettes, weighing more than a ton and valued at more than a million francs. As they were preparing to cross the Siamese border, they were arrested and brought before the Pnom Penh court, where they were convicted.

Although the account in *Le Journal* added a number of flourishes—notably gratuitous references to the assiduousness of a certain metropolitan Police Commissioner named Caron—it was essentially a restatement of these "facts." However, its tone was hostile to Malraux personally, alleging that he had not hesitated to "completely sack a temple, breaking statues, pulling apart bas-reliefs, and making off with more than a ton of booty." The story in *Le Matin*, headed "Gentleman Fop Sentenced to Three Years in Prison," was a far more vicious personal attack. The circumstances of the theft were dismissed in a few lines; the bulk of the article was a diatribe against Malraux's personal habits, his liking for cubist and African art, his strange friends, and his vain attempts "to attract attention to himself" by publishing weird novels. It was indeed salutary, concluded the anonymous columnist, that the Pnom Penh court had seen fit to "put an end to [his] love for exotic art and publicity." This outpouring was apparently motivated by a conservative's deep antipathy for the whole group of avant-garde artists and writers, his abhorrence of the way they lived as well as their aesthetic beliefs.

The biographical information in these last three articles was common knowledge among Parisian intellectuals, but where had the newspapers obtained the gross misstatements that they had printed as the "facts" of the theft? The *Journal* story had specifically noted that the Governor General's office in Hanoi had cabled to Paris only the judge's sentence, nothing more. Malraux subsequently pointed out that the mailboat from Indochina took a minimum of twenty-three days; consequently, a courtroom report from Pnom Penh could not have been available to Paris newspapers before mid-August at the earliest.[43] Evidently a local source had furnished the details upon which the erroneous August 3 accounts were based. That source could only be the Colonial Office, which still had in its possession the bulky dossier compiled by the police as well as the records of its own pre-trial administrative inquiry, based on Crémazy's report. Thus, what was presented to the public was not the truth but rather the Colonial Office's biased and uncorroborated version of the truth.

Had it not been early August, the attacks in *Le Journal* and *Le Matin* would have provoked an immediate chorus of rebuttals from Malraux's many friends. But, during the late-summer doldrums, the reaction was delayed. Fortunately, one of those who had remained in Paris was Malraux's first employer, René-Louis Doyon. Astonished when no one rose to the young man's defense, Doyon sent to Léon Treich, a friend who wrote a literary column in *L'Eclair*, a long and eloquent letter urging him to "present a reasoned defense for one of our colleagues, an artist of taste, an author after all, and a young—*very young*—man." [44] Doyon vehemently condemned the injustice of "the comments that the press has abundantly bestowed upon him, augmenting an uncommonly severe sentence." He concluded with the hope that Treich would support "this appeal for justice on behalf of a poet and someone of real distinction." Triech did not agree with Doyon's view, but he published the letter in his August 9 column under the heading "Plea for André Malraux." It was the first move in what Malraux later referred to as a "campaign of rectification."

Clara Malraux, who had returned to Paris to be ready for just such a contingency, immediately thanked Doyon for his help and then set out to "arouse everyone and every milieu" on behalf of her husband and his friend.[45] The poet Max Jacob, one of Malraux's oldest and closest literary friends, was among the first she contacted. Jacob was vacationing in Brittany and apparently did not learn of the newspaper reports until several days later. He wrote to Malraux's mother at the time: "I was informed too late about our misfortune to be the first to act; I was merely the sec-

ond." [46] His protest—like Doyon's—took the form of a letter to
L'Eclair, and it was published in Treich's August 15 column. After
expressing his gratitude for the newspaper's fairness in the "unfortunate affair of the poet André Malraux," Jacob joined Doyon in
asking leniency and sympathetic understanding for the young
man:

> Although averse to amoral behavior, one can ask for indulgence from
> the judges and from the press on behalf of an active intelligence and
> someone of rare distinction. Keen tastes and talents are a source
> of excitement that a very young man resists with difficulty. The
> Pnom Penh judges were perhaps unaware of this kind of extenua-
> ting circumstance and of the caliber of the man whom they con-
> demned. Those who have esteemed him and also those whose own
> youth was somewhat 'spirited' should hope that the case of the
> poet André Malraux will be examined by magistrates in Paris.[47]

Meanwhile, Malraux's friends at the *Nouvelle Revue Française*,
led by Gide and Edmond Jaloux, had also decided to take action
on his behalf. They drew up a petition—subsequently printed on
the front page of the August 16, 1924, issue of *Les Nouvelles
Littéraires*—and circulated it among their colleagues. When an impressive number of signatures had been obtained, the document
was forwarded to the Ministry of Justice, the Ministry of the Interior, and the defense lawyers preparing the appeal in Saigon.
The text was brief and to the point:

> The undersigned, aroused by the sentence handed down against
> André Malraux, have confidence in the concern that the courts
> usually have for those who contribute to the intellectual patrimony
> of our nation. They are eager to attest to the intelligence and
> genuine literary value of this individual, whose youth and present
> achievements permit very great hopes. They would vigorously deplore
> the loss resulting from the imposition of a punishment that would
> prevent André Malraux from accomplishing what everyone had a
> right to expect from him.[48]

Among those who signed it, in addition to Gide and Jaloux, were
François Mauriac, Maurois, Rivière, Roger Martin du Gard,
Gallimard, Fels, Louis Aragon, Pia, Breton, and Marcel Arland.
The grand old man of French letters, Anatole France, went so far
as to write and sign a personal note across the bottom of the docu-

ment: "To André Malraux, with all my sympathy in these difficult hours." Malraux later acknowledged that he was very proud that nearly fifty of the foremost literary figures in France had joined in this appeal.[49]

Unfortunately, many conservative *littérateurs* and columnists were not so charitable, and as time went by Parisian literary gatherings buzzed with unsavory rumors.[50] One story said that the Prime Minister of Belgium had been at Angkor in December and had seen Malraux arrive at the local Governor's residence with his cartloads of booty.[51] Roland Dorgelès, a member of the Goncourt Academy, told friends that while he had been touring Cambodia in January, he had seen Malraux in Pnom Penh being "led off between two policemen." [52] He made no secret of his hope that the young lawbreaker would be dealt with severely. It was rumored that the Malraux case had caused a dispute between two highly placed government officers—Albert Sarraut, the Colonial Minister, and Philippe Berthelot, a young politician who greatly admired Malraux's intelligence and energy. However, in the light of later developments, the most interesting tale maintained that Malraux had been involved with an Indochinese political group agitating for liberal reforms and eventual independence for the colony, and that the Colonial Administration had been severe with him in order to discourage such harmful activity.[53]

As a result of these stories and of Clara's requests, several more of Malraux's friends were aroused to protest his treatment. The August 25 issue of *L'Eclair* carried a letter, signed by Marcel Arland, André Breton, François Mauriac, and Jean Paulhan, protesting "the condemnation of André Malraux and the more or less base commentaries with which certain newspapers greeted it." The writers earnestly requested the support of other intellectuals so that at the appeal hearing, account would be taken of his "intelligence and genuine literary value." [54] A short time later, André Breton, who had signed several of these petitions even though he did not know Malraux personally, issued a long personal declaration, "For André Malraux," which appeared on the front page of the September 6 issue of *Les Nouvelles Littéraires*. Three years in prison for the "rape of two or three stone dancers" was excessively severe, he argued, particularly for a writer of Malraux's talent. His two works, *Paper Moons* and *Written for a Trunked Idol*, were "part of today's most esoteric intellectual activity . . . remarkable experiments in a laboratory where the mass of the public is not admitted." It was precisely Malraux's poetic modernism and his "understanding of cubist painting" that had been largely responsible for his heavy prison sentence, because most people regarded such leanings as clear "evidence of immorality."

The most moving plea for Malraux was the introduction that Marcel Arland wrote for two excerpts from *Written for a Trunked Idol* published in his review *Accords*. After praising the courage and probity of "one of the finest of today's young leaders," Arland explained that his friend Malraux had undertaken an "adventure" in the jungles of Cambodia because he was filled with torment, an anguish that literature—the manipulation of words—could no longer assuage. He continued:

> If one can speak of anguish, it is certainly in connection with this man who at the age of twenty-three has lived more, thought more, suffered more, than most of those who are officially elders. His admirable intelligence intensifies this torment; it has flung him toward all the possibilities that presented themselves to him one after another; he envisions them, often gives in to them; but he retains the lucidity that nurtures him until the end—an intensity that makes an artist of him, and a restlessness that ceaselessly pushes him forward.[55]

Malraux later disclosed that these petitions had been initiated without his knowledge or consent. However, when the Paris newspapers finally reached Saigon by mailboat and he saw the slanderous articles, he declared: "Now that I have read them, I can only be infinitely grateful to my friends for having acted without consulting me and for having defended me against what were truly the attacks of lackeys—whose courage in attacking someone in absentia is equaled only by their complete ignorance of the facts." [56]

The press in Indochina was as vicious as that in Paris. Shortly after the judgment was handed down in Pnom Penh on July 21, Malraux and Chevasson went to Saigon to begin preparing their appeal, scheduled to go before the Saigon court on September 23. The principal Saigon newspaper was *L'Impartial*, an ultraconservative daily, unofficially subsidized by the Administration. Its editor was a corrupt man named Henry Chavigny, self-styled de la Chevrotière.[57] He liked to pose as the champion of virtue and public morality, especially if it meant attacking a "Bolshevik," his label for anyone with a liberal idea.

Chavigny had shown an early interest in the case with his inflammatory editorial on "Vandals and Pillagers of Ruins" a few days after Malraux's arrest. Later, he had dispatched a "special correspondent" to Pnom Penh to cover the proceedings in detail. A long account appeared on the front page of *L'Impartial* on Monday and Tuesday, July 21 and 22. Only two-thirds of the story was a factual report of what had happened in the courtroom; the remaining paragraphs were an attempt to bolster the newspaper's earlier contention that Malraux's theft was in reality a huge financial exploit. After praising the beauty of the sculpture, the article insinuated that some "rich English or Yankee connoisseur" had been waiting to acquire them for "a sizable figure in dollars." The reporter noted that it had long been the custom for antique dealers to make annual visits to ruins in the Angkor area, where they "collected" numerous pieces of sculpture. One such dealer, a Mr. Bing, had carried off a number of carved heads from Angkor some three years earlier. These pieces, although less beautiful than Malraux's, ultimately had been sold to the Cleveland Museum for well over $8,000 each. The implication, of course, was that Malraux's booty had been worth a great deal more.

Chavigny himself, apparently feeling that his correspondent had failed to develop the financial motive sufficiently, wrote a companion front-page editorial headed "Let Us Protect the Artistic and Archaeological Treasures of Indochina" and accompanied by four large photographs. In it, Chavigny bitterly attacked the two "vandals," "unscrupulous collectors," who had stolen priceless works of art from the Angkor ruins. He lamented that "thefts of this type are unfortunately more frequent than is supposed, and we can only regret not having been able to record more numerous arrests. . . . How many pagodas in Cambodia, Laos, and Annam have been stripped of their buddhas! The time is not long gone when veritable boatloads of buddhas went down the Mekong to end up enriching some collections, if not just to enrich shrewd local fanciers." Happily, Malraux and his accomplice had been arrested before they could make off with their "tidy little fortune," and an example should be made of them so that such thefts would cease. The archaeological sites must be preserved intact, Chavigny concluded, "for the future of tourism in Indochina." This obsession with the mercenary aspects of the case provides an interesting insight into the values of this man. That Chavigny was acting in bad faith was flagrantly evident from the photographs that accompanied his editorial. Three showed sculpture from Banteay Srei that had figured in the trial—but the fourth was of the great temple at Angkor Wat. Obviously the intent was to mislead readers into believing that the sculpture had been taken from that famous site rather than from a ruin half-buried in the jungle.

In view of this, and the fact that on September 5 *L'Impartial* had published the harsh article from *Le Matin,* it is difficult to understand why Malraux consented to give a long interview to Chavigny's newspaper a little more than a week before his appeal was to be heard. He even went to its offices to be photographed.[58] He may have hoped that his cooperation would mollify Chavigny, or that firsthand knowledge of his side of the case would cause the editor to print a fairer report of the appeal proceedings. Perhaps it was simply an act of bravado by an impetuous and haughty young man. Whatever the reason, it soon became clear that granting the interview had been a mistake; it only furnished Chavigny with more material for his diatribes. Since Malraux was very voluble, the reporter came away with a sheaf of notes. These were reduced to a column-long account that was published on the front page of the September 16 issue of *L'Impartial* under the deliberately misleading heading "The Affair of the Angkor Statues—The Pronouncements of M. André Malraux."

"Swept-back blond hair, a pale complexion, eyes by turn flaming bright, then clouded by melancholy, perhaps also with regret"— this was how the young "man of letters and art lover" appeared to the Saigon newspaperman. When the reporter asked about the insulting articles that had appeared in *Le Journal* and *Le Matin,* Malraux replied archly that they were "foolishness, concierges' gossip" bearing little relation to the truth. The furnishings of his Paris home were not "wildly cubist," nor did they include "copies of the Angkor sculptures." He disclosed that these slanderous attacks would soon be balanced by a "campaign of rectification" to be undertaken by two other dailies, *L'Eclair* and *L'Intransigeant.* Moreover, he had learned that "French intellectual circles are being aroused by my fate" and that petitions were being circulated on his behalf.

Questioned about charges that he had pillaged a temple of more than a ton of statues, Malraux replied that it was difficult to characterize as a temple "a pile of stones whose height does not exceed four feet," and added the half-truth that the ruin had yielded nothing but "a few mutilated bas-reliefs." Contrary to what several newspapers had tried to suggest, the Angkor ruins were not involved at all: "It was not a question of the temple of Banteay Srei located twelve miles from Angkor, which at the present time is a very holy pagoda, but rather of a group of destroyed temples of the same name indicated by a certain Lieutenant in his circuit report. We had to travel nearly forty miles by ox cart in order finally to reach it." Asked to give reasons for his arrest and for the unrelenting attitude of the local authorities, Malraux could suggest only that perhaps it was believed—because of his father's position and his own earlier activities on the Paris stock exchange—that he was in Indochina on a secret commercial mission. Evidently some people even thought that he was somehow working for the Germans; at the Pnom Penh trial he had been called a *boche*.

The interview as it appeared in *L'Impartial* made Malraux seem somewhat of a fop. For example, he was quoted as having said: "I am rich and am able to indulge myself in literary efforts as well as to collaborate on periodicals," and as boasting that his father was "in charge of the affairs of one of the biggest oil companies in the world." However, since raising objections to the article's misrepresentation would only bring down more notoriety on himself just before his appeal, Malraux probably would have remained silent, if Chavigny had not appended a final paragraph of editorial comment to the interview. These remarks suggested, among other things, that the forthcoming *Eclair-Intransigeant* campaign would be a blatant attempt to influence the judges of the Court of Appeals in Malraux's favor. This gratuitous statement brought an immediate and lengthy reply from Malraux. Under French law, Chavigny was forced to print it on the front page of the following issue, on September 17.

Malraux explained that the articles in *L'Eclair* and *L'Intransigeant* were to be part of a "campaign that has nothing to do with the sentence and is limited to correcting calumnies by the French newspapers that concern me personally." As for any attempts by newspapers to influence the legal decision, everyone knew that on this count *L'Impartial*, the "newspaper of the government," was a model of integrity. It was a newspaper that never

attempted to lead people to believe that the impounded sculpture had been taken from Angkor; that did not publish—at the same time as the account of the trial—a photograph of Angkor Wat; that did not on the same day publish an article asking for an exemplary sentence, just as if that article represented public opinion—said public opinion being about as interested in Banteay Srei as in the man in the moon; that even today did not entitle its interview "The Affair of the Angkor Statues," even though neither statues nor Angkor is involved; and that is not going to try—in replying to this answer—to instigate a further polemic for purposes that are clearly disinterested.

Chavigny, in publishing this biting letter, accompanied it with several paragraphs of editorial comment calculated to embitter the dispute further, just as Malraux had predicted. After vigorously denying that *L'Impartial* was a government paper and affirming his personal objectivity, Chavigny wrote:

I note . . . that M. Malraux does not fear . . . publicity centering on his person. This man of letters, who doubles as an art collector, knows how to keep public opinion interested, and his trial will most certainly not pass unnoticed. . . . In any case, he seems to us to be the sort of man to profit from the situation, if only by writing the adventures of an art collector at the Angkor site.

This immediately brought forth another angry retort from Malraux. His second open letter to Chavigny was published on the front page of *L'Impartial* the following day, Thursday, September 18, under the heading "M. Malraux Protests Again." After accusing Chavigny of deliberate provocation, Malraux observed that there was considerable risk for him in engaging in such polemics: "Have I anything to gain . . . by replying to you? Certainly not. I may even lose a great deal. However, sir, this is perhaps not sufficient reason for me to keep silent." Returning to the editor's motivation for attacking him so intemperately, he asked Chavigny how he would have felt if—during the editor's 1916 trial for bribery and blackmail—a local newspaper had tried to "create a hostile public opinion" as *L'Impartial* was presently doing. "Since you know that this matter is to be responsibly adjudicated right here, why don't you wait for the trial?" Malraux demanded. Referring to Chavigny's remark that he, Malraux, would one day use the whole episode as the basis for a novel, he concluded: "I shall not relate the adventures of an art collector at Angkor, first of all because the collector of whom you speak didn't have any adventures at Angkor, and second because I do not write adventure novels." Malraux evidently intended that *The Royal Way*, the book he had already begun to write about the Banteay Srei experience, would not be an adventure novel in the usual meaning of the term.

Chavigny was furious at Malraux's reference to his criminal record, which of course he was compelled to print, and he appended a bombastic but totally unconvincing essay of self-justification. He then dropped the subject until the following Monday, September 22, the day before Malraux's appeal was scheduled to be heard. The front page of *L'Impartial* carried an article that filled two columns, plus several photographs, to recall details of the case to the Saigon public. The text was a slight reworking of Pnom Penh correspondent's account published on July 21, but the blaring headline—"The Malraux-Chevasson Affair—The Theft of the Bas-Reliefs from Angkor"—was another attempt to inflame public opinion by misleading statements. Malraux later charged that when the Court of Appeals convened the following morning, Chavigny had had "distributed in the courtroom, during a trial supposedly about bas-reliefs" the article that he had written against the accused.[59] Fortunately for Malraux, the maneuver backfired. This blatant effort to influence the judicial process caused the judges to grant Malraux a postponement of two weeks so that his case could be heard in an atmosphere less prejudicial to him; his hearing was rescheduled for the morning of Wednesday, October 8, 1924. The court evidently warned Chavigny about his conduct, because *L'Impartial's* reporting of those proceedings is remarkably moderate in tone.

Both of Malraux's letters to *L'Impartial* referred to the legal basis on which this hearing before the Court of Appeals had been granted. He had remarked that "the prosecution was no more satisfied than the defense" with the outcome of the trial in Pnom Penh and that both parties had requested a review of it. Chavigny stated that the public prosecutor, "judging that the sentence was too lenient," was seeking to have it increased. He also suggested that the defendants were hoping to obtain "the pure and simple dismissal" of their sentences. Strictly speaking, neither of Chavigny's statements was true. Both prosecution and defense appeals were based not on the sentence but rather on a point of law —the relevance of the Colonial Office's decrees. In his reply to Chavigny's allegations, Malraux refused to comment on his own position, but he took pains to point out that the government's petition was "an *unspecified* appeal. . . . Far from leading—as you believe—to a request for an increase in the sentence, this appeal instead places the whole trial in question before the appellate court." The legal point raised was so interesting and important that a number of Saigon lawyers came to hear the final summation by Malraux's attorney at the appeal hearing.

The first two sessions took place on October 8. That day, *L'Impartial* carried a very short notice about "The Malraux-Chevasson Affair," noting only that the morning had been given over to a long and detailed recital of the facts of the case by the presiding judge, M. Gaudin. During the afternoon, the government prosecutor, Moreau, made a three-hour presentation, which was reported at length the next day. Moreau first attempted to show that the crime had been premeditated and to "prove that in all circumstances it had been Malraux who had played the primary role." He called the latter "vainglorious, and a liar," and not the educated scholar he claimed to be. He commented in detail on each aspect of the adventure, from the authorization of the expedition by the Colonial Office to the loading of the stolen sculptures onto the riverboat for Saigon.

Turning to the point of law involved, Moreau argued that a theft had indeed been committed, because the ruins were not "abandoned property." Siam, formerly their owner by right of conquest, had ceded that ownership to France in a 1907 treaty that surrendered all Siamese claims to the provinces of Battambang, Sisophon, and Siem Reap. In turn, the French Government had—by a decree of the President of the Republic—ceded these territories to the King of Cambodia. Although the precise legal status of the ruins in these areas was not absolutely clear, it was certain that they belonged to someone—either the French Government or the Cambodian Crown—and that Malraux and Chevasson had committed a theft and should be punished. Moreau asked for Chevasson simply a confirmation of the judgment of the Pnom Penh court. For Malraux, however, he asked not only that the Pnom Penh sentence be upheld but that the residence prohibition be increased to the maximum permitted by law, and that the young man "forfeit his civil rights."

The court reconvened the following afternoon to hear the summations of the two defense lawyers, which were reported at great length in the October 10 and 11 issues of *L'Impartial*. Since the central part of the defense was based on a question of law concerning the ownership and status of the Banteay Srei ruins, some two hours—most of the session—were given over to an exposition of this problem. Malraux's lawyer, M. Béziat, undertook this task. He conceded that the area in which the Banteay Srei ruin was located had been given to France by the 1907 treaty with Siam, and further, that, by order of the Governor General of Indochina, a week after ratification of this treaty the territory had been turned over to the Cambodian Crown, an act confirmed by a decree of the French President some eight years later, in 1915. But since only the French legislature was legally empowered to dispose of French territory, it followed that any subsequent government decrees could affect only its *political* status. Legally, it remained a part of France, subject to French laws and to the French executive authority, not to the directives of the Colonial Office. These points were delicate, and as the *Impartial* reporter pointed out, they could have far-reaching legal consequences.

Béziat cited a number of precedents and decisions in French law that established the government's obligation to issue a decree specifically naming a monument or national treasure before it could be considered legally "classified." Banteay Srei had not been so classified. Therefore, the acts attributed to his client did not "fall under the provisions of any law" on the books. He pointed out that it would have been a simple matter for the appropriate French executive authority to protect the temple remains in question. As early as 1916, Parmentier had visited the ruin and drawn up a survey of it. This study "made its classification marvelously easy. A decree citing M. Parmentier's work would have sufficed. It certainly appears that no one was further interested in these dilapidated buildings . . . isolated in the jungle." In any event, since they had not been classified by a competent authority, they were legally *res derelictae*, available to anyone who wished to take possession of them.

Béziat then undertook to discredit the prosecution's contention that Malraux was simply a rapacious adventurer, that he could not be of any intellectual stature since he had only a high-school education. From his bulging brief case, he drew a series of letters and articles attesting to Malraux's literary and intellectual gifts. His writings had been praised in critical studies by Henry Bordeaux and Edmond Jaloux, members of the French Academy, and by various other authors, including François Mauriac, André Breton, Pierre MacOrlan, André Maurois, Henri de Régnier, and Guy de Pourtalès. Gide had written Malraux a letter in which he had lauded his study, published in *Action*, of *Les Nourritures Terrestres*, telling him that it gave evidence "of singular penetration and insight." Charles Maurras had written to ask him to prepare an introduction to his *Mademoiselle Monk*; Salmon had sought his opinion on the literary talent of an unknown young writer. Marcel Arland had sent an open letter which he spoke of his great personal admiration for Malraux's work and affirmed its influence on other writers of the young generation. Finally the Gide-Jaloux petition, with its impressive list of nearly fifty names, was introduced to support the contention that Malraux was indeed a writer of great promise.

Counselor Gallois, Chevasson's lawyer, spoke briefly since the major points of law had been developed at length by his colleague Béziat. After outlining his client's involvement in the affair, he painted Chevasson as a sober and hard-working young man. He maintained that neither he nor Malraux merited the label of "highwayman" that the prosecution had gratuitously applied to them. Moreover, if these two young men were to be imprisoned for taking the sculpture from Banteay Srei, should not the same penalty be exacted from the various Governors, High Commissioners, and administrators of Indochina who had done the very same thing to similar monuments? When enormous frauds involving public funds and even murders of Indochinese were dealt with so lightly in the colonial courts, why should this peccadillo be blown up out of all proportion and punishment for it be so severe? "We should not thus exaggerate the importance of an act committed by two adolescents who, after all, have their youth as an excuse. Reduced to its true proportions, the affair does not justify —far from it—the commotion made about it." Moreover, was it not strange that the Government, which had allegedly delegated agents to spy on the young archaeologists and therefore knew what they were doing, had not warned them of the danger they were running, instead of waiting until the crime had been committed? In any event, he concluded, "Haven't we, after all, in the very recent past settled other such affairs amiably, even when they involved thefts of greater value?"

The documentation and eloquence of the defense lawyers apparently had at least some influence on the three magistrats of the Court of Appeals. Their ruling, handed down three weeks later, on October 28, reduced Malraux's punishment to one year in prison, Chevasson's to eight months, and granted both prisoners the right to petition for a suspended sentence. However, the judges upheld the order of the Pnom Penh court requiring that ownership of the sculpture be ceded to the state.[60]

Malraux immediately announced that he and Chevasson would appeal to the Court of Cassation in Paris, the highest court of appeal in France. Not only was a point of honor involved; he was determined to recover possession of the sculpture from Banteay Srei. He remained stubbornly convinced that legally and morally he had a greater right to it than did the State. Unfortunately, Malraux never obtained a conclusive decision. When the School restored Banteay Srei in 1925, Malraux's sculpture was simply taken from storage in the Pnom Penh museum and replaced in the temple wall, where it still is today. The final disposition of the theft charges remains obscure, but it is generally believed that sometime in the 1930's they were either dropped entirely or that the sentences were reduced to a minimum and suspended.[61]

III

Indochine is Born

Four days after the Court of Appeals handed down its decision, Malraux sailed from Saigon aboard the *Chantilly*.[1] He was returning to France to prepare his appeal to the Court of Cassation in Paris, the highest appellate court in France. He had other pressing business, too. He had never been concerned with political matters before coming to Indochina, but, during his stay on the peninsula, he had come to realize the oppressiveness of the system under which the natives in the colony lived. What he had suffered at his trial made him all the more conscious of the injustices that the Colonial Administration was inflicting on those under its control. He did not hesitate to make his feelings known, and he soon met a few others, both Frenchmen and Indochinese, who shared his anger and disgust. The group decided that the most effective weapon against the abuses of the government was an opposition newspaper, and Malraux was commissioned to make all the preliminary arrangements for the venture during his trip to Paris.

Malraux's principal collaborator in this project was an outstanding lawyer, newspaperman, and politician from Saigon, Paul Monin. He had come to Pnom Penh probably in the late winter or early spring of 1924, either for political reasons—he was a member of the Colonial Council, the highest elective body in the colony—or to defend some "unpopular" client.[2] It was not surprising that he and Malraux should meet and quickly become friends. Lawyers like Monin had long been among the most vociferous opponents of the Colonial Administration's suppression of civil liberties.

Later in the spring, Monin went to France on political matters. He did not return to Saigon until October 16, 1924, a few days before the Court of Appeals decision on the Malraux-Chevasson case.[3] Talking with political friends in the metropolis had convinced Monin that an opposition newspaper was an indispensable preliminary to any reform of the arch-conservative government of Cochinchina. Since Malraux was leaving for Paris and had many contacts in literary circles there, Monin asked him to make the necessary publishing arrangements for the proposed newspaper. In the two weeks before the sailing of the Chantilly, plans were completed and a sizable sum of money was contributed by Monin's Annamite supporters. It was understood that any additional funds required would be raised by Malraux in France.[4]

The *Chantilly* docked in Marseilles during the last week in November, 1924. Malraux immediately went to Paris.[5] There he called on everyone who had come to his support at the time of the trial, to proffer his heartfelt thanks. Among the literary personalities he saw was Daniel Halévy, director of the successful *Cahiers Verts* series put out by the publishing firm Grasset.[6] When Halévy in 1920 had agreed to organize this project, he had made it clear to Grasset that he wanted to publish not only novels by promising young writers but also "those forms of intellectual expression that seemed to be declining—the essay, the letter, the political tract, the dialogue." [7] Halévy was therefore interested to learn that Malraux had partly finished an essay, "a rather special work touching on metaphysics" (evidently a preliminary version of *The Temptation of the West*), and he agreed to publish it.[8]

Malraux made several trips to see his father and stepmother in Orléans.[9] On one of these visits, he stopped off to see the man who had first recognized and encouraged his literary talent, Max Jacob. The older man had retired from the intellectual life of Paris to the seclusion of Saint-Benoît-sur-Loire, a few miles east of Orléans. During the ensuing visits at Saint-Benoît, Malraux urged Jacob to go to the Far East with him on his return. He even made Jacob the generous offer of $3,000 and expenses to undertake a lecture tour in China. Their discussions about the Orient were mainly literary and philosophical, rather than political; Jacob was surprised that Malraux made no mention of "prisons, revolutions, ransoms, famine, etc." [10]

In his seven weeks in France, Malraux may have had some contact with the many groups, both French and Annamite, that were agitating for political reforms in the colony. He may even have talked with some government officials. However, he spent much of his time obtaining material for the proposed newspaper. He and Monin had resolved at the start that not only would their publication be a liberal organ for local causes, but that it would also be of the highest quality, since the intellectual level was incredibly low in almost all the French-language papers in Saigon. In Paris, Malraux first contacted A. Fayard and Co., publishers of the recently founded French weekly *Candide*, to which a number of important French writers regularly contributed. During December and early January, he had several discussions with the directors of Fayard, and finally obtained exclusive rights to publish in Indochina "all articles, short stories, tales, news items, etc. . . . or in general all the texts that make up our weekly *Candide*." For these rights, he was to pay in advance $6,000 a year, in quarterly installments.[11] He then entered into negotiations with the Messageries de Journaux, a branch of the publishing house of Hachette that specialized in special supplements for daily and weekly newspapers, and finally accepted their terms. A confirming letter, dated January 22, gave his newspaper the distribution rights for a number of supplements, including *Miroir des Sports, Canard Enchaîné, Merle Blanc, Dimanche Illustré*, and later, *Petit Echo de la Mode*.[12]

In the middle of January, 1925, barely seven weeks after his return to France, Malraux and his wife went to Marseilles, where they took third-class passage on the mailboat for Indochina.[13] It is not clear why they chose to travel third class, but financial considerations apart, it may have been because they wished to avoid the offensive French colonials in first and second class. The long trip gave them an excellent opportunity to meet many Indochinese returning home, and to learn from them more about the political situation in the colony.

Malraux's activities during the next four months are obscure. After the ship docked in Saigon, in mid-February, 1925, he apparently traveled widely over the whole peninsula. In late April or early May, he was in Annam. Monin telegraphed him there to ask for help in obtaining the release of a Chinese friend arrested for being a member of the Kuomintang, the Chinese Nationalist Party.[14] Malraux thereupon went to Hanoi, where he eventually succeeded in obtaining at least one interview with the *chef de cabinet* of the Acting Governor General, Monguillot.[15] Later events clearly indicate that he became involved in anti-government

political agitation during these months before he began to publish
his newspaper, but no precise details are available.

The years 1924 and 1925 were a period of considerable political
activity in Indochina, most of it directed against the reactionary
Colonial Administration. In spite of constant harassment by the
Sûreté and frightened local Annamite administrators, nationalist
movements were growing in Tonkin, Annam, and Cochinchina,
the three coastal sections of French Indochina. In Saigon, the demands for governmental reform were particularly insistent. Bui-
quang-Chieu, head of the Indochinese Constitutionalist Party;
Nguyen-phu-Hai, editor of the recently closed independent paper
Tribune Indigène: Phan-boi-Chau, a famous patriot; Dejean de
la Batie, a reporter on *L'Echo Annamite;* and above all, Nguyen
An Ninh, editor of *La Cloche Fêlée,* an "organ of democratic
persuasion"—men like these kept the question of political reform
very much alive. Their articles and speeches are invaluable indi-
cators of the frustration and anger felt by the whole native community. The Colonial Administration was not interested in reforms, however; its only concern was to silence these agitators as
quickly as possible.

The general attitude of Annamite intellectuals toward French
rule is exemplified by Nguyen An Ninh, one of Monin's closest
friends. In a speech that later appeared as an article in *La Cloche
Fêlée,* he castigated the French for what they had done in Indochina.[16] By sending out greedy "louts" to govern the colony, instead of enlightened intellectuals, the Colonial Office in Paris had
greatly lowered the cultural level of the Annamites in a very short
time. By a series of repressive actions, short-sighted and authoritarian colonial administrators had reduced the native peoples to
complete servitude. To call these colonials "bearers of light" and
"miracle workers in Asia" was a supreme irony. As for the economic development of the peninsula, one could only cite a series
of financially ruinous enterprises that had bled the country white
to the exclusive profit of Frenchmen.

Ninh felt that this program of "unbridled exploitation," organized by a veritable army of civil servants, was not in keeping with
the traditions of French civilization, which, he was convinced, was
a great civilization and one which could play an important role in
the transformation of Annamite culture. In fact, the elite among
the native peoples were truly eager to have France bring its intel-

lectual heritage "to contribute to the nurturing of our scholars and creative artists." However, he pointedly concluded, for this alien culture to be successfully assimilated, it was necessary to permit the Annamites to have "freedom of choice, absolute freedom. All coercion brings on indigestion, and indigestion can be fatal."

It was evident that Ninh was opposed not to the civilization of France but to the French colonial government. He developed his position further in an article that appeared in the liberal Parisian review *Europe:* [17] to remain in control of their colony, the French administrators constantly reiterated the shibboleth of European superiority; no Annamite, however gifted, could ever be the equal of a Frenchman. In his homeland, even the rare native who obtained French citizenship was treated like a conquered subject. Was this dominance of Europeans based on any real moral or intellectual superiority, asked Ninh? Did the French Administration remain in power because it was *better* than any Annamite government could have been? Obviously not. The whole colonial system, as the French "louts" understood it, was based on physical force, primarily the coercive power of the political police, the Sûreté. Such a regime was quick to curtail any activities that might endanger it, and consequently, the colony had become an authoritarian state in which the basic French laws were inoperative.

One of the most flagrant abuses of civil liberties in Cochinchina was the muzzling of the press. A loophole in local regulations permitted a group of Annamites to establish a French-language paper if they could find a French citizen to act as its guarantor, but such a paper would reach only the French-speaking minority of the population. As Ninh pointed out, the Vietnamese who knew French were usually government employees, and it was easy for their European superiors to prevent them from reading such "subversive" writings until the Administration could find a pretext on which to shut down the paper permanently. However, a newspaper in *quoc-ngu*, the romanized form of the Annamite language, could reach a large part of the native population because in most towns there was at least one person literate in this script who could read the news to his neighbors. Government regulations therefore made it virtually impossible to start such a dangerous enterprise. The prospective editor was required first to obtain preliminary authorization from the Governor of Cochinchina. After this, he had to bring each issue to the official censor for approval *before* it could be printed. Finally, he must agree never to discuss any political matters. The last two conditions were largely academic, since the Governor never gave preliminary authorization to any newspaper that did not promise unequivocal support to his Administration.

The government similarly prohibited printers from publishing any unauthorized manuscripts, under threat of prison. If a book was political, excuses always were found to delay the necessary permission indefinitely. It was forbidden to import books freely into the colony, especially those written in Chinese characters. Even translations of French authors like Rousseau or Montesquieu came under this ban. Needless to say, Annamites were not allowed to make "dangerous" speeches or meet to discuss any questions that were even remotely political. Moreover, the kinds of organizations that they could form or join were severely restricted.

The government had issued a series of directives designed to prevent Annamites from moving freely within their own country, and to go abroad required a dossier of documents, including a special visa from the police. This visa was rarely given, especially if the Annamite requesting it wanted to study abroad. Ninh cited the editor of the conservative *Courrier Saigonnais,* who had observed that the more education these young Asians received, the more anti-French they seemed to become. They were the ones, the editor said, who were constantly bringing before their countrymen such improper demands as the right to be represented in government councils by freely elected representatives. It was obvious to Ninh that most of the *colons* were convinced that the political status quo must be maintained by any necessary means if France was to continue to exploit her colony.

In view of the injustices of the French regime, it is amazing that the vast majority of Annamite intellectuals continued to agitate for its *reform,* rather than for a revolution that would oust the Europeans. As Ninh summed up the situation:

> Annamites molded by French schooling desire for their people a slow but sure evolution, under French sovereignty, toward the constitutional form of government of European nations. Some among them, enlightened patriots, have even devoted their efforts to trying to show the masses the dangers of revenge and the advantages of a patriotism that accepts evolution, under French sovereignty, toward political liberty as promised in official pronouncements. They believe that collaboration between Frenchmen and Indochinese is possible.

But if the colonials stubbornly continue to deny elementary liberties
to the Annamites, they cannot blame the masses for any violence.
Let France remember all this repressed power.[18]

This was the fundamental position of Malraux and Monin.

Malraux must have worked closely with nationalists like Ninh
during the first four months after his return to Indochina. As a
man of action, he felt strongly compelled to do something more
positive and direct than just writing articles for a newspaper, and
he set about organizing the nationalist program into a political
movement. His group was called Young Annam (Jeune Annam)
obviously after a similarly named organization in China. It was
semi-secret and illegal, and little is known of it, but in a letter he
wrote from Saigon in the autumn of 1925, Malraux called himself
the "head of the Young Annam Party." [19] Several years later, he
stated unequivocally that he had "organized the Young Annam
movement." [20] Among the Annamites associated in it with him
were Ta-thy-Thau and Nguyen-Pho.[21]

In addition to pursuing political activities, Malraux worked with
Monin in the spring of 1925 on their forthcoming newspaper, to
be called *Indochine*. To obtain support and subscriptions, they
printed a brochure which was circulated by French and Vietnamese volunteers in Saigon and in the provincial areas of Cochinchina. The pamphlet announced their program of closer Franco-
Annamite cooperation and plans for an intensive investigation and
exposure of corruption in government. It cited a number of "very
prominent political figures" as sympathetic to a far-reaching reform of the whole Colonial Administration. Finally, the variety
and literary excellence anticipated for the projected newspaper
were underlined, for these qualities would clearly put *Indochine* in
a class well above that of all the other Saigon papers.[22]

Since the two men did not have sufficient capital to purchase a
printing plant, they had to locate a printer who would agree to put
out their paper. This was not easy, since the Administration had
suggested that anyone who helped them might find himself in
difficulties with the Sûreté. But a printer was finally located—
Louis Minh, a French citizen of mixed blood. He published the
Malraux-Monin newspaper until it was closed, for the first time, in
mid-August.

The first issue of *Indochine*, 5,000 copies of which were printed,
appeared on Wednesday, June 17, 1925. Like the following two

editions, it was distributed free in Saigon, Hanoi, and many provincial centers, probably by anti-government patriots belonging to
Young Annam.[23] Malraux and Monin had chosen their moment
well. A new Governor General for Indochina was about to be
named, and a few issues of a crusading newspaper sent to the right
places in Paris might have far-reaching effects. In any case, at least
one strong voice would tell the new appointee arriving in Indochina that the old colonialism was under attack, a fact carefully
concealed by the government-supported papers of Saigon.

The law required that a French citizen be legally responsible for
the paper and that his name be listed on the back page as the
manager. He was to receive the publishing authorization delivered
by the Colonial Administration, and he had to sign the copy of
each issue that, by law, was sent to the Bibliothèque Nationale in
Paris. The manager of *Indochine* was E. Dejean de la Batie, a
métis (of mixed blood) whose father had been a minister plenipotentiary in the colony.[24] It was probably because of his father's
position that the Administration did not dare invent excuses to
refuse an authorization to *Indochine*, even though it was clearly
going to be an opposition paper.

Dejean de la Batie had long been an active reformer in the
colony; the great nationalist leader Phan-chau-Trinh, on returning
to Saigon after a political exile in France, greeted him almost like a
son.[25] An ardent Annamitophile, he had previously been one of
the chief contributors to the French-language Annamite paper
L'Echo Annamite. There, with a number of other Annamites and
métis, he had struggled to obtain justice for "the race from which
my mother comes." [26] His leaving the exclusively Annamite paper
to become associated with two "real Latin Frenchmen" caused
some unfavorable comments among his Vietnamese friends, but
in the sixth issue of *Indochine* Dejean eloquently justified his
move. He also made clear the esteem in which the Malraux-Monin
paper was held by the leaders of the nationalist movement:

> If I have left an exclusively Annamite paper, it is precisely to better
> serve the [Annamite] cause, since now I have powerful means at my
> disposal to bring about its success. I would perhaps have failed in
> my duty if I had refused my assistance to Frenchmen who rush to
> meet the Annamites, their arms outstretched, their hearts open, and
> resolved to make themselves the champions of the legitimate
> demands of the natives.[27]

He remained faithful to this commitment all during the life of *Indochine*, in spite of threats against himself and some of his Annamite relatives.[28]

The guiding force behind *Indochine* was Paul Monin, Malraux's co-editor. Monin had a great reputation among the Annamite intellectuals. Dejean once wrote proudly, "Just the name of M. Monin is a sufficient guarantee of the pro-Annamite character of *Indochine*." [29] A lawyer from Lyons, he was only slightly older than Malraux. Wounds suffered at Verdun apparently had left him partly crippled, as he occasionally had to walk with a cane. He had come out to Indochina after the war and—like Malraux—had evidently contracted a fever or intestinal sickness. Photographs of him show a very thin, angular face and an almost emaciated frame.[30] He joined a French law firm shortly after his arrival in Saigon but resigned in mid-1923, probably to be completely free to defend the Chinese and Annamite communities against governmental injustice. He went into partnership with one Léon Pacès and took offices at 97 Rue Pellerin. A fairly successful lawyer, he purchased a building in Saigon sometime before 1923.

Monin had become involved in politics almost immediately after arriving in the Far East, and in the 1919 elections he ran as an opposition candidate for a seat on the Colonial Council, the highest elective body in Cochinchina. Defeated, he campaigned even more vigorously in 1922 and was elected in spite of strong opposition from the conservatives, led by Chavigny. Although the Administration-controlled leadership of the Council tried to bury the young lawyer in the innocuous Livestock Committee, they could do nothing to silence him during the General Sessions. There Monin always spoke out strongly against governmental abuses, and in the Council voting he usually sided with his Annamite colleagues. Sometimes he even led them, notably in their fight against giving members of the Sûreté special rewards based on the number of smugglers or political agitators they arrested. He opposed this practice because it had led to extensive abuses and "frame-ups." [31]

French parliamentary elections were scheduled for mid-1924, and it was evident that Monin would be a very strong candidate to represent Cochinchina in the Chamber of Deputies in Paris. His articles in *Vérité*, an "independent republican newspaper," and his courageous actions in the Colonial Council were bringing him firm support from the more enlightened residents of the colony.

He announced in July, 1923, that he was not planning to run against the incumbent, the ultra-conservative, Chavigny-supported Ernest Outrey, but changed his mind early in 1924 and entered the contest.[32]

Chavigny was furious. In Paris, he had already spread the rumor that Monin was a Communist, and now he began a similar campaign in *L'Impartial*. He crowded its pages with articles full of slanted facts and outright lies, highly inflammatory and calculated to win blocs of votes from Monin. He opened his attack with the "damaging" information that Monin had received the "approbation of the Central Committee of the League of the Republic," the Parisian liberal group of which Paul Painlevé was president. With the approach of election day—May 11, 1924—the tone became violent. Typical headlines were "CIVIL SERVANTS: MONIN HAS BETRAYED YOU"; "MONIN HAS LIKEWISE BETRAYED THE COLONIALS AND THE BUSINESSMEN"; "PAUL MONIN COMMUNIST: FACTS, DOCUMENTS, PROOF." [33]

The Communist charge came down to two points. First, according to *L'Impartial*, Monin had obtained a loan of 35,000 piasters ($70,000) from the Chinese Merchants' Bank and had gone to France with the money. In Chavigny's mind, the bank was Communist simply because it was Chinese. It was later proved in court that Monin had not taken the money to France but had used it to cover a note he had signed for a fellow war veteran.[34] Second, Chavigny accused Monin of actively associating with Communists and other revolutionaries. Hadn't the young lawyer returned from a trip to France with "a notorious Communist, Léon Werth, in his baggage"? As Werth indicates in the preface to his book *Cochinchine*, Monin had indeed urged him to come to Indochina to see for himself the conditions there. Moreover, the highly informative book that Werth wrote after the trip fully substantiated the charges of oppression and corruption subsequently made by Malraux and Monin in *Indochine*.[35]

Monin's leftist associations seemed dangerous to the conservatives, who were even more alarmed by his aggressively pro-Annamite ideas. As Chavigny wrote during the election campaign: "In reality, Monin is the candidate, the champion of an Annamite group whose leaders are Bui-quang-Chieu, Nguyen-phu-Hai of *La Tribune Indigène*, and Nguyen-an-Ninh of *La Cloche Fêlée*. It is this Annamite group, the enemy of French influence, that supported Paul Monin." [36] It is certainly true that Monin was an enemy of the "French influence" represented by such corrupt Frenchmen as Chavigny and his associates. However, Monin's *Vérité* articles and, later, those in the *Saigon Républicain* and *Indochine* were eloquent proof of the extent to which he was pro-French as well as pro-Annamite.

In the 1924 campaign against Outrey, Monin had the support of the few independent newspapers of the peninsula, notably *La Voix Libre, L'Indépendant, La Tribune Indigène, Le Journal de l'Extrême-Orient,* and *La Cloche Fêlée,* as well as of his own paper, *Vérité.* The elections showed that he had surprising strength, especially in Saigon. Out of 2,440 votes cast in Cochinchina, where only French citizens could vote and very few Annamites had been able to obtain such citizenship, Monin got by far the second largest number, 626.[37] But, typically, French *colons* in the provinces were very conservative. They, together with the numerous Indians in government employ who were French citizens, gave Outrey a winning 1,555 votes.

In France, the 1924 elections marked a victory for what the editor of *L'Impartial* called a dangerous "leftist bloc." In his view, it was this success that encouraged some of the more outspoken pro-Annamite publications in Indochina to become increasingly insistent in their demands for reforms.[38] Several incidents—notably the attempt by a "Communist" Vietnamese patriot to kill Governor General Merlin with a bomb in Canton—strengthened the hand of the colonial conservatives, who renewed their efforts to silence the independent papers.[39] They were very successful. With the exception of *La Voix Libre,* all of the newspapers that had supported Monin against Outrey in 1924 had suspended or ceased publication by the time the first issue of *Indochine* appeared in June, 1925.[40] Monin's paper, *Vérité,* was closed in June, 1924. He then joined Camille Delong and Hippolyte Ardin, the local head of the combined Radical Radical-Socialist Party (of which Monin was a director), to found the *Saigon Républicain.* He resigned from this paper—and from the political organization—shortly afterward, when he became aware that Ardin had been bribed by the Administration and was softening his attacks on its corrupt practices.[41]

It was not only Monin's political and journalistic activities that made him suspect to the local Administration; he was also known as a social agitator. Early in the 1920's he had—according to Chavigny—provoked a "strike of Navy conscripts" and had "paraded the red flag in Saigon." [42] Moreover, it was common knowledge that, contrary to a 1908 ordinance, he had organized a number of unions among the workers in Cholon, the port city of Saigon. Not surprisingly, Chavigny also saw this as part of a Communist plot:

> Thanks to Paul Monin, at the present time we have in Cholon the jewelers' union, the laborers' union, the factory workers' union, the masons' and carpenters' union, the union of restaurant workers and musicians, etc. Paul Monin has thus laid the groundwork for the strike he hopes to unleash at the right moment, at a signal from him. . . . It is the working class set against management.[43]

Although the specific basis of these accusations is obscure, it is significant that in *L'Impartial*'s view, unionism, a fundamental tenet of French socialist belief, was equated with Bolshevistic Communism.

Chavigny was equally suspicious of Monin's activities on behalf of the Chinese minority in the colony. The young lawyer was one of the first to denounce a proposed law giving a French group a monopoly on the port facilities at Saigon—an arrangement that would have deprived hundreds of Chinese firms of their livelihood. He sent protests and documents to the French League for the Defense of the Rights of Man in Paris, and the resulting scandal caused the government to drop the idea.[44] Chavigny, who would have profited enormously from the proposed monopoly, was even more incensed when Monin shortly afterward came to the defense of a Chinese named Huynh-vi-Khanh and precipitated a *cause célèbre* in the Colony.

On April 12 and 13, 1925, members of the six provincial committees of the Chinese Nationalist Party of Cochinchina, which was affiliated with the Kuomintang in China, had met with the Saigon-Cholon Chinese community for ceremonies to commemorate the death of Sun Yat-sen. The Administration of Cochinchina had authorized this patriotic demonstration. The following day, the provincial delegates had been summoned to a special private meeting to discuss, among other matters, the means of raising 10,000 piasters ($20,000) to purchase an airplane "in memory of Sun Yat-sen" to be given to the Republican government of China. Each provincial representative had agreed to raise 1,000 piasters.

Shortly after his return home, the delegate from Baclieu, Huynh-vi-Khanh, had been seized by the Sûreté. He had had in his possession some pamphlets urging the Chinese of the colony to contribute money for the airplane and a number of special Kuomintang stamps to serve as receipts. Although Huynh had been taken immediately to Saigon and questioned at length, technically he was never arrested. Chavigny wrote in his bland version of the incident that Huynh "had simply been kept at the disposition of the investigator at the police station." [45]

An ardent Sinophile, Monin led the protests raised against Huynh's detention. He twice cabled Acting Governor General Monguillot in Tonkin to inform him of the matter, and he sent a wire to Malraux in Annam, asking him to go to Hanoi to intercede personally. In addition, Monin contacted groups in Paris.[46] Since he was a member of the Colonial Council, his protests carried considerable weight. The vice president of the League for the Rights of Man was one of many who lamented the treatment given this Chinese Republican.[47] "The inquiry having been completed," as Chavigny put it, Huynh was released. Malraux commented sarcastically that the whole incident simply proved that "Cochinchina is the only French territory where it is forbidden . . . to profess republicanism." [48] Monin's action on behalf of this Chinese nationalist, just before *Indochine* began publication, bolstered conservative opinion that he was a dangerous and irresponsible revolutionary.

These, then, were the three young men primarily responsible for *Indochine*: a *métis*, an ailing politician, and an "art thief." Dejean held a number of jobs. He supervised the make-up of the paper, and was also important because of his understanding of the Annamite mentality and his intimate contacts in the Indochinese community. Monin, with the analytical mind of a lawyer and the experience of a legislator, often dealt with legal and financial abuses in Cochinchina. Malraux, who had proudly called himself a *"littérateur"* at the time of his trial, used his talent for biting sarcasm or passionate eloquence to arouse readers about the corruption that was being uncovered. Together, in the months between June, 1925, and February, 1926, they produced a remarkable newspaper.

The first issue of *Indochine* came out on June 17, 1925, and except for holidays, the paper appeared regularly thereafter, six days

a week, until August 14, a total of forty-nine issues. Like most of
the other Saigon papers, it had eight pages. The usual layout was:

Page 1: Editorials, news bulletins, and political news.
Page 2: International dispatches from "our special correspond-
ents."
Page 3: International wire-service and radio bulletins.
Pages 4, 5: Advertisements and serial fillers.
Page 6: Local events.
Page 7: The elite page.
Page 8: Miscellaneous—photographs, crossword puzzles, run-
over of front-page articles, documents reproduced in connection
with various exposés, etc.[49]

The first and last pages, which served as a cover, contained the
major political editorials, but much of the material on the unnumbered inner pages was also worthy of note. By carefully selecting
articles, the editors sought not only to document their political
ideas and proposals, but to maintain a high literary standard. This
is especially evident when one compares *Indochine* with the inane
Opinion and the pompous *L'Impartial*, the two principal Saigon
newspapers.

The fourth and fifth pages of *Indochine* were the only ones that
carried advertising, and they were often filled out with half-page
serials or literary columns. Evidently, local firms were reluctant to
purchase space in the paper, since, with few exceptions, the
advertisements are for companies in France. They were obtained
by a contract with a Parisian publicity agency called the French
Exporter. (By comparison, *L'Impartial* carried at least four full
pages of paid advertisements for a variety of French and colonial
firms.) Later, a few Indochinese or Chinese establishments bought
space in the Malraux-Monin paper, but probably the threat of
government reprisals discouraged the remainder of those who were
sympathetic to the reform cause.

With negligible advertising revenues and no government help,
how did *Indochine* remain solvent? There were undoubtedly some
sustaining gifts from wealthy Annamite and Chinese liberals as
well as from political organizations such as Young Annam and the
local Kuomintang, but most of the paper's income must have
come from subscriptions. The first issue carried an order form, and
subsequent numbers frequently pointed to the excellence of the

news coverage and the quality of the various features to encourage prospective subscribers. As *Indochine* became the most outspoken advocate of reform in Cochinchina, it drew increasing support from Indochinese all over the colony. Despite constant police harassment, the number of subscribers grew steadily.

Each of the four inside pages without advertising had a special heading to indicate its contents. Although there was often a run-over from another page, the layout and content remained fairly constant. Page seven, the "Page de l'Élite," was the most literary. Its articles, which were usually continued on other pages, were bought from *Candide* and were of high quality. The two main elements in the literary sections of French newspapers are the *feuilletons,* or serialized articles, and by-lined columns. The principal serial carried by *Indochine* was "Anatole France at the Bechellerie: Remarks and Reminiscences, 1914–24," by Marcel Le Goff. The opening installment appeared in the first issue of the newspaper, and it ran in every edition until the last. Since Malraux was a friend of the author of *The Opinions of M. Jerome Coignard,* it is not surprising that this new book was chosen as the main *feuilleton.* In the two months before the newspaper's publication was interrupted, a number of shorter serials also appeared, as well as stories by such authors as Pierre Bost, Miriam Harry, Lucie Delarue-Madrus, René Benjamin, Pierre Benoit, Emmanuel Bove, and even Tolstoi.[50]

Many regular columns from *Candide* were also carried by the Malraux-Monin paper. Pierre de Colombier wrote about exhibitions and other events in the Paris art world, and Emile Vuillermoz discussed music. Sacha Guitry contributed theater reviews, reminiscences of life in the theatre, and comments on the contemporary scene. Book reviews were frequent. Controversial material often appeared in a column called "Nos Grandes Reportages," or "Our Big Stories." In the first issue of *Indochine,* it carried an account of the "Communist Outrage on Rue Damrémont," by Edouard Helsey. Next came an exposé of a recent grain speculation that had caused great hardship in France. Later there was an article on life in Soviet Russia by Jean Priel. The most interesting of these "Big Stories" was a series by André Foucault, beginning July 3, on the war in North Africa. In an introductory paragraph, the editors of *Indochine* pointed out "the great importance of the events in Morocco" and proudly noted that their paper was the only colonial publication—except for *L'Echo d'Alger*—to give an extensive firsthand account of the situation.

The page that usually preceded the literary "Page de l'Élite" was headed "Local Events." This sixth page carried ship sailings, exchange rates, administrative promotions, and official announcements, along with detailed accounts from the police calendar of the previous day. Items about the provinces of Cochinchina were listed under separate "Chroniques," and frequently there were features giving supplementary information about the front-page scandals. In its "Review of Local Newspapers" section, Malraux —and occasionally his co-editors—wrote diatribes against other Saigon newspapers and their editors. The comments, which ranged from puerile sarcasm to biting wit to subtle insult, reveal an unexpected side of Malraux the writer, and we shall deal with them in more detail below.

World-news coverage in *Indochine* was usually extensive. On the third page, labeled "Du Monde Entier" or "World-Wide" (a title later used by Malraux for the series of foreign-novel translations he directed at NRF), appeared items furnished free to all Saigon papers by the semi-official Agence Radiophonique Internationale de Presse (ARIP). These were never up-to-the-minute bcause they had to undergo government censorship before being released. The ARIP items carried by *Indochine* frequently differed from those appearing in the other Saigon papers, which ignored or cut stories on the social and political unrest in the non-European world. These editors seemed especially reluctant to print favorable stories concerning China.

Indochine sought to fill this void. On the "Du Monde Entier" page were published as many items about the non-European world as could be obtained from official sources, together with any other materials that underlined the need for closer cooperation between East and West. In this connection, Malraux made effective use of several in a series of interviews with outstanding literary figures by Frédéric Lefèvre, which was syndicated in the Paris paper *Les Nouvelles Littéraires*. By reprinting those discussions, in which respected Westerners interpreted the civilizations of the East for their countrymen, he sought to reinforce the *Indochine* cause of Franco-Annamite reconciliation.

Two interviews were especially noteworthy. One was "An Hour with Sylvain Lévi," a four-installment article devoted to the brilliant Indian scholar and professor at the Collège de France; it opened in the fifth issue of *Indochine*. Lévi emphasized that it was the duty of the French as humanists to make "an effort of compassion and understanding in order to comprehend foreign civilizations in their past and present . . . [especially] our great colonies of Asia." This duty was all the more imperative since the French Government was guilty of interfering in these civilizations, usually without the consent of the native people, and had by its intervention "jeopardized all their traditions." Unfortunately, Europeans had not been equal to their responsibility, and colonial peoples everywhere were turning against them. Lévi maintained that because the Russian Revolution was a major attack on the capitalist civilization of the colonialist West, it was understandable that Orientals should envisage the Communist Party as a means of obtaining national independence and social change. As he saw it, the only solution for the French in Indochina was to abandon the old colonialism: "Wherever we are, let us step forward and act as friendly collaborators who expect and hope for collaboration." [51] This was exactly the position of the editors of *Indochine*.

Paul Claudel was the subject of the second serialized interview.[52] Because he was French Ambassador to Japan and—in *Indochine's* somewhat exaggerated evaluation—"the only great and invincible poet of our time," his statements were expected to carry great weight. Although his discussion was largely concerned with the contemporary French literary scene, he did make several comments on important movements in Japanese letters and arts, concluding that "all these young people have a sincerity, an enthusiasm . . . that is a pleasure to see. There is great strength for the future there." He took pains to point out that his work had been greatly influenced by Asian ideas and said that he had been able to "draw upon the books of the Orient with profit." Such an attitude was, of course, detested by conservatives in the colony, who were constantly denigrating everything that was not Western.

Another regular feature of the "Du Monde Entier" page was the "Review of French and Foreign Newspapers." Most of its items, which were reprinted from newspapers throughout the world, dealt with Asia and its problems. For example, in the late July issues of *Indochine*, there was an essay on "Gandhi and Annamite intellectuals"; an exposé of corrupt elections in French Guiana and oppressive government practices in Martinique; an article on intellectual movements in contemporary China; and an interview with Li-Tchuin, of the Chinese legation in Paris, on Chinese nationalism and the crisis in Shanghai.[53]

"Du Monde Entier" was also the heading for the second page of *Indochine*. Here were found some *Candide* features, notably the "Revue de la Presse Humoristique Française" and cartoons by Emile Paul, as well as drawings by local artists and jokes about events in the colony. Occasionally, runover from articles or editorials on the front page was carried here. More than half of page two was marked off for a department headed "Dispatches from Our Special Correspondents," which included regular feature columns and a long section of news dispatches, some continued from page one.

Especially interesting to liberal Annamite readers were firsthand reports from other parts of the Far East—such as the "Courrier du Siam," the "Courrier du Japon," and the "Courrier de Hué." The latter began with a forthright attack on the puppet Emperor of Annam and his court.[54] This article drew letters from a number of Vietnamese intellectuals, and on June 26, the editors announced that a new column, the "Annamite Readers' Forum" would afford their readers an opportunity to air legitimate grievances against the French Administration.

The series began with some pointed remarks by T. Tan on deteriorating Franco-Annamite relations, and subsequent articles or letters discussed such topics as the difficulties of obtaining a foreign-study visa, the poverty of the heavily taxed local farmers, the double-standard in wages paid to French and Annamite civil servants, the exportation of Annamite workers for slave labor in other French colonies, and the total absence of personal liberty for Indochinese everywhere on the peninsula.[55] Several Annamite intellectuals even dared to set down their thoughts on such forbidden subjects as the revolution in China, illegal land expropriations at Camau, and the political organization of the colony, notably the "Empire" of Central Annam. This latter question in particular was hotly debated in a number of "Forum" columns.[56]

Since *Indochine*'s raison d'être was to bring about political reform, the first page always featured political articles—sometimes editorials, sometimes exposés, sometimes interviews with important men. In tone they varied from serious, almost scholarly discussions of subjects like international finance and political philosophy to violent exhortation, personal insult, and even possibly libelous diatribe against certain administrators of Cochinchina. The material often ran over onto the second page or onto the back cover page, which also carried reproductions of photographs and documents that supported positions taken in the lead editorials. As co-editor, Malraux had a large role in preparing these two pages. Out of some thirty-one major signed pieces that appeared on them, he was responsible for nearly half.[57]

The six-column format of the front page was firmly established by the third issue. The first two (occasionally three) left-hand columns were devoted to the lead political editorial, interview, or article. Next came the three-column "Dispatches from Our Special Correspondents," short items printed in large type. A note at the bottom of this column referred readers to page two, where longer stories appeared. If the sixth column was available, it usually carried two or three short provocative paragraphs—sometimes bearing Malraux's initials—about local issues or personalities. They were similar in tone to his comments in the "Review of the Local Press."

The front-page dispatches and similar items on the second page contained the kind of disturbing news that most Saigon newspapers preferred to ignore. There were accounts of the labor movement in England, the activities of Mussolini, and revolts in Serbia, Russia, and Morocco. Of more immediate interest to Annamites were items concerning events in Asia. These ranged from an account of Moscow's sympathetic interest in local nationalist movements and the Russian plan for a trans-Siberian railway, to a detailing of strikes in Singapore and riots in British India. News from China was especially extensive. Malraux and Monin chose to feature news of social upheavals in various parts of the world, a subject considered dangerous or "defeatist" by the other Saigon newspapers, because of a conviction that only by making far-reaching social and administrative reforms in its colonial empire could France remain in the Orient. Events of the last twenty years have abundantly testified to their foresight.

IV

A Strident Welcome

Indochine, as its editors doubtless intended, was an immediate sensation. In the very first issue, on June 17, 1925, conservative Saigon readers were shocked to see blatantly "subversive" ideas in a front-page interview: "Does not an increasingly close collaboration between colonials and natives constitute the very base and purpose of a well-conceived colonial policy, such as ours ought to be?" "It is the duty of Republicans to contribute with all their strength to the realization of this collaboration. This is the very essence of our colonial task, as the parties of the left conceive of it." The exchange had occurred in an interview granted several weeks earlier to *Indochine*'s Paris correspondent, Jean Bouchor, by Paul Painlevé, soon to be named President of the French Council of Ministers.

Thus, the first issue of the new paper dropped a political bombshell in the colony. The pro-Annamites were delighted, the *colons* scandalized. Not only did the editors apparently have the ear of the most powerful executive in the French government; more important, Painlevé's comments showed him to be in complete agreement with Malraux and Monin and very much in disagreement with those who held power in Cochinchina. As Monin put it in a short paragraph of introduction, "The thoughts that the new President of the Council of Ministers expressed to us are a noteworthy change from the aggressive snarling of certain little men in petty local politics." Painlevé's views were shared by many political figures in France, but in ultra-conservative Cochinchina, such sentiments were anathema.

After flatly stating his belief—and that of his party, which was

71

very powerful in the Chamber—in the type of close Franco-Annamite collaboration proposed by the new Malraux-Monin newspaper, Painlevé pointed out that a fundamental means of achieving such an end was education: "Integrated education is the best and most complete means of assimilation between different races. There is no understanding or agreement without an inter-penetration of minds. . . . Access to our educational system, at all levels, should be open to Annamites." This would create a native elite that could take an increasingly larger part in the administra-tion of their country, preparing for an increasingly democratic and representative government. Painlevé urged "the development of native councils" and wanted the local population "always to have a consultative voice in deliberations concerning the welfare of the colony. The people always ought to be able to make their aspira-tions known to the government."

Although in principle he was in favor of an Annamite represent-ative in the Chamber of Deputies, Painlevé, as its former Presi-dent, was aware that one individual in that body could do little to further the cause of the huge numbers of his native electors. The latter would quickly become disillusioned. Painlevé saw a more effective way of achieving the same end: "Cooperation between the native councils, increasingly active as they assimilate the French mentality, and the Government of Indochina should bring about more appreciable results. This is the task of the present and of the future, the end result of an evolution that we should en-courage, protect, and guide." Such an evolution implied the more frequent granting of French citizenship to educated members of the Annamite community.

Painlevé concluded his interview by wishing success to the pro-jected newspaper that Bouchor represented. In the evolution of the Indochina colony, he said, "the press, your newspaper for ex-ample, should render outstanding service. The French and native press *must* be free. Otherwise, it will not speak out. . . . The free-dom to express one's opinion is, after all, at the base of all civiliza-tion."

As *Indochine* repeatedly pointed out in the eight months of its intermittent existence, the highest officials of Cochinchina were constantly striving by every means possible to keep the French and Annamites divided as masters and servants. They rigidly controlled the press and thwarted the formation of any educated native elite that would jeopardize this master-servant relationship. Their acts may have occasionally been prompted by political conviction, but as the scandals unearthed by Malraux and Monin amply demonstrated, the primary motivation was nearly always financial.

Malraux and Monin had presented the basic ideas guiding their newspaper in a serious article appearing in the first issue, but something more than abstract discussions of political principles, however "revolutionary," was necessary to arouse and hold the attention of Indochinese readers. The editors knew that the average Annamite or minor French official would be more interested in following a campaign of personal diatribe or dispute, especially if the individuals under attack had long been his oppressors. Malraux had a wide and well-deserved reputation for sharp wit and brilliant conversation. He was responsible for most of the invective that so heavily spiced the pages of *Indochine* during its first weeks. Such items ranged from very short statements of "correction," to long columns minutely dismembering an opponent's statements, to inflammatory front-page editorials. Many are quite amusing. All convey his deep anger and bitterness.

It would be a mistake to dismiss this aspect of Malraux's campaign as little more than a personal vendetta by an embittered young man seeking revenge for a personal humiliation. If he was angry, it was not so much because of what had happened to him; it was because of what was being done to the hapless Indochinese. If he felt the bitterness of frustration, it was not so much because he was unable to exact personal revenge; it was because he was powerless to correct the abuses and injustices that he saw all about him. Certain of his *Indochine* editorials give ample evidence that he could write constructively—and in eloquent, sober prose—when the occasion demanded. He deliberately made more frequent use of ridicule, parody, and sarcasm, for he realized that in an Asian country—even more than in France—these weapons would wound his opponents.

By being made to appear ridiculous, the sacrosanct rulers of the colony lost face. This encouraged the native peoples to become less reticent about demanding reforms and more aware that the Administration did not hold power irrevocably and by divine right. To be sure, a barbed tongue could not slay the bureaucratic behemoth, but it could at least goad it into making some reforms. Perhaps if sufficiently infuriated, the monster might one day even destroy itself. In the meantime, *Indochine*'s readers would be entertained and subtly encouraged to act.

Malraux's first editorial, a trenchant attack against Maurice Cognacq, the authoritarian Governor of Cochinchina, appeared in the second issue of *Indochine,* in the front-page columns that had carried the Painlevé interview the day before. His piece eloquently affirmed his fundamental position "that one doesn't govern men at all; that one may—with great tact—direct an evolution; that to guide it is a worthy role." Written as an imaginary "First Letter from Jacques Tournebroche to Jérôme Coignard," the editorial in style and tone skillfully mirrored Anatole France's work *Les Opinions de M. Jérôme Coignard.* One can imagine the delight of the oppressed Annamites and the fury of the Governor on reading it.

The letter presented Tournebroche's gentle reminiscences of "the sweet bygone days" when his master, Coignard, was wont to "gently caress Catherine the lace-maker, in a bower, while slowly drinking a select wine." Since that happy time, many "encounters" had marked Jacques' life. Some of those in France had been beautiful and strange, but none had equaled one which had taken place "in this strange land where magpies really talk and where it is women who wear the pants"; namely, his meeting with "Gouverneur Je-Menotte" (Governor I-Handcuff).

At the mention of this name, Jacques becomes bitter; the tone of his letter becomes increasingly caustic and ironic. The hatred which the Annamites felt towards their Governor had led him to expect to meet a monster, but—he writes facetiously—"you aren't . . . any more ugly than anyone else who isn't handsome, and the reputation for violence you have made for yourself is not at all reflected in your face, nor in your little turned-up nose." Appearances are deceiving, however, because in the "rather long period" that he has ruled Cochinchina, Je-Menotte has succeeded in exasperating and infuriating everyone by his actions. The Governor was supposed to be the top *administrative* official in the governmental hierarchy. His duties as outlined by the law were to encourage the Colony in an evolution towards a certain degree of economic and political independence. Guiding an emerging nation along such a road should have been done gently and tactfully. Unfortunately, maintains Tournebroche, the Governor has a quite different idea of his function. He is too short-sighted to see that "anyone who tries to direct men against their wishes only directs phantoms and vain shadows;" he insists on forcing those in his charge to do exactly as he wishes. Although largely motivated by a desire for personal gain, this coercion is publicly justified by the

Governor in the name of "order." It is most blatantly exercised at the time of elections when Cognacq is able to transform the voting process "into a struggle between Negroes in a tunnel."

The technique of his fraud is simple, writes Jacques. Some 500 minor civil servants in the Colonial Administration are Indians from French enclaves on the subcontinent. Unlike the vast majority of Indochinese, they have long enjoyed French citizenship, and so are entitled to vote in Indochinese elections. However, they are completely dominated by the Governor because they are poor and owe what little they have to his favor. It is understandable, says Jacques, that they should vote as he directs. In this manner—as well as by outright illegalities—Cognacq runs the colony like a personal fief, always justifying his actions by "the principle of order."

In the final analysis, Jacques concludes, the only principle that the Governor represents is that of authority, his *personal* authority. He permits no opposition, and the only right that he grants Annamites—especially those educated in the French tradition—is "the right to shut up." In the face of widespread injustice and political unrest, it is ridiculous for this aggressive official to maintain that his rule is bringing order and prosperity to everyone. However, as Tournebroche notes in an ironic parting comment to the Governor, there will be a reward for such an administration: "My very dear child, you will be blessed down through the years. And your soul, filled with music and song, shall long rejoice: for in the celestial hierarchy, among the Angels, Archangels, Thrones, Virtues, and Dominations, God will certainly not grant you Virtues; but He *will* give you Domination."

This editorial was a biting statement of Malraux's fundamental objection to the philosophy of "rule by domination." His subsequent articles in *Indochine* developed his position further and dealt with specific abusive practices adopted by the Governor to maintain his totalitarian control.

The tone of *Indochine* was clearly established by its first two issues, which contained both a serious attack on the ultra-conservative principles of the Colonial Administration and a mordant personal indictment of the Governor who headed it. Other newspapers in Saigon were quick to react to the strident new voice in their midst. The liberal *Echo Annamite* immediately welcomed the newcomer warmly: "Let us sincerely wish long life and prosperity to the newborn, because it is a newspaper whose pro-Annamite tendencies are significantly indicated by the name of M. Monin, who is co-editor with M. Malraux." The editor of *L'Echo Annamite*, Nguyen-phan-Long, emphasized that *Indochine*, as a truly pro-Annamite newspaper, put freedom of the press at the top of its list of necessary reforms. Rigid government censorship by officials who wanted to "reign without incidents" had often been known in history, he admitted, but the control of the press in Indochina held "the record for stupidity, because it doesn't even need to *appear* intelligent to the natives; the invoking of authority is enough to make them carry out the most arbitrary decisions." [1]

Surprisingly, the conservative government-supported *Courrier Saigonnais* was the first non-Annamite paper in the city to greet *Indochine*. A curious front-page notice wishing the new newspaper "long life and prosperity" appeared on June 17, the date of *Indochine*'s first issue.[2] The *Courrier*'s native printers had evidently slipped it in without the knowledge of their French employers. Not unexpectedly, an angry "Correction and Clarification" was published the following day. Violently disclaiming any responsibility for the offensive item, the editors stated emphatically that it expressed—

> exactly the contrary of our hopes, because we here know too well what a regrettable anti-French undertaking *Indochine* wishes to prepare, the atmosphere of harsh criticisms with which they will surround us, and the half-concealed calls to revolt that they will issue. . . . So will our readers forgive us and please remain assured that we are still what we have been in the past, firm believers in order and in legitimate authority, rejecting any appearance of common cause with fishers in troubled waters and instigators of discord.[3]

A full investigation of the entire incident was promised.

This article was echoed by other conservative Saigon papers. Malraux and Monin did little to encourage moderation with their gibes and their documented revelations of collusion between the Governor and the four principal Saigon dailies that were attacking *Indochine*: the *Courrier Saigonnais*, the *Progrès Annamite*, the *Saigon Républicain*, and *L'Impartial*. Monin and Dejean occasionally contributed to the attack on the puppet press, but Malraux spearheaded the assault, often in the "Review of the Local Press."

The *Courrier Saigonnais*, a daily founded in 1888, had been successful enough to acquire its own plant, which often did printing for the government. Although basically conservative, the *Courrier* had shown a certain independence in the past, notably during Malraux's trial, when the editor, Camille Devilar, had steadfastly refused to join in Chavigny's intemperate attacks. Unfortunately, shortly before *Indochine* appeared, the *Courrier* had been purchased by Cognacq's associate, M. de la Pommeraye.[4] Thereafter, its editorial policy was virtually identical with that of *L'Impartial*.

The insulting remarks published by the *Courrier* in its June 18 "Correction" gave Malraux and Monin an excellent opportunity to obtain additional publicity for their paper and reveal the type of men opposing them. They dispatched seconds to challenge to a duel the individual responsible for the comments. The terrified managing editor, a Dutchman named Staadt, assured them that the new editor-owner was ultimately to blame for the offensive remarks. Hurriedly reached by telephone, that gentleman disclaimed any involvement and refused even to receive the representatives from *Indochine*. Malraux wrote that he found particularly dishonorable actions of men like de la Pommeraye who "not only don't have [the courage] to fight but *don't even have enough to acknowledge what they have written.*" [5]

The fourth and sixth issues of *Indochine* carried two caustic front-page open letters assailing de la Pommeraye and Staadt. The *Courrier* had called the editors of *Indochine* "anti-French" and had violently rejected the program of closer Franco-Annamite relations proposed by Painlevé. Malraux noted sarcastically that because Staadt was Dutch and had spent many years in Indonesia, his opinions were especially worthy of consideration; the colonial administration in Indonesia was widely admired for its efficiency, "bolstered by those graceful rattan canes that an indulgent nature has placed on Java within arm's reach." He concluded in cavalier fashion: "It would perhaps not be undesirable if M. Staadht [*sic*] were to go elsewhere to express his Javanese ideas. For . . . isn't he afraid that between his backside and a French or Annamite foot there will occur one of those regrettable collisions which, once a century, take place between wandering and vagabond planets? Comets attract comets." [6]

However, it was not Staadt but the new owner of the *Courrier* who was the main object of Malraux's ire in these two letters. The powerful de la Pommeraye—Malraux never once used his first name—was President of the Chamber of Commerce, director of the government-subsidized Société des Grands Hôtels, and an administrator of the lucrative Société des Distilleries de l'Indochine. Fat and venal, he had begun his career as a reporter on a Tonkin newspaper and had later come south to Cochinchina. There he had quickly become rich through a series of business swindles, usually involving public monies. As Malraux wrote bluntly: "His entire fortune has been built with subsidies granted him by the Governor or by the Municipal Commission, which never acts unless in accord with him." Some of his frauds were really only questionable business deals, such as a government contract under which he bought film in France for 30 francs a meter and sold it to the Colonial Administration for ten times that sum. Others, such as the infamous "affaire Calendrier," were so utterly indefensible that they brought protests from even the most obtuse colonials.[7]

However, the swindle that most incensed Malraux concerned Saigon's "theatrical season." Because of his position as President of the Chamber of Commerce, de la Pommeraye had succeeded in getting himself appointed director of an ambitious program that was to include concerts, theatrical performances, and even a rodeo. In his greed, he pocketed such a huge part of the 80,000 piasters ($160,000) allocated for the series that little was left with which to hire adequate performers. The result was an incredible fiasco. Malraux noted with typical sarcasm:

> M. de la Pommeraye is gifted with a picturesque and charming imagination. He recomposes the universe with grace, and without effort he ushers us into a country which used to be the realm of the fairies. There, tenors are mute, which spares us from hearing false notes; the youthful leading ladies are replaced by a few well-preserved mummies. . . . Only the piasters are real. Illusion has always been queen in the theater. Let us pay tribute to this imaginative man who . . . had three different organizations reimburse him for his trip to Shanghai as an impresario.

De la Pommeraye answered Malraux's taunts with a vehement denial that he was dishonest or that he had anything to do with the *Courrier Saigonnais.* In his reply, he could not resist a passing reference to the "scandalous rumors" associated with one of the editors of *Indochine.*[8] This provoked Malraux to write a second front-page "Letter to Monsieur de la Pommeraye" three days later. After comparing his opponent's writing style to "that nonchalant grace which enchanted Baudelaire when he gazed upon young elephants," Malraux ridiculed de la Pommeraye's denial of ownership of the *Courrier:*

> What! You bought a newspaper, you haven't sold it, and those fellows [from *Indochine*] go so far as to believe that you are the owner of it? I understand why you don't understand.
>   A voice in the wings: All those fellows
>   Are not intelligent. . . .
> You don't even express yourself in polished language. Rather, you write like a broom. . . . The next time you reply to us, sir . . . for heaven's sake, change your broom. The one you are using is unsatisfactory. Don't make any more allusions to "scandalous rumors." Although those words may signify what you want them to say, it is preferable to use them to refer to little-known events. Those which you have in mind were, on the contrary, so public that they raised protests even in the *Chicago Tribune*.

Although de la Pommeraye's corrupt career was a vulnerable target for the editors of *Indochine*, they were even more aroused by the anti-Annamite policy of his newspaper. In the "Review of Local Newspapers" of June 24, *Indochine* reprinted some comments due "to the solid good sense and sure judgment of M. Staath [*sic*]." (Staadt had publicly ridiculed Annamite demands for an expanded educational program in the colony.) "What," wrote the editors in mock reply to an imaginary Vietnamese malcontent, "you are not being educated quickly enough? . . . Don't you have a university from which there emerges each year a handful of minor civil servants for the Administration? What more do you want!" Of course, such protests from Annamites or Frenchmen were "dangerous," noted Malraux, and if they were to continue, Staadt "with all his characteristic authoritativeness would once again call us agitators and accuse us of being anti-French and of fishing in troubled waters, etc. Only MM. Staath and de la Pommeraye are true superpatriots. And they have certainly shown us so!"

The second Saigon newspaper with which the editors of *Indochine* became embroiled was the *Progrès Annamite*, a daily founded in 1924 to appeal to the French-speaking Annamites of Cochinchina. It was directed by a Dr. Le-quang-Trinh, who was typical of those Annamites through whom the Administration sought to control the native people. His ludicrous autobiography, *A Stormy Life*, reveals him to be an incredibly pompous and con-

ceited man.[9] Once, after alluding to his father's position as a court
mandarin at Hué, he boasts that in several fist fights he himself had
singlehandedly overcome French soldiers twice his size. Nick-
named "Love's Doctor," he enjoyed a certain fame in Saigon because he had been publicly spanked by several prostitutes for
improper behavior during one of his frequent visits to a brothel.
His countrymen despised him and sometimes jeered or spat at
him.

A man like Trinh was particularly useful to the French Administration. When high officials from Paris or from the Governor
General's office in Hanoi came to Cochinchina on inspection
visits, Trinh was presented as the official spokesman for the
Annamite community. He naturally sang the praises of Cognacq's
Administration. Moreover, when sufficiently rewarded, he could be
counted on to uphold the government position both in his newspaper and in the Colonial Council, of which he was one of the
Vice Presidents. Only a few Annamites dared to voice their disgust
openly at being represented by this degenerate. *Indochine* published a detailed letter from one of Trinh's constituents, accusing
him of having done absolutely nothing to fulfill his campaign
promises. The writer also noted that although Trinh was nominally the delegate from Hatien, he had not set foot in that province for nearly three years. "Under such conditions," the writer
asked him, "how can you know the needs and aspirations of its
inhabitants?" [10]

Since Trinh's *Progrès Annamite* faithfully supported every oppressive policy of the government, Malraux and Monin made his
newspaper one of their primary targets. In their second issue, a sarcastic passing reference noted that *Progrès* had a total of five
readers, one of whom was a condemned criminal whom the judge
had ordered to read it in order "to increase his sentence." More
seriously, *Indochine* assailed Trinh's efforts to denigrate the leaders of nationalist movements in Asia. Near the end of June, for
example, he had written an unflattering piece on Gandhi, whose
popularity among Annamite intellectuals was growing rapidly.[11]
Malraux replied heatedly that Trinh was incapable of compre-
hending the greatness of the Indian leader because Trinh "admires
only his dear protectors—for example, M. Darles of the Thai-
Nguyen scandal, M. Fontaine of the food swindle, M. Cognacq of
the Camau fraud. *Those* are great men, heroes before whom the
Annamites should make a deep bow! But Gandhi? Bah!" [12]

Native nationalists were even more dangerous, in Dr. Trinh's view. When *Indochine* gave wide coverage to the anti-government remarks of the Annamite patriot Phan-chau-Trinh, Trinh retorted that such demands and protests could only "add to the unrest already stirred up by a certain newspaper run by notoriously ambitious individuals who, by their insolent scolding, have only succeeded in halting the reforms which France was ready to grant us." [13] In the same article, he was careless enough to refer to Malraux as a thief. Shortly afterward, Trinh received a visit from the "thief" and was subjected to an assault that was no less savage for being purely verbal. According to the complaint that Trinh subsequently lodged with the police, Malraux had stalked off without waiting to hear his explanations, but the *Progrès'* account predictably told a quite different story. It was sprinkled with phrases such as "I told him . . . I pointed out to him . . . I indicated to him. . . ." Malraux characterized this recital as "grotesque" and thereafter paid little heed to Trinh and his newspaper.[14]

Indochine's dispute with a third paper, the *Saigon Républicain,* was longer and far more bitter. This was the publication that Monin, with Hippolyte Ardin and Camille Delong, had founded in 1924 as the organ of the Radical-Socialist party and from which he had soon resigned on learning that his co-editors had sold out both the newspaper and the political organization to Cognacq. As he later wrote, "The *Saigon Républicain* is not at all the organ of the Radical Party but rather the newspaper of M. Ardin, printer." [15] Whatever its party label, the daily soon revealed its loyalty to Cognacq's regime and joined the other Saigon newspapers in attacking *Indochine.* In one issue, Ardin and Delong devoted three articles to an attempt to discredit *Indochine's* interview with Painlevé.[16] In another, they questioned the legitimacy of the financial backing for the new, liberal paper. Malraux retorted that the financial record of the *Saigon Républicain* was "as simple as Ubu and as clear as a jug of wine [a slang term for bribe]." In passing, he commented that Delong's writing was "like a bouquet of poppies and onions: his readers either cry or fall asleep." [17]

This barb was particularly wounding, for Delong evidently had literary pretensions. He had told numerous friends in Saigon that he was writing "something along the lines of Nietzsche, Epicurus, and Spinoza but with what was lacking in all three of them." [18] He angrily warned Malraux that he would not tolerate any further derogatory remarks and that if the young man dared continue, "he would find someone to whom he must answer." Malraux responded with his customary verve: "Answer you, M. Delong, that I might still do; just don't ask me to *read* you. . . . But here, right off, is what I think of you: You aren't Nietzsche, Spinoza, and Epicurus improved; you're Prudhomme, Homais, and Pecuchet worsened. And if that were to seem to you to be an insult, I would be delighted." [19]

In the course of the next few days, Delong hurled a long series of epithets at his antagonist: "Fugitive from the lap of André Gide, hesitating between literature, business, burglary, and prostitution . . . callow youth . . . fashionable thief . . . emptying into his newspaper the filth that he has in his heart . . . pastiche of France and Voltaire." Malraux retorted caustically that "not everyone can write naturally like Joseph Prudhomme and M. Delong" and cut off the exchange with blunt finality: "Ingenious, shrewd, subtle, clever, astute, wily, inventive M. Delong accuses me of youthfulness. Well, M. Delong, forty years of stupidity have never produced intelligence." [20]

Ardin, Delong's co-editor, also annoyed Malraux by his clumsy use of the French language,[21] but his betrayal of republican principles outraged the younger man even more: "M. Ardin tells whoever will listen to him that Dr. Cognacq is a reactionary Governor, a specialist in arbitrary acts, and that he is waiting for the said Cognacq to be replaced by a republican Governor in order to continue to participate in politics. *We dare him to print that in his newspaper*." [22] A few issues later, Malraux observed that Ardin had taken the dare: "After some days of reflection—and a few orders received—he has printed that M. Cognacq is terrific." [23]

The Malraux-Ardin quarrel almost became a brawl. Shortly after Malraux had accused Ardin of taking a bribe from Cognacq, the two men had a violent encounter on the terrace of the Continental Hotel in Saigon. Malraux denounced Ardin's hypocrisy in permitting a man like Cognacq to support a supposedly republican paper. Ardin retorted viciously that only an "Isaac" like Malraux would insinuate that there were irregularities in his newspaper's accounts. "Not everyone can be named Judas," answered Malraux.[24]

A few days later he took up Ardin's anti-Semitic remark directly:

I am not Jewish. Even if I were, it would be of little concern to me. But in any case, I am not. And since the epithet "Isaac" may allude

insultingly to a woman who is close to me . . . I would be obliged
to you if you would explain yourself. Otherwise, I regret that I
shall have to repeat to you that I consider a man who seeks to hurt
the woman because he cannot get at the man is a bugger; and I
intend this not in a newspaper sense, necessarily attenuated, but in
the fullest meaning of the word.[25]

Few references to the *Saigon Républicain* and its editors appeared in *Indochine* after the above remarks. But when Ardin and
Delong boasted that Malraux and Monin no longer dared answer
their attacks, a brief note was inserted in the "Review of Local
Newspapers" column of August 6: "We repeat that we have not
replied, that we are not replying, that we shall not reply to the
Saigon Républicain as long as it has only thirty-three readers."

In his acrimonious exchange with the *Saigon Républicain*, Malraux had remarked that it was his principle never to be the instigator of a personal dispute: "I insult only those who have insulted
me." On the whole, he held to this policy. His restraint regarding
Chavigny was remarkable because that editor had done everything
possible to ensure an unfavorable verdict for Malraux's appeal in
Saigon the previous year. Moreover, Chavigny's newspaper was
one of the Administration's most powerful weapons in keeping the
colony under strict control. During its first three weeks of publication, *Indochine* printed only three brief items involving the ultra-
conservative editor of *L'Impartial*. The first, which appeared on
June 20, ironically called attention to the possibility of a duel between "two notable descendants of crusaders"—de la Pommeraye
and Chavigny—over a question of government subsidies for private businesses: "The place chosen for the combat is said to be the
stage of the Eden-Cinema. Blue blood will flow, alas."

Three days later, Chavigny published a short paragraph suggesting that Malraux had never received encouragement for his liberal
paper from officials in Hanoi as he had claimed.[26] *Indochine*
printed a humorous rebuttal in fairly moderate terms the next day,
June 24, and dropped the matter until the end of the month,
when the newspaper published an item that was clearly intended
to undercut slanderous rumors against Malraux that were circulat-
ing among Chavigny's ultraconservative friends.

A bold front-page heading in the June 29 issue of *Indochine*
proclaimed "The End of a First-Class Joke," over a brief article
announcing that Malraux's appeal to the Court of Cassation in

Paris had been successful. He had just been informed by cable that the October, 1924, ruling of the Saigon court had been set aside: "By decree of June 25, the Court of Cassation in Paris has set aside the decree of the Saigon court adjudicating the Malraux-Chevasson affair because of the presence of coded items—not translated—in the dossier. Which proves that it is imprudent to plot little schemes and make up dossiers 'not to be communicated to the defense by reason of their confidential and political character' in a matter that is supposed to be one of common law." In point of fact, this was not quite true. The Court of Cassation had not examined the question of the coded items because the trial was invalid for a more fundamental reason, a purely technical legal flaw. The Saigon court recorder had neglected to indicate specifically that the hearing had been open, as was required by law.

From the colonial viewpoint, the greatest threat posed by *Indochine* was represented by the report in the first issue that Painlevé supported a number of liberal reforms in the colony. As Chavigny later admitted, the backing of so powerful an official lent considerable weight to the Malraux-Monin demands, and was liable to "diminish the authority of the local Administration and . . . profoundly discourage the healthy segment of the Cochinchinese population." [27] Chavigny felt that it was absolutely essential to discredit this interview, and as soon as he had read it he cabled François de Tessan, a friend in Paris, explaining what had happened and asking him to make some inquiries. He decided to remain silent until an answer came. Exchanging insults with his opponents would only give them publicity for their paper, and they were already getting enough in the pages of the *Courrier Saigonnais*, the *Progrès Annamite*, and the *Saigon Républicain*.

On Saturday, July 4, Chavigny finally received an answer from de Tessan. He published it on the front page of the Monday issue of *L'Impartial* under the banner headline "M. Paul Painlevé's Denial to the Newspaper *Indochine*." The cable read:

> In conversation with Painlevé on subject new Saigon newspaper Council President told me knows absolutely nothing of actions Monin Malraux never authorized them to use his name absolutely repudiates any such use that may be made without his authorization stop Painlevé denies most categorically having ever been involved in such affair in any way whatsoever authorizes me to declare so publicly. Tessan.

In his editorial, Chavigny observed that it was a common technique of unscrupulous journalists to obtain money from a credulous public by vaunting the "imaginary support of men in high
places" and suggested that *Indochine* was a blatant fraud. The
truce was over. This item was the opening salvo of a battle between Malraux and Chavigny that was to last as long as Malraux
remained in Indochina.

On the following day, July 7, Chavigny published a long editorial entitled "Will Indochina Become the Prey of Brazen
Adventurers?" Monin was scarcely mentioned; Malraux was the
more appealing target. After referring to a flood of "brazen adventurers" descending upon the hapless colony, Chavigny related how
one day Indochina had seen arrive on its shores "a certain Malraux
accompanied by a few accomplices." These thieves had come "for
the sole purpose of stealing a part of the artistic treasures" of the
ancient Khmer civilization, which they planned eventually to sell
to a group of international art dealers. The editor of *L'Impartial*
marveled that the chief culprit, sentenced to prison for his crime,
now dared return to the scene of his exploits to join with another
unsavory individual, Paul Monin, in establishing a political newspaper.

Posing as "impeccable arbiters of virtue, honesty, and righteous-
ness," Chavigny charged, these two agitators hoped to sow discord
in the colony and make trouble for the government. In order to
bolster their destructive program, they had fraudulently claimed
the approbation of important political figures in France. Happily,
their nefarious plans would be frustrated, concluded Chavigny
with typical bombast, because "there still exist here a majority of
honorable people; there is in this land a healthy press, a press
firmly resolved to block their path."

The reaction of the *Indochine* editors was immediate. On July
7, under a huge banner, they charged that after trying every other
form of pressure to close down their paper, the friends of the
Colonial Administration were undertaking "a little campaign of
defamation" that was more ignoble than anything they had done
before. Since the *Indochine* issue carrying the Painlevé interview
had not yet had time to reach Paris, wrote Malraux, "it was therefore solely on the basis of M. de Tessan's biased gossip that M.
Painlevé had had to make a statement—if indeed he had made
one." As soon as the President of the Council of Ministers received the document, *Indochine* would publish "his acknowledg-

ment and approval of this text." In the meantime, Bouchor's signed original of the interview was on exhibit in a shop window on a main Saigon street to disprove the Chavigny-Tessan charge. This brief rebuttal in *Indochine* ended with the announcement: "Tomorrow: First Letter to M. de la Chevrotière (as a beginning). We're really going to have some laughs." Chavigny had stirred up a hornets' nest. He was to regret it bitterly.

Two-thirds of the front page of the July 8 *Indochine* was given over to the "First Letter to Monsieur Henry Forward-to-the-Rear, stern moralist and healthy journalist." The long editorial, accompanied by a caricature of Chavigny, was signed "André Malraux, brazen adventurer and unhealthy journalist." It was the first of four attacks that Malraux wrote to expose this man, who posed as the epitome of virtue and civic responsibility. The basic facts —carefully corroborated by legal records, court transcripts, and official documents—justified the fervor and vehemence of the editorials. To Malraux, this corrupt journalist and politician typified all those who held power in the colonial society and government of Cochinchina.

Malraux began his open letter by saying that he understood perfectly why Chavigny had become a moralist: "Everything led you to it, particularly an immaculate past. On seeing you, everyone asked: 'Who is that virtuous virgin?' And in your wake, the perfume of orange blossoms long floated." He then set forth the specific details of a most unsavory history.[28] The self-styled Henry Chavigny de la Chevrotière was born plain Henry Chavigny in Saigon on September 11, 1883. His father, Eleutère, was a mixed-blood Frenchman from Senegal, and his mother was Vietnamese. As a young man, he had worked for newspapers in Hanoi and Saigon in "public relations." About 1905, he married a Vietnamese woman named Marie Do and had six children by her. A flagrantly unfaithful husband, he abandoned his family completely after he became involved with a notorious and demanding Frenchwoman in Saigon.

His newspaper salary was quite insufficient for his life of debauchery, and in order to earn extra money Chavigny became a police informer. On one occasion, he went so far as to encourage a Vietnamese woman to offer a bribe to an official of the local draft board to pass over her son, knowing that he would receive half of the confiscated bribe for denouncing her. The woman could raise only part of the sum required, and so Chavigny generously lent her the balance. He found an excuse to make her laboriously copy a note in French—she was literate only in Vietnamese—that tended to incriminate an innocent Army officer. This proved to be Chavigny's undoing. The Sûreté arrested the woman, but the military authorities conducted their own investigation and subsequently demanded that Chavigny be charged. At his trial before the military tribunal, he protested that he could not be condemned for having encouraged the woman to commit a crime because this was a legitimate part of his work as an informer. As Malraux later wrote sarcastically, such an "apotheosis of the stool pigeon is a pleasing allegory and a fine decorative effect. I propose having it engraved on the bills of some bank or other against a background of bits of paper embellished with threats and subsidies." [29] The legal proceedings were reported at length in the local papers, and no one was surprised when Chavigny was found guilty. He spent three months in the Central Prison of Saigon.

Early the following year, 1917, this man who was by turns an "ordinary stool pigeon and a *provocateur*," as Malraux put it, became involved in another compromising incident. France was suffering great losses on the battlefield and had begun to call up more classifications of men for military service. Chavigny was terrified at the idea of going to war, and he seized the only straw that he could find—a 1916 regulation that granted exemption to men with large families. On March 6, 1917, he filed an affidavit stating that he was paying the equivalent of $200 a month for the support of six children, ranging from three to twelve years of age. The military commander of the Saigon area ordered an inquiry into the allegation. Chavigny threatened his wife several times in order to force her to back up his claim, but when the investigating officer appeared, she told the truth: She was supporting the children on her meager salary; Chavigny contributed practically nothing. "It was not until there was a possibility of his being drafted that my husband seemed to want to take care of his children, and this was for the purpose of not being drafted," she said.[30] She produced a threatening letter from him that bore out her story. Her employer fully corroborated it, adding that it was a truly ignoble father who would spend money for "pleasure parties . . . and cozy dinners at the Continental Hotel" while his family was in need.

Undaunted by this unfavorable report, Chavigny resubmitted his request for exemption on May 4, perhaps in the hope that friends in the Sûreté would use their influence on his behalf. He was unsuccessful again, however, and shortly afterward found himself aboard a ship returning to France. After the vessel left Singapore, he feigned illness and was taken off at Colombo, Ceylon, to be returned to Saigon. There, on October 20, he finally obtained exemption from military service for the rest of the war. This was the man who subsequently referred to Malraux and Monin as traitors and "anti-French."

Following his "recovery" from the illness acquired after leaving Singapore, Chavigny decided to establish a newspaper. In view of the frantic campaigns that *L'Impartial* subsequently waged on behalf of certain conservative political figures—notably Ernest Outrey, the Cochinchina Deputy to the French Chamber—it seems probable that the financial backing for this venture came from such people. Malraux intimated that Chavigny had perhaps obtained money by using his publication for blackmail. In any case, when Maurice Cognacq was named Governor of Cochinchina after the end of the war, Chavigny's fortunes began to rise rapidly. *L'Impartial* soon became the semi-official government organ, and he, a constant companion of the Governor's, obtained several high posts in the Administration.

These facts about Chavigny and his paper were revealed in the opening half of Malraux's "First Letter." However, the young man did not intend to overlook the innuendoes about his trial the previous year that *L'Impartial* was printing, and so he devoted the second half to refuting them. Chavigny had written that "the affair of the theft of the bas-reliefs is going to come before our Court of Appeals again." He had failed to mention that the earlier sentence had been set aside by the Court of Cassation, thus deliberately implying—as Malraux pointed out—"that it is because I am so guilty that I am going to be sentenced twice. Yes sir, twice, to teach me a lesson! But," he continued, "it is not a question of any 'affair' or 'theft' or 'bas-reliefs' or 'Angkor.' . . . *I* was found guilty in a matter that was so clear that it was necessary to put together a dossier of items 'not to be communicated to the defense because of their confidential and political nature,' some of them coded. . . . When I was sentenced, the fifty greatest writers of France came to my defense." Chavigny, on trial before a military court, could muster in his behalf only such grotesque caricatures as Sosie, Captain Fracasse, Matamore, and Tranche-Montagne.

Malraux heartily agreed with the editor of *L'Impartial* that

Indochina should not be permitted to become "the prey of adventurers." Would it not be well, he suggested, for the honest, pious community leaders—i.e., those involved in the various scandals currently being exposed by *Indochine*—to form an "Academy of Virtue" under the leadership of Chavigny? The main difference between adventurers and moralists like Chavigny, de la Pommeraye, and Trinh, he concluded, was that the former, "after they have been condemned by the explicit order of people whose power is not unknown to them," nevertheless attack them head on in the courts, while the latter just "voluptuously lick their boots."

To bring the dispute to a head quickly, Malraux deliberately called Chavigny "a grotesque coward" in his editorial, and in a sarcastic item on the second page called attention to his cowardly "Colombo illness." According to the unwritten code of the colony, a man who had been insulted so deliberately must seek satisfaction of his honor by a duel. Malraux later wrote that he thought dueling was "completely out of date" but that it was good for a newspaperman to be "called upon to answer with his sword for what he had affirmed with his pen." [31] He waited for seconds to be sent by Chavigny, and when they failed to appear, he published on the following day, July 9, more insulting remarks on the front page: "Since M. de la Chevrotière specializes in pistol duels with short-sighted people and in sword fights with one-armed men, I'm looking for a surgeon who would be good enough to reduce me to the condition of a man-trunk on the day before I must once again point out to Monsieur Henry Chavigny de la Chevrotière that he is perhaps a bit of a coward."

Chavigny beat a hasty retreat from this challenge, saying that he planned to continue his "clean-up campaign" against Malraux and Monin but that time was needed to complete his research. He asked his readers to be patient and give him "a few days' respite." Meanwhile, in an obvious effort to embarrass Malraux, he announced a special contest. *L'Impartial* published a large photograph of one of the pieces of sculpture that had figured in the Malraux trial the previous year, and accompanied it by the following paragraph: "It seems that this has nothing to do with any bas-reliefs, or theft, or Angkor. . . . We ask our readers to elucidate the mystery. To the first one who replies, a free subscription to *L'Impartial*." [32]

Malraux could not let such a chance go by. He wrote the following answer to the "mystery," published on July 10 by both *L'Im-partial* and *Indochine*: "Sir: Given a prize as appealing as a year's subscription to *L'Impartial* (let's not bankrupt ourselves), I am unable to restrain my desire. I shall therefore confess to you . . . that your photo represents a high-relief (see the arm), not result-ing from a theft (see the Court of Cassation), and not coming from Angkor (since I discovered it at Banteay Srei). . . . Receive, sir, the assurance of my slight respect." Chavigny wisely decided to drop this line of attack; he made no further reference to Malraux's trial until late September, when he published the text of the de-cree from the Court of Cassation.

Although Chavigny's abusive personal assault against Malraux had provoked the young editor into a vehement rebuttal, it is evi-dent from his "First Letter" that the Chavigny newspaper was his primary target. In his July 8 editorial, he ridiculed Chavigny's pompous style, in which he detected numerous unintentional ob-scene *double-entendres* and blatant errors in basic French usage. How could such a badly written, inane newspaper remain alive and profitable enough to satisfy a voraciously greedy editor? The an-swer was simple, Malraux explained to Chavigny: "You made a few cronies understand that a newspaper like yours, highly objec-tive and full of greatness of soul (in the space left free by rubber stamps), should be aided." This "aid" took the form of 1,800 "Administration subscriptions," an income of nearly 400,000 francs ($80,000) a year. Thanks to this help, Chavigny had be-come a "healthy journalist . . . because health begins at 1,000 Administration subscriptions." Malraux thus began his docu-mented exposé of the illegal but effective method by which the Colonial Administration maintained tight control over most of the press in Cochinchina. The entire back page of the July 8 *In-dochine* was devoted to proof of these charges.

The government was forbidden by law from subsidizing news-papers because it was felt—rightly, of course—that a subsidized press would soon become the tool of those who held the purse strings. Yet the technique for getting around this law was simple. The Administration had under its control a vast army of civil serv-ants. In some instances, these functionaries were specifically told what newspaper to read, and their superiors saw to it that each of them ordered and paid for a subscription. But in the vast majority of cases, department heads simply sent in subscriptions for all those employed under them, concealing the expenditure in different sections of their individual budgets. Provincial and communal administrative centers followed a similar procedure.

Although the government vehemently denied these accusations, Malraux was able to prove his charges. *Indochine* had obtained a printed form that had been used to enter an Administration subscription for someone in the veterinary service in Saigon. This document, reproduced photographically in a later issue of the newspaper,[33] must have been furnished by a sympathetic Vietnamese nationalist who worked in the offices of the Governor. From an order number on the form and from other information he had obtained, Malraux calculated that *L'Impartial* received some 1,800 such subscriptions a year. At twenty piasters each, this produced an annual revenue of 36,000 piasters, or nearly $75,000. Any advertising income was in addition to this sum. What were *L'Impartial*'s expenses? Exclusive of printing costs, Chavigny had to pay out only about seven piasters a month—well under $250 a year—to put together his publication. Malraux unfolded the details of the operation.

As in all the other conservative Saigon papers, the world-news cables published in *L'Impartial* came exclusively from the semiofficial press agency, ARIP. After a preliminary government censoring, these bulletins were furnished gratis to any newspaper that wanted them. Chavigny obtained longer news items by subscribing to the Associated Press. This cost him only three piasters a month, according to the AP catalog that Malraux cited at length. This catalogue also revealed that other materials were available to subscribers, in most cases at no additional charge, including novels, short stories, by-lined columns like "Aunt Rosalie's Chats," and cartoons. Malraux pointed out that these items made up the bulk of *L'Impartial*. It was clear that Chavigny's newspaper brought him a huge income with practically no overhead costs.

L'Impartial was not the only Saigon paper to benefit from governmental largess. In a subsequent editorial, "Freedom of the Press," [34] Malraux charged that there were nearly 4,000 Administration subscriptions in Cochinchina. Among the French newspapers, *L'Impartial* headed the list with its 1,800 subscribers, but *L'Opinion* with 1,200 and the *Courrier Saigonnais* with 400 were prospering, too. Three conservative French-language Annamite papers—*Progrès Annamite*, *Voix Annamite*, and *Reveil Saigonnais* —accounted for the remaining 600. These costly subsidies were especially unfortunate for the colony since its budget was far in the red, but they were absolutely essential to Cognacq's Administration, whose survival depended on concealing the true political situation in Cochinchina. As Malraux bitterly concluded:

> Thus, in order to make himself admired in an appropriate manner, M. Cognacq, Governor of Cochinchina, takes from the treasury of Cochinchina, without having the right to do so, a million and a half [francs] per year. . . . When one is sure of representing nobility, grandeur, truth, justice, and plenty of other things besides, one takes (preferably by the collar) a Chavigny in the right hand, a Trinh in the left hand, and shows them to the people saying: "Harken well, ye peoples, to these unprejudiced gentlemen dangling from our two fists. They are going to speak." And the gentlemen say: "The countries of France and of Annam are behind us!" It's true. They are behind them, filled with disgust, assiduously booting their backsides.

L'Impartial and the other pro-government papers could not reply effectively to these documented charges. Moreover, Chavigny and his colleagues were being made a laughingstock by Malraux's barbs. It was obvious that the conservative forces in the colony had to find—and quickly—a way to silence these two "brazen adventurers" and their crusading newspaper.

V

Governor Cognacq and Rule by Corruption

Although the editors of *Indochine* devoted a considerable amount of space to attacks against the Saigon newspapers, the paid defenders of Cognacq and his regime, their principal target was Cognacq himself. Not only was he the symbol of all that was wrong in the colony; he was the primary source of the vast stream of corruption. Malraux's first editorial, the witty imaginary letter from "Jacques Tournebroche," had ridiculed the Governor and indicted his Administration for illegalities and oppression. Cognacq was infuriated by the article, and early in the week following its appearance, he ordered the young writer to be brought in to see him. Intimidation was his preferred way of dealing with any opposition. It was his custom to arrange personal meetings with recalcitrant individuals like Malraux so that he could bellow threats at them, face to face. Invariably present at these interviews were two of his most feared aides—André Arnoux, head of the Sûreté, and Darles, the "butcher" of Thai-Nguyen, infamous throughout the peninsula for his brutality, Cognacq's close friend and chief associate.[1] Malraux's second editorial, "To Monsieur I-Handcuff," published on Thursday, June 25, was a caustic account of this meeting with the Governor. Accompanied by a caricature of Cognacq's bloated features, the article was an unmistakable gesture of defiance.

Cognacq began his talk with Malraux on a conciliatory note in spite of his anger. He evidently considered Monin the more dangerous opponent—because of his prestige among the Annamites and because of his important political contacts in Paris—and he offered to be lenient with Malraux if he would agree to implicate his co-editor in a fictitious political plot against the local Colonial Administration. Malraux of course indignantly refused the proposal. The Governor then tried a bribe. When this, too, was emphatically rejected, he lost all patience and began shouting threats of police harassment and prison. Proud and sharp-tongued as always, Malraux replied airily that the Governor had spent so much of his youth "in reading about the adventures of the Argousin tribe" (a euphemism for prison guards) that he had retained "something of their customs." Cognacq sputtered that *Indochine* was a seditious paper which he intended to silence. Free discussion of political questions in such a publication was dangerous and harmful to the colony since the native people were too simple to understand what was really involved. If Malraux wanted to preach social reform, he bellowed, why didn't he go to Moscow! "The seed that you are trying to sow in this country will never sprout!" In any case, he boasted, as Governor he had the support of the vast majority of Frenchmen in Cochinchina. They approved of his Administration, and they stood squarely behind him because he maintained "order."

This lie was too much for Malraux. He retorted that for the first time in any French colony a group of leading citizens, including the President of the highest elected body, the Colonial Council, had openly formed a committee to work for the removal of the Governor. This clearly indicated a widespread and deep-seated dissatisfaction with the Administration. The reasons for this were to be found in the Governor's peculiar conception of the duties of his office, Malraux explained heatedly: "You have injected politics into the Administration where it has no business to be. You've tried to run everything by yourself. That is a defensible policy, but one that you also approved by yourself. Your elected officials . . . are now clearly adopting policies opposed to those of your friends. It is possible that in Europe notice will be taken of these . . . developments."

Cognacq, furious at not being able to browbeat Malraux, ended the interview with dire threats: "Wherever you go, you will find Dr. Cognacq. . . . My people will inform me of your slightest moves. . . . All Cochinchina obeys me and . . . if you persist, Dr. Cognacq is prepared to take extreme measures." He must have been even more incensed when shortly thereafter he found this exchange related in detail on the front page of *Indochine*.

It was not strange that a movement against Cognacq was gaining momentum in the colony despite his energetic efforts to stop it. Few men could have been less qualified to govern an overseas possession of France in the difficult postwar period. Originally a member of the Colonial Health Service in the Antilles, he had been transferred to an administrative position in the Indochina Medical Corps shortly after the final pacification of the peninsula. When it was later decided to establish a native university at Hanoi to discourage Annamite contact with "Bolshevik" student groups in France, Cognacq used his long familiarity with the workings of the government bureaucracy to obtain an appointment as head of the rather makeshift program of medical studies. (The level of instruction was far inferior to that in France, and graduates were called "auxiliary doctors" or "native doctors" to indicate that they had not received European training.) An indifferent physician, he soon distinguished himself in his new office by his blatant venality. He missed no opportunity for financial gain, going so far as to award contracts for textbook procurement on the basis of how large a bribe he had been offered.[2]

When the war ended, Cognacq was already nearing the relatively young age when he would be eligible to request his pension and return to France. In the Colonial Service, as in many bureaucracies, it was not uncommon to give substantial promotions to men approaching retirement. The doctor somehow convinced the Colonial Office that he deserved to end his career in the important and sensitive position of Governor of Cochinchina, and he was appointed to that post in 1922, with the official grade of Lieutenant Governor. Although until then he had been little known outside Hanoi, the conservative *colons* of the south immediately recognized him as a kindred spirit, because his first public statement on the complex colonial question was the shibboleth "We don't need any intellectuals in this country."[3] His clash with Malraux and Monin was inevitable.

Malraux, in his account of his interview with I-Handcuff, reported that the Governor had bragged that he enjoyed the support of all the elected chambers in Cochinchina, including the Municipal Council of Saigon. Malraux immediately pointed out to Cognacq that this statement was ridiculous because the Saigon Council was headed by a newly elected and honest Mayor who had just revealed the "tricks, weighted dolls, shuttlecocks, and Chinese puzzles at which you played with such skill over the municipal subsidy and the Khanh-Hoi land tracts." The Mayor's report on the Khanh-Hoi scandal and related articles by several lawyers were featured in the next few issues of *Indochine*.[4] Soon all of Saigon knew the details of Cognacq's swindle.

Ever since the end of the war, the Municipal Council had been considering plans to enlarge and improve the port facilities of Saigon-Cholon. The city had made numerous attempts to acquire the necessary land, but the owners had always asked exorbitant prices. Then, on June 3, 1923, the Khanh-Hoi Realty Company contacted the President of the Municipal Council and offered to give the city parts of an unimproved 900,000-square-meter tract of land (about a third of a square mile), ideally situated adjacent to the harbor. As it was subsequently proved, the realty company at this time did not exist legally—the articles of incorporation were dated June 29, 1923—and did not own the land it offered. The title transfer of the tract was not carried out until June 30. The Council President was apparently quite uninterested in these legal niceties. He quickly reached an understanding with the director of the Khanh-Hoi Realty Company, a M. Eutrope, who was Inspector for Political Affairs in Cochinchina and a close personal friend of the Governor's. However, no written contract was signed at the time, probably because it was feared that this legal step would immediately bring the matter to public attention.

The agreement stipulated that the city of Saigon would undertake—*at its own expense*—a number of "improvements" on the company's land. These were to include filling in marshes, laying out and paving streets, and building a market hall and a municipal center. In return, the company was to cede to the municipality the land required for the streets and public buildings. It was estimated that the necessary improvements would cost the city a minimum of 300,000 piasters, over half a million dollars. The parcels of land that would be turned over to the city to compensate for this large expenditure had cost the secret owners of the company, Cognacq and his friends, the paltry sum of 3,600 piasters. Thus, after work had been completed, they would be in possession of desirable property which had been improved at no cost to themselves.

Work on the site began almost immediately and continued more or less steadily for more than a year, even though no contracts had been signed. The President of the Council, in league with several of his colleagues, apparently was sure that he could eventually force the majority of the other Council members to ratify the secret agreement, especially if it was presented as a *fait accompli*. Unfortunately for them, a decree suddenly arrived from France ordering municipal elections to be held on May 3, 1925. If new councilors and a new mayor took office, it was probable that the irregularities of the Khanh-Hoi scheme would be exposed. The company hurriedly drew up an agreement that was signed by the President of the Council on April 23.

It was an incredible fiscal contract since, as *Indochine* put it, "the city promised everything, the company nothing." It was even more incomprehensible from a legal point of view because there was no clear title to the land. As early as the spring of 1924, the original owners had instituted legal proceedings against the company for fraud, and the matter was still pending when the contract was signed with the City of Saigon. In the event of an unfavorable decision, the municipality would sustain a huge loss because it would be unable to reclaim the funds that had been invested in land improvements. As a subsequent editorial in *Indochine* asked pointedly: "What overriding motive could have impelled the President of the Municipal Council to pledge the city treasury in such a risky business?" [5]

In spite of vigorous opposition by the company, the Saigon municipal elections of May, 1925, brought into office an honest Mayor named Rouelle. One of his first official acts was to launch an inquiry into the Khanh-Hoi affair. When he learned of the flagrant illegality of the undertaking, he ordered all work at the site stopped until the situation had been clarified in the courts. He then wrote a detailed account of the facts to explain his action. Rouelle did not specifically name the men behind the Khanh-Hoi Realty Company, but his exposé, published in its entirety by *Indochine*, strongly suggested to Malraux that Cognacq had secretly engineered the highly profitable scheme. As a result of Rouelle's investigation, Malraux noted, "like some nymphs—but prettier—struck down by a terrible fate, you are left, arm and leg upraised, to contemplate with a melancholy eye the broken pieces of your game, which evoke innumerable memories. O time forever gone by! Land of Plenty! El Dorado!" [6]

The unexpected opposition successes in the May elections together with the Khanh-Hoi scandal had weakened Cognacq's hold on the Saigon Municipal Council, but he still retained tight control of the three other major consultative bodies in Cochinchina: the Chamber of Commerce, the Colonial Council, and the Chamber of Agriculture. Only by keeping these groups powerless could he maintain his authoritarian, one-man rule of the Colony. Malraux boldly declared in an editorial: "We have declared here on several occasions that the first of Governor Cognacq's illegal acts consisted in governing, not with the help of the elected assemblies whose activities he is supposed to coordinate, but on the contrary, without taking the slightest account of their wishes. In short, he is an excited cerebellum who takes himself for a brain." [7] A scandal in the Chamber of Agriculture soon gave the editors of *Indochine* another opportunity to attack Cognacq's dictatorial rule.

The Chamber of Agriculture was composed of some dozen members, of whom at least two were Annamites. Several delegates were apparently appointed directly by the Governor, but the majority were biennially elected to four-year terms by the French citizens of the colony. For some time, the President of the Chamber had been a *colon* named Labaste. He had first won a seat in the Chamber in 1908 and had been re-elected in every subsequent contest. He would have had to run again in 1924, but because a reorganization of all the chambers of agriculture in Indochina was in progress, the Governor General in Hanoi had temporarily postponed the elections. Any expiring terms were automatically extended until the reorganization could be completed. At the time the scandal broke in Saigon in the late spring of 1925, Labaste's elected term had been prolonged for more than seventeen months.

The Chamber chose its officers every two years by a simple majority. If a majority was not obtained on the first ballot, a revote was authorized, with a limit of three ballots. In the 1922 contest for the presidency, the incumbent—the Cognacq-supported Labaste—was vigorously opposed by the more liberal Blanquière. The first ballot was inconclusive, but Blanquière received a majority of the votes on the second. However, by some undisclosed maneuver, Labaste forced a third and then illegal fourth ballot, after which he proclaimed himself elected. A number of the Chamber members strongly protested this. They immediately drew up papers questioning the legality of the election and sent them to the Governor, as prescribed by their bylaws, for eventual forwarding to Hanoi. However, Cognacq was determined to keep his supporter Labaste in office, and he held up the incriminating documents until the statutory time limit for contesting the election had expired. Reluctantly, the dissenting members accepted the situation.

All this changed abruptly in late 1924 or early 1925. The Treasurer of the Chamber, a close friend of Labaste's, died suddenly, and a successor was elected from outside the Cognacq clique, M. Arborati. After a long and bitter struggle culminating in a direct appeal to the Governor General in Hanoi, Arborati finally forced Labaste to surrender the official financial records of the Chamber, which he had illegally impounded. It soon became clear why the President had been so unwilling to turn over the books. The new Treasurer reported at the May, 1925, meeting that a number of expenses for which Labaste had been reimbursed were either illegal or patently inflated. Moreover, several large sums of money were utterly unaccounted for—notably some 20,000 piasters, or more than $40,000, withdrawn by the President for two "missions." After these revelations, a majority motion by the Chamber requested that Labaste permit the Vice President to act as presiding officer until the matter could be cleared up. This was perfectly fair, especially since Labaste's original term had long since expired and his re-election as President had not been without chicanery. However, Labaste angrily refused, adjourned the meeting, and stalked out, ordering the two Annamite members to leave with him. The rest of the group, with the Vice President presiding, remained behind to continue their discussion of the matter. They finally decided to attempt to elect a new President at the next monthly meeting, on June 19.

The June meeting took place as scheduled, but President Labaste did not attend. Cognacq sent as his personal representative Eutrope, his Inspector for Political Affairs and the director of the Khanh-Hoi Realty Company. That gentleman informed the Chamber in no uncertain terms that anyone who tried to take over its presidency would be subject to "legal prosecution for usurpation of authority." Nevertheless, voting was held and Lacouture, a lawyer from Saigon, was chosen to replace Labaste as president. His first act was to send a wire to Hanoi to inform the Governor General of the situation. This telegram was reprinted in *Indochine* on June 24, and the following week Malraux and Monin began their exposé of the situation. As they succinctly pointed out in one of their editorials, the Labaste-Cognacq collusion involved a major question of principle:

The top civil servant of Cochinchina, the representative of the executive branch who is responsible for ensuring the strict and complete application of the law, is the first one to violate it when his personal interests or those of his friends are involved. How much longer will the Government of the Republic stand for such a scandal, which is enough to demoralize the country? [8]

Indochine subsequently revealed some amazing facts that clarified Cognacq's actions. As President of the Chamber of Agriculture, Labaste had appointed himself a delegate to the Colonial Council. There he had been very useful to the Governor. Not only had he helped push through a number of questionable money grants for him, including a $20,000 credit for a new car, but he had faithfully supported every scheme from which the Governor and his friends could profit. In several instances, notably the port-monopoly project, he had even voted *contrary* to the express instructions of the Chamber of Agriculture. This loyalty did not go unrewarded. Thanks to collusion by the Administration, Labaste had paid no taxes since before the war. Even more serious, he had been granted a number of loans by the Bank of Indochina that ultimately reached the staggering total of nearly 1½ million francs, or $300,000. Because he had had these loans classified as agricultural they were guaranteed by the French Government and bore a very low rate of interest. The largest sum, nearly 800,000 francs, had been obtained in 1923, during Cognacq's regime. However, the law clearly stated that the total of government-guaranteed agricultural loans to any one individual could not exceed the value of one-third of the yearly harvest from his land. Did this mean, queried an *Indochine* editorial of July 2, that Labaste's rice crop brought him the fantastic annual income of nearly 4.5 million francs? Or was this arrangement simply another example of Cognacq's disregard for legality where his friends were concerned?

Labaste was a close associate of Chavigny, and as was to be expected, *L'Impartial* gave front-page space to his long, rambling letter of reply to the charges leveled by *Indochine*. It contained few facts. Labaste began with several paragraphs of pompous self-praise for his long years of struggling against tremendous material difficulties, "fearful reefs where my colonial bark was often damaged, indeed almost sank, while leaving . . . honor high and dry." [9] The remainder was primarily an unimaginative and irrelevant litany of personal invective directed against the editors who had exposed him. He accused *Indochine* of confusing the law-abiding

Annamites by its "deliberately defamatory opposition" and its "unpunished call to impertinence, to revolt, to lawbreaking, to Bolshevism." He appealed for conservative support in the coming Chamber of Agriculture elections, asserting that a vote for him would be a vote against "these opportunists, these sowers of discord, colonials of the rear guard." He ended with the ringing cry, "Throw out the false colonials!"

Indochine continued to feature the Labaste story to keep the matter fresh in the minds of the voters. The editors knew that Cognacq's hold on the Chamber of Agriculture had been seriously weakened, both by the scandal and by the Administration's subsequent high-handed attempts to conceal the facts.

In mid-July an even greater malfeasance involving the Governor came to light: investigations by Malraux and Monin into the land swindle at Camau revealed that Cognacq was directly involved in the fraud.

Cochinchina was a very fertile province, but until the coming of the French, only part of its arable land had been under cultivation. The Annamites had sought to produce only enough food for their own consumption. France, however, wanted an export surplus, and the Colonial Administration had vigorously encouraged farmers to open up the undeveloped areas. This was an arduous and dangerous task. To provide a strong incentive, the government had long permitted the peasants to become owners of any virgin lands they cleared. An Annamite farmer could request title to his fields after he had worked them for at least three years and had paid taxes on them. Sometimes he was granted the whole acreage free, but most often he was given 25 acres outright and allowed to buy the remainder at a nominal cost. The price was fixed by the authorities and paid in yearly installments. In the event that several peasants claimed the same piece of land, the government had the option of auctioning it to the highest bidder.

A system that empowered the Colonial Administration to decide who was to get what land and at what price obviously lent itself to abuses. A number of suspicious incidents involving small tracts of land were reported in the early issues of *Indochine*. In one newly opened area, the peasants were told by local authorities that *none* of their land would be given them free and that they would be permitted to buy only half of what they had cleared. The remainder, the choicest plots, had been set aside for an unnamed government official.[10] In another area, the French administrator informed the farmers that the government ordered them to cede their lands to his close friend and collaborator, the local Annamite delegate to the Colonial Council.[11] The peasants repeatedly protested these injustices to authorities in Saigon and Hanoi, but their pleas went unheeded. Moreover, the government-controlled press in Cochinchina refused to print their letters; only *Indochine* took up their cause. At first there was little hope of implicating the Governor directly, but an unexpected turn of events suddenly revealed Cognacq "with his hand in the till," as Monin put it. The Camau story broke in the July 11 issue of *Indochine* and was featured for the next two weeks.[12]

In late April and early May, 1925, Governor Cognacq had made an inspection tour of the newly cultivated sections of Camau, the richest agricultural area of Cochinchina. The government papers celebrated the event with lyric abandon, noting that "he saw everything, listened to all complaints, satisfied all petitioners." He made it a point, they said, to put everything in order so that the illiterate farmers could not be exploited by "certain sharks or speculators." Shortly after Cognacq's trip, a discreet item appeared in the *Bulletin of Commerce*, indicating that an auction sale of land in Camau province would take place on July 27. Contrary to usual practice, the announcement gave no indication of the acreage to be sold or the minimum bid required. However, the appropriate register in a government office in Saigon showed that 26 parcels of land, varying in size from 520 to 2,335 acres, were involved. The total area to be auctioned was about 37,000 acres, and more than three-fourths of it was already under cultivation. The authorities had fixed the minimum bid at ten piasters per hectare (about $50 per acre), a ridiculously low figure since the *yearly* income from the rice crop grown on this land was more than $400,000.

At first glance, the auction rules set forth in the register appeared to be the usual ones, but closer inspection revealed two highly unusual clauses. The first required anyone wishing to take part in the bidding to have in his possession enough cash to cover his bid or a certificate from the governor of his province stipulating the maximum figure at which he was solvent. In any case, the president of the auction had the prerogative of deciding which bids to accept and which to refuse. He could exclude anyone from the bidding without explanation. As Malraux pointed out, this gave unusual—if not illegal—power to the person directing the auction.

The second departure from standard auction conditions was the apparently harmless provision that "at the request of buyers, several contiguous lots may be grouped in order *to be put up together for bidding,* on condition, however, that each of the lots for which grouping is requested has a minimum area of 500 hectares." Fourteen of the twenty-six plots to be auctioned were more than 500 hectares in area, and an examination of the surveyor's map revealed that these fourteen were all contiguous. Moreover, they were the most desirable lots in the sale. Thus a huge expanse of some 10,000 hectares (about 25,000 acres), more than two-thirds of all the land to be sold at this auction, could be formed, simply on the request of a prospective buyer, *before* any bidding was allowed on separate plots. This was contrary to the usual procedure, which did not permit lots to be joined in one parcel until *after* each of them had been bid on and purchased individually, the selling price for the entire parcel being the sum of the prices realized for the individual lots. Some Annamite landowners in Camau could perhaps put up the opening price for a plot of 500, 700, or even 1,000 hectares, but certainly none of them could furnish the minimum of $200,000 required to make an initial bid on the 10,000 choice hectares. Only a buyer representing some powerful financial group could have such a sum at his disposal. Unopposed in the bidding, he could acquire a huge tract of excellent land for the ridiculously low minimum price—and both the colonial treasury and the farmers who had cleared the land would be cheated.

The first *Indochine* editorial on Camau appeared in the twenty-second issue, dated July 11. The hard facts presented there showed clearly that the two special clauses had been drawn up in order to permit someone to circumvent the standard safeguards against fraudulent practices. A flood of letters from farmers in Camau poured into *Indochine*'s editorial offices. A particularly informative one came from one of the French planters in the region, a M. Beauville. His letter was published in the next issue, which came out on July 15, immediately after the three-day holiday. According to Beauville, everyone in the province had long been aware of the Governor's efforts to "build himself a very sizable fief of rice fields" by all kinds of illegal means. However, the attempt to manipulate the coming land auction for the benefit of the "consortium behind which M. Cognacq prudently takes cover" was a fraud on a much larger scale than anything he had dared undertake in the past. By citing precise figures on the annual rice crop,

Beauville demonstrated how absurdly cheap the government-fixed
purchase price was. He concluded by forcefully pointing out that
there was no Bolshevism in the colony, as repeatedly claimed by
L'Impartial, but that there most certainly was a widespread movement of social protest—the direct result of the "general discontent
of the Annamites . . . who curse M. Cognacq and his zealous administrators, who do not scorn to buy rice fields cheaply." [13]

Two days later, on July 17, the front page of *Indochine* carried
a copy of a letter written by a greatly respected Camau mandarin
named Nghia to M. Fays, President of the Colonial Council and
the highest elected officer in the colony. (The original document
had been "lost" in the mail.) Nghia confirmed all the irregularities
that Malraux and Monin had uncovered and pointed out, as they
had done, that the two special clauses "more than suffice to
eliminate—purely and simply—the original owners who wish to
repurchase lands that they have improved by their own efforts, and
I am very much afraid that this affair is going to result in many
murders."

Nghia's testimony was impressively supported, three days
later, by another mandarin from the same area, Tran-van-Dang,
formerly a provincial councilor. His letter on behalf of the "dispossessed landowners of Camau" was published on the front page
of the July 20 issue of *Indochine,* followed the next day by copies
of the telegrams that he had sent to Cognacq, Fays, acting Governor General Monguillot, and the Minister for Colonies in Paris.
From these documents and the more than thirty affidavits that
they had received from the local farmers, Malraux and Monin acquired additional information on the fraud. It appeared that the
lands of an entire town were in jeopardy. Some farmers there had
been working the same rice paddies since as early as 1913; none
had arrived later than 1920. All had receipts to prove that they had
regularly paid their taxes. Though they had repeatedly requested
title to their plots, which had long since been officially recorded by
government surveyors, they had received no answer. When they
appealed to Cognacq during his spring tour, the Governor had
promised them that their ownership would soon be confirmed. In
any case, since none of the fields in the area was claimed by more
than one farmer, it was clear that an auction at Camau was completely unjustified.

Faced with the continuing silence of the Administration as the
auction date of July 27 drew ever closer, the unhappy Annamites

and their French supporters renewed their protests to the Governor General. The law stipulated that he must specifically authorize any sale of public lands involving more than 1,000 hectares, and it was doubtful that Cognacq had obtained approval for the Camau auction. Editorials, telegrams, and letters were sent to Hanoi, urging Monguillot at least to postpone the sale and investigate the matter for himself. Malraux made a blunt appeal to him on behalf of the long-suffering Annamite farmers: "Monsieur the Governor General will perhaps wish to take into consideration the fact that all of these men are poor, that if their lands are put up for sale and are bought by others they will lose all reason for living, and that the surest way of protecting them against spoliation . . . is to grant them title to these lands whose entire value they have created." [14]

Monguillot drove into Saigon on an inspection visit on July 23, a scant four days before the auction was scheduled to take place in Camau. On the preceding day, Malraux had brought the whole matter to a head with his scathing "Third Letter to M. Henry Chavigny Forward-to-the-Rear, Professor of Refinement," a front-page editorial obviously timed to catch the attention of the arriving Governor General. After a number of sarcastic comments on the personal probity of Chavigny, Malraux mentioned the three major scandals in which the editor of *L'Impartial* had been involved with Cognacq—the port-monopoly scheme of 1924, the Khanh-Hoi land swindle, and Camau. In all three frauds, the Colonial Administration had maneuvered so that a private financial group would profit from the spoliation of some poor Annamites. The exploiters were successful only because most of the newspapers were in collusion with them, a collusion that usually took the form of silence. In the present case, wrote Malraux angrily, except for *Indochine* "not a single French newspaper in Saigon has carried the letter from the dispossessed landowners of Camau that we ran. . . . It is remarkably moderate in tone. It is moving. It is based on a solid point of fact. No other newspaper has published it."

Chavigny was very quick to accuse others, notably the editors of *Indochine,* of undermining the French cause on the peninsula by building up ill will against France among the Annamites. Yet Chavigny and Cognacq deliberately turned their backs on poor farmers who were pleading for justice. Malraux's indignation and deep concern over these flagrant social and legal injustices lift his final paragraphs to an angry eloquence. Addressing Chavigny directly, he wrote:

> These farmers . . . came and settled in Camau a very long time ago. They were poor. Little by little, they transformed the bush into a fertile land. I will not speak to you of heat or fever. They are exceptionally severe . . . but they are such old friends that no one pays attention to them. I will only ask you to look at their faces. All the suffering of the Annamite farmer is written there, and the toil of their fathers has branded them with pitiful deep scars.
>
> You and your cronies who covet their lands, you do not mistake this. You see all their toil, all their suffering, in the magnificent rice. You can visualize, beneath each field, the dead man who cleared it. You imagine him, of an evening, counting the piasters he has earned—the value of his land. *You count along with him*. . . .
>
> You will tell [the protesting farmers]: "French law has anticipated everything. If this dispossession does indeed take place, you will not lose from it. Your work will be evaluated by an expert, and you will be paid its value."
>
> But before this is done, they will have to institute legal proceedings in the Disputed Claims Court. Then referral to the Council of State. Before the end of the proceedings, they will be dead. And France—too far away, alas—will extend her long, sad shadow across their tombs.
>
> To be sure, you will still say: "Their death shows how well they understood their duty. Their lands are richer than ever, and the rice grows thick over their graves. The most beautiful fields of Cochinchina, those through which the wind passes with the sound of tinkling money, are those where were laid out countless vanquished sufferings, countless hopeless bodies. . . ."
>
> Especially, sir, if they were *lean* ones.

For Cognacq, all this uproar about Camau was especially embarrassing, coming when Monguillot was in Saigon. Accordingly, the government-controlled press, so long silent on the matter, was instructed to begin a concerted effort to vindicate the Governor. The primary aim of the articles that subsequently appeared in these newspapers was either to discredit the protestors who had written from Camau or to "prove" that the Administration was acting for everyone's best interests in organizing the auction. The editor of *Opinion* called the protests of the two mandarins from Camau nothing but "sick imaginings" and expressed his confidence that the Administration would give them "a most categorical denial." Another pro-government newspaper, the *Voix Anna-mite*, asserted that Councilor Dang did not even exist! *Opinion* contradicted this notion several days later with a deliberate attempt to confuse the issue by misidentifying Dang as a minor functionary named Doan.[15]

The editors of *Indochine* were not interested in this petty bickering. Monguillot was in Saigon, and it was essential that he be informed of the true facts about Camau. To this end, Malraux gave a detailed summary of the matter in his July 25 editorial, "Camau —The Thirty Protests." The Administration maintained that the rights of the farmers had been protected, that their cultivated land had been excluded from the sale, he wrote. However, the official plan of the area clearly showed that scarcely one-tenth of such land had been so reserved. Why had the peasants waited so long before protesting the injustice of the auction? The answer was simple: On his visit to the area, Cognac had solemnly assured them that they had nothing to fear, that their lands would soon be granted to them. "It is obvious that he kept his word," Malraux commented sarcastically. A few land titles had been officially recognized, but according to the more than thirty affidavits in the hands of the editors of *Indochine*, payment of huge bribes had been necessary. The entire scandal, concluded Malraux, turned on one question, to which the government and Cognacq should be forced to give a clear answer: Was there an unusual clause in the sale terms that would permit unification of adjoining 500-hectare lots into a single parcel? "Yes or no—*does that extraordinary clause* appear in the record of specifications? For whose profit?"

This editorial appeared on Saturday, July 25. It was *Indochine's* last word before the auction, which was scheduled for the following Monday. Unknown to the two young editors, Cognacq at that very moment was making some hurried last-minute changes in the conditions of the sale. Malraux and Monin received this welcome news just before their newspaper went to press on Monday, July 27, and they hastily made room on the front page for a preliminary announcement of victory: "The conditions of the Camau sale have just been modified, which, as Chavigny says, demonstrates the good faith of the head of the local Administration. . . . The Camau farmers will not be dispossessed."

During the following week, the various government-supported papers made garbled efforts to "explain" the Camau affair and to extricate Cognacq from his predicament. The longest of these lame rationalizations was an editorial that appeared in *Opinion* on July 28. The following day, the back page of *Indochine* reprinted the ridiculous article, liberally sprinkled with barbs by Malraux; the front page carried an account of the auction.

Late the previous Saturday, Cognacq had announced that he was immediately dispatching to Camau his trusted Inspector for Political Affairs and auctioneer, Eutrope. The Governor took special pains to make it very clear that this unexpected trip was *not* the result of any newspaper articles written by notorious and ambitious anti-Frenchmen, but rather the product of his personal desire to see that justice was done. Eutrope arrived in Camau on Sunday morning. The 387 protesting farmers were scattered over a large area. To consult with even half of them would involve traveling some 150 miles and would take several days. Yet that very evening, Eutrope announced that he had completed his "inquiry" and that the auction rules were to be modified. Not only was the clause permitting the grouping of 500-hectare lots removed, but the choice area already under active cultivation by the farmers was withdrawn from the auction and reserved for them.

Since these were the two fundamental abuses about which *Indochine* had protested most vigorously, the editors were delighted. Moreover, they pointed out, these changes incriminated Cognacq even further. Since Eutrope had no authority to modify an administrative directive issued by the Governor of Cochinchina, he must have had Cognacq's rescinding order in his possession *before* he left Saigon to make his twelve-hour "inspection." This appeared to them to be conclusive proof that "Cognacq was in on the whole affair and that it was he who had ordered the offensive against the poor farmers of Camau, just as it was he who ordered the retreat, today turned into a rout." [16]

Once the unjust clauses had been rescinded, the auction at Camau went smoothly. The 9,652 hectares remaining after the withdrawal of the choice land were sold in fourteen lots. Nearly 280,000 piasters, or about $560,000, were realized for the government treasury, far more than the 100,000 piasters that the Cognacq group would have paid for the same land under the original terms of sale. This figure was all the more noteworthy since it represented payment for the least desirable, non-reserved lots.

Malraux's paean of victory took the form of another entertaining "Letter from Jérôme Coignard to Monsieur Maurice Cognacq," published on July 29. It is quite reminiscent of the first edi-

torial piece that he had written for *Indochine* some six weeks
earlier. After relating the Camau debacle, Coignard-Malraux concluded his epistle to Cognacq with customary verve:

Do not say . . . that nothing was changed and that the sale took
place according to the pre-established conditions. For the official
statement, which you had the infinitely judicious prudence not to
communicate to the unhealthy Bolsheviks, states that 4,876 hectares
were set aside, precisely the fifteen lots about which these fishers in
troubled waters were speaking, who—admit it, my son—did indeed
find a rather dirty business on the end of their line.

Do not say—oh mad mortal in the clutches of an evil demon—
that since no one took advantage of the possibility of grouping the
lots, your good faith is proved. If no one dared to do it, it is
because the show had been given away, unlike the coveted lands,
which were not. But call together your Academy: Chavigny, known
for his subtlety; Staath, the clever Dutchman; de la Pommeraye, the
very appropriate defender of the public treasury, which he knows
intimately; Ardin and Delong, sleeping the same sleep for four
thousand years. . . . And ask all these clever individuals what they
would reply if they were told: "An unprecedented clause was inserted into the record of specifications. A newspaper divulged it.
Consequently no one dared to make use of it. Isn't it true that
that clause was inserted *by accident?*"

For the sake of prudence, my son, rattle a few Administration
subscriptions. Their sound is sweet to the ears of healthy journalists.
It delights their soul unto beatitude and admits into their eyes
and ears naught but *revealed* truth.

Thus, all will answer: "It was by accident."

Then you will add: "Never have we sought to wrong anyone. From
all eternity, the cultivated lands were reserved."

And if a voice says: "But, my good sir, if they were reserved, why
did you put them up for auction?" You will say, waving your
Administration subscriptions: "The whole bundle to the one who
answers!"

And you will perhaps finally get a reply, which, alas! is very, very
slow in coming. . . .

Camau made it clear to the Annamites that the new newspaper
was seriously interested in defending their interests and in putting
an end to the blatant corruption of the colonial government in
Cochinchina.[17] However, both Malraux and Monin were aware
that tabloid activity—scandal, diatribe, and ridicule—was essentially negative in character. It made entertaining reading and had

proved to be a potent weapon against Cognacq's Administration, but this was not enough for them. Their purpose in creating *Indochine* had been, and would continue to be, centered on a positive ideal.

VI

Toward a New Colonialism

The title banner of *Indochine* proclaimed that it was a "newspaper for Franco-Annamite reconciliation." This was the fundamental tenet of their colonial credo, and Malraux and Monin gave it most of their energies and most of the space in their newspaper. The front page of the first issue had featured Jean Bouchor's interview with Painlevé on the subject of colonialism. In it, the President of the Council of Ministers had expressed his liberal views on such controversial topics as higher education for Annamites, greater participation by Indochinese in the government of their own country, and the right of native populations to enjoy insofar as possible the same personal and civil liberties granted to Frenchmen. He had affirmed that increasingly close cooperation between the native peoples and the French colonizers was "the very essence of our colonial task."

During the next two months, *Indochine* featured, almost weekly, a number of similar statements by outstanding French political figures. Among those whom Bouchor interviewed in Paris were Marius Moutet, Deputy from the Rhône area and a member of the Chamber's Commission for Colonies; Maurice Violette, the farsighted Governor of Algeria, formerly a member of the Budget Commission; Henri Simon, who had been the Minister for Colonies in an earlier Cabinet; and Ferdinand Buisson, President of the powerful League for the Rights of Man. All these men made the same points again and again. They insisted that the economic, intellectual, and moral prosperity of the peninsula demanded that Frenchmen and Annamites become *partners* in its development. Simon put it bluntly: "We cannot continue to

111

appear—in the eyes of the natives whom we govern or whom we protect—as invaders, preoccupied only with the advantages that they can derive from their conquest, hostile or simply disdainful of the rights and interests of the populations who live on a territory of which they were the first occupants." [1] Moutet seconded this view, pointing out that "we should no more act like invaders than the Annamites should act like rebels in a perpetual state of revolt." [2] Violette added that since "there is no race superior to another," there was absolutely no excuse for depriving the native populations of their rights.[3]

To encourage a necessary social and political evolution, educational facilities in the colonies should be extended; gifted Indochinese must be urged to come to France for their university studies. After being trained, these young men should be given teaching and government posts in the colony at the highest levels commensurate with their abilities. Frenchmen could not long continue to administer by themselves a vast and developing colonial empire in the Far East, and this kind of partnership between conqueror and conquered would bring about a stronger union and increased stability in the area.

Freedom of the press was an indispensable part of the "reconciliation" program, and Buisson was emphatic in pledging support for this element of *Indochine*'s campaign.[4] Personal freedom was no less important, and the four men interviewed all urged removal of the restrictions imposed on the native population. Annamites should be allowed to travel freely, both within their own country and to France. They should be encouraged to form societies and organizations for various purposes, including political discussion, and should be permitted to participate directly in the government of the whole colonial area through their elected representatives on the councils of the Administration.

Moreover, since it was "inadmissible that only the voice of Frenchmen should be heard in Parliament," Indochinese should have a representative in the Chamber of Deputies in Paris. Finally, naturalization should be liberalized so that many more of them could obtain full French citizenship. All of these reforms could be justified on purely selfish grounds, Moutet contended. By treating the Annamites more equitably, the French could make sure that in the future the natives would have "their hearts and their minds turned toward us rather than toward a native nationalism, doubly dangerous, both for us and for them." [5]

"Bolshevism!" screamed the government-supported newspapers in answer to each of these suggestions, and this cry soon became the shibboleth of most colonials. In rebuttal, Malraux and Monin published lengthy statements by Rouelle, the newly elected liberal Mayor of Saigon, and by Gallois-Montbrun, the widely respected senior member of the Saigon bar.[6] As a long-time resident, Gallois-Montbrun had a particularly intimate knowledge of the political situation in Cochinchina. As he saw it, the ultra-conservative colonial mentality was the product of historical evolution. In the early days following the conquest, when capital was urgently needed for development, entrepreneurs were encouraged to come to Indochina. They were granted special privileges and were warmly welcomed because they were needed. Unfortunately, they were subsequently followed by "operators." These men had continued to pour in, "more and more numerous, their teeth sharper and sharper," determined to exploit their favored position to the utmost. They had gradually obtained fiscal and political control of the colony, and now they vigorously rejected every suggestion for modifying the *status quo*, for restoring national dignity to the conquered Annamites. Unhappily, Gallois-Montbrun commented prophetically, "their policy is perhaps the one that could best foster Bolshevism in this country through widespread discontent, through the awakening and aggravation of nationalist feeling. . . . In Asia as in Europe, the propertied classes are really doing everything possible at the present time to help the extremists' game."

The editors of *Indochine* believed that financial exploitation of the colony, whether by questionable business agreements or by outright corruption, must be stopped. To this end, they gave full coverage to any such irregularities uncovered in the local Administration. However, because of his experience in the Paris stock exchange, Malraux realized that the unrealistic piaster-franc exchange rate, fixed by law in favor of the franc, produced even greater economic injustice. The French Government, as well as a number of knowledgeable private manipulators, was deriving huge profits from this arrangement, which was subtly bleeding the colony white. In order to make the indigenous economy viable, it was absolutely essential to stem the outflow of capital. Annamites had made little complaint about the exchange rate because they were not aware of the damage that it was doing to their country. A new and more equitable exchange law had come up for discussion in the Paris Chamber at about the time *Indochine* began publication, and in the second issue Malraux announced that "we shall examine the law that is under consideration and we shall publish the opinions of all qualified authorities."

Two days later, an interview with Caillaux, the French Minister of Finance, set forth the basic issue: should the value of the Indochinese piaster be based on the French paper franc, on gold, or on silver? [7] The discussion was rather technical, and Malraux apparently felt that many Annamite readers would not grasp its importance. He therefore wrote a sarcastically humorous "Open Letter to M. de la Pommeraye," which ran in an adjoining column. In it he reduced the problem to very concrete terms, pointing out that the President of the Cochinchina Chamber of Commerce had been able to build a huge fortune on exchange manipulations as well as on outright frauds. In succeeding weeks, some seven front-page articles by Bouchor dealt with the piaster. Among those interviewed on this subject were a former budget commissioner and a member of the legislative committee studying fiscal reform, as well as presidents or directors of the Banque de France, the Banque de France et des Pays-Bas, the Banque de l'Indochine, the Banque Industrielle de la Chine, and the Crédit Foncier Indochinois.[8] These financial experts all agreed that something had to be done, but unfortunately they differed on what the best solution would be.

In spite of this extensive coverage, it is doubtful if most Annamite readers became very concerned about high finance. They were much more interested in correcting a number of political abuses that touched them in a more immediate and tangible manner. One of the most irritating of these was Cognacq's suppression of news. Because of Malraux's exposés, people were becoming aware of the system by which the Governor controlled most of the French and Annamite publications of Cochinchina and silenced local criticism of his regime. But they did not know about the surreptitious censorship that Cognacq exercised over "dangerous" publications arriving from metropolitan France. Less than two weeks after its birth, *Indochine* set out to expose this illegal practice.

On Saturday morning, June 27, Paul Monin went to the public library of Saigon, accompanied by a notary. The latter's account of what happened was featured in *Indochine* the following Monday. After a preliminary search through the public catalogue, the young editor asked the librarian on duty to give him the "request book." This was the register in which readers entered the titles of any limited-circulation publications that they wanted to borrow from the library archives. The director of the library was summoned, and after a short discussion, he handed over the record. Monin proceeded to call the notary's attention to a number of requests for liberal newspapers. Several French professors from the Ecole Normale in Saigon had asked for *L'Oeuvre, Le Quotidien, L'Humanité,* and *L'Ere Nouvelle;* two Annamites had requested *L'Echo Annamite* and *Indochine.* These requests dated back from as early as October, 1924, to June 21, 1925, just a week earlier. In the column of the notebook labeled "Response," the head librarian had written a series of unequivocal No's. The professors had objected. One had inserted a "Why No?" after the librarian's refusal. In reply, the librarian had noted succinctly: "The library's newspapers are newspapers of information." Evidently it had been decided that *L'Oeuvre* and *Le Quotidien* were not bona fide publications but propaganda organs. As Monin subsequently maintained, this was a spurious justification for their having been illegally "laid under an interdict by M. Cognacq, Governor of Cochinchina." Indicative of Cognacq's bad faith was the absence of restrictions on "propaganda" publications of blatantly conservative hue, such as *L'Homme Libre* and *Le Progrès Annamite.*

To circumvent this censorship and obtain wider exposure for the liberal viewpoint, Malraux and Monin began reprinting articles from the forbidden French and Annamite newspapers in *Indochine.* The 5,000 daily copies of their newspaper assured these reprints a wide circulation, which was further increased through the cooperation of semi-secret reform groups like Malraux's Young Annam. Letters and comments from all over the province began to pour into the editorial offices on the Rue Taberd. To stimulate further serious discussion by Annamites of their various problems and complaints, Malraux and Monin established a special daily feature called the "Annamite Readers' Forum." [9] From this column, as well as other sections of the newspaper, it is possible to determine rather accurately the major elements in the nascent Annamite program of political and social reform.

The first article in the "Forum" appeared on June 26; it was a general statement of the problem of Franco-Annamite reconciliation from an Annamite point of view. Essentially, the author—T. Tan—did little more than restate the Malraux-Monin position in slightly different terms. However, after condemning the oppressive

acts and what he called the medieval Spanish colonial ideas of
Governor Cognacq, he praised the courageous stand of *Indochine*'s editors:

> The pro-Annamite Frenchmen who—true to the generous ideas of
> France—work for the reconciliation of the protector and the pro-
> tected peoples, are called anti-French by the false Frenchmen, by
> those masters of the destiny of a weak people, those authoritarians
> who want to free themselves from the metropolitan govern-
> ment in order to reign as all-powerful despots. They label anti-
> French those who are concerned about the Annamites, who remain
> independent, who defend Indochina against sharks.

Subsequent "Forum" columns discussed in detail some of the oppressive acts of these authoritarians.

In the liberal view, the creation of a highly educated native elite
was absolutely essential if Indochina was ever to emerge from its
colonial bondage. Thus the cream of the Annamite youth must be
sent to France for advanced technical and university studies. According to official regulations, this was fairly easy to do. The only
requirement was that certain papers be obtained and validated
prior to the issuance of a passport and an exit permit. Moreover,
the Administration was apparently eager to encourage such study;
it stressed that the colony was not "a prison, either for the natives
or for Frenchmen. Everyone is free to leave it or to enter it, nay, to
re-enter it, as he pleases." [10] However, a number of letters from
readers of *Indochine* revealed that this was not at all the case.
The seemingly reasonable requirements were in reality a device by
which the government arbitrarily controlled all movement out of
the colony. Several Annamites cited their frustrating efforts to obtain passports to go to France for study.

The preliminary papers that had to be obtained and validated
included a birth certificate, a certificate testifying to "sober life
and habits," a police report, a medical certificate attesting that the
applicant was "fit to stand the climate of France," a family financial statement, a pledge by parents or family to pay for the return
trip from France, and, finally, an educational certificate.[11] These
documents were obtained from various officials in the applicant's
home province, but before being sent to the Sûreté in Saigon, the
whole dossier had to be approved by the local province chief. Before giving his approval, he usually ordered a secret inquiry to determine if there was anything even remotely political or "anti-

French" in the background of the applicant or his family. If there was, or if appropriate bribes were not given, approval was delayed indefinitely. *Indochine* demanded angrily whether it was fair that qualified Annamites who wanted to go to France to complete their education "have not been able to leave their native village because of their failure to sufficiently grease the palms of officials, or because one of these had some kindly motive for bearing a grudge?" [12] Even if the province chief gave his permission, the dossier still had to pass through the hands of the Sûreté in Saigon and the Governor of Cochinchina. Either could exercise a surreptitious veto if he so chose.

Another injustice that was very vexing, particularly to Annamite intellectuals, was the difficulty of becoming a French citizen. In the older French colonies—notably the Indian enclaves—educated natives could obtain this citizenship virtually upon demand. This was not at all the case in Indochina, where the law was so restrictive as to make naturalization virtually impossible. A number of French lawmakers realized the injustice of the situation, and new legislation was being discussed in the Chamber of Deputies. As was to be expected, many colonials were vociferous in their opposition. Some went so far as to maintain that citizenship should *never* be granted to Annamites. As Le-Hoang-Muu pointed out in a "Forum" article headed "French Naturalization," [13] this was particularly galling to Indochinese because most of the Indians living among them were French citizens and could therefore vote in Indochina! It was obvious, he wrote, that the opposition of the colonial reactionaries was inspired by the fear of seeing "Frenchmen reduced to a minority in the various elective bodies and eliminated from the various local assemblies." However, if the French governed justly, did they have any more reason for fear in Indochina than in their other colonies, where large groups of natives had been given the right to vote?

The desire of many Annamites to obtain French citizenship arose in part from their realization that enfranchisement would permit them to correct—by democratic means—some of the most glaring governmental abuses in Cochinchina. Even more important, however, as Frenchmen they would be protected by French law. Certain personal liberties would be guaranteed to them, rights that even a Cognacq would hesitate to violate. There was, for example, the question of freedom of association and assembly; for, as Truong-Nguyen stated in another "Forum" col-

umn,[14] the local government "is opposed to the formation of any
new society whatsoever . . . nor does it welcome the presence in
the various associations of 'Bolsheviks,' that is to say, anti-French
men . . . those who assume the right of judging its acts and
deeds." The Governor had not hesitated to take illegal measures to
suppress such groups and to silence Annamite leaders. However,
he certainly would have hesitated to try and abridge the freedoms
of Frenchmen so blatantly. Moreover, Annamites were openly encouraged to use opium, and their villages were obliged by decree to
buy a certain quantity of liquor from the State Alcohol Monopoly.[15] Could such ruthless measures be taken against French citizens? The books and personal papers of the Annamite scholar
Nguyen-van-Ninh were seized by the Sûreté on his return from
France on the grounds that they contained Communist propaganda. The incriminating materials turned out to be two tracts by
Jaurès and some pamphlets distributed by the League for the
Rights of Man.[16] Possession of such documents certainly would
have been insufficient to justify a similar action against a French
citizen. Another Annamite, Phan-chau-Trinh, commented in a
"Forum" column: "Grant us the same law as Frenchmen, and we
shall ask nothing better than to live under the aegis of France.
French law for everyone!" [17]

French citizenship and French law would also help protect the
Annamites from exploitation and oppression by the mandarins,
the vestiges of the old indigenous ruling class. Abuses by the
mandarinate were evident on a provincial and town level almost
everywhere on the peninsula, but they were especially severe at the
court of the Annamite King-Emperor, at Hué. It was there that
the reformers aimed their main attacks.

The French, as they completed their conquest of the Indochina
peninsula in the second half of the nineteenth century, assumed
direct control over Cochinchina in the south. However, they permitted the former overlord of the whole eastern half of the peninsula to continue as titular ruler of its central section, called
Annam, with a vague suzerainty over the northern province of
Tonkin. Although this ruler, surrounded by French "advisers," was
now no more than a powerless puppet, his imperial dignity provided a convenient shield for the wrongs committed by his venal
courtiers. During the spring of 1925, Emperor Khai-Dinh fell seriously ill; in mid-June, the first issue of *Indochine* reported the
rumor that he was dying. A week later, on June 25, the newspaper

published a long article written by Nguyen-Phong from Hué, the capital of Annam.[18] It suggested that the Emperor was already dead, but that the French Administration of Annam "for grave reasons of a political nature is doing everything to keep secret the death of His Majesty." Evidently the problem of succession had not yet been solved.

A royal son named Vinh had earlier been designated heir apparent, but it was subsequently discovered that the Emperor was not his father. The French advisers were reluctant to support his accession to the throne. It was suspected that the French were secretly seeking a way to install a more amenable prince of a collateral line as leader of the country. According to Nguyen-Phong, the problem could be simply solved by "abolishing the monarchy in Annam and joining this country directly to the French Administration." He concluded his article by stating bluntly that such a step "would be looked upon favorably by the educated natives of the midlands, even by the old scholars of the ancient tradition, because of the abuses committed by the mandarins under cover of the sham supreme power set up on behalf of the 'Son of Heaven.' "

Subsequent articles in the "Forum" discussed some of the abuses committed by court mandarins and by local notables, both in Central Annam and in other parts of the peninsula.[19] Among the most reprehensible were various types of indenture. In some cases, rich landowners, in return for a fee, would lure or force a number of young farmers into signing contracts with French firms. These hapless victims were then shipped to work as virtual slaves on French plantations in the New Hebrides or New Caledonia. In Indochina, impoverished peasants could obtain modest loans from wealthy notables only by agreeing to pay exorbitant interest. It was customary for the creditors to insist that the peasants give one or more of their children in bondage until the debt was repaid. As most rural families made a marginal living at best, this servitude was usually for life. One Annamite accurately observed that such arrangements were nothing more than thinly disguised slavery.[20] Since this type of cheap labor was one of the main sources of the mandarins' wealth, they were obviously against any moves to abolish it.

Nguyen-Phong stated in the "Forum" that the Annamite ruling house was made up of decadent incompetents who were utterly incapable of change. He subsequently elaborated on his opinion:

"The whole court, from the King down to the eunuchs, is a troupe of comedians, and as such is a useless luxury." As long as the monarchy remained, "the mandarins and their acolytes remain and . . . their palms must be greased, under penalty of being thrown into prison and mistreated in the worst way." [21] This delicate matter was touched upon in several columns before it was abruptly brought to a head during the first week in August.

Sometime in July, an Annamite patriot named Nguyen-van-Pho arrived in Saigon from Tonkin. He was on his way to France to purchase printing equipment so that he could set up a publishing business. Before booking passage for Europe, he decided to arrange for the immediate publication of a pamphlet that he had written on the Annamite monarchy. The text, in the Annamite language, was fairly short, and the Saigon firm of Portail agreed to print it in both the *quoc ngu* romanization and in Chinese characters. When Pho came to pick up his order, he was greeted by men from the Sûreté. They arrested him on the charge of having incited to revolution.[22] On August 6, three days after Pho's arrest, *Indochine* printed a French translation of his pamphlet in the "Forum" column so that everyone in Saigon could judge the falseness of the Administration's accusation.

The opening words of the pamphlet indicated its tone and contents: "Proclamation to the People by a Group of Annamite Patriots: The Emperor is dying. The heir apparent is not certain of succeeding him. This fine opportunity to do away with the monarchy must not be allowed to pass." Pho recalled Annam's long line of kings, some of them good, some bad. He conceded that in other circumstances, continuation of the monarchy might be desirable: "If there had been no contacts at all between Europe and Asia, if the French protectorate had not been established in our country, if the world had not been flooded by a wave of democracy, finally if we had had valorous kings to guide us, we would ask nothing better than to serve the monarchy." However, contact with the modern European world had wrought a profound change in Indochina, and the whole monarchial system had become an enormous liability. It was the King-Emperor who protected the mandarins, the group most actively opposing every effort to bring the country into the twentieth century. The imperial institution, Pho wrote, encouraged vainglorious Annamites to expend their energies in seeking titles and empty court honors rather than in rendering worthwhile service to the new nation. The situation was all the more ridiculous because the present reigning family, a collateral line of the ancient imperial house, elicited from most Annamites neither the veneration due tradition nor the respect due integrity. It was maintained in power by the French, who supported it simply because it was relatively easy to control.

Pho ended by ridiculing the protectorate system of Central Annam. He felt that it was particularly absurd to argue that a democratic republic like France could guide and "advise" an authoritarian monarchy founded on diametrically opposed principles. His solution, paralleling the one offered earlier by Nguyen-Phong, was an interesting indication of how a number of Annamite reformers envisioned the future of the peninsula:

> Without distinction as to Annamites or Tonkinese, we should have the same attitude and the same position, asking for the abolition pure and simple of the monarchy, the placing of Tonkin and Annam under the same administrative regime as Cochinchina, the union of the three countries into a single French colony, the formation of a chamber of native deputies participating jointly with the government in carrying on the country's affairs, with a view toward future autonomy.

It was clear from the "Forum" column of *Indochine* that most Annamite leaders had a very high opinion of French political institutions and traditions. The respected patriot Phan-chau-Trinh, for example, believed that it was quite unnecessary for his countrymen to resort to violence in order to bring about changes in the colonial regime. Public opinion in France, properly informed, would be so aroused that the abuses would have to be corrected: "Be united as a single man in demanding your legitimate rights. Write in the newspapers, set forth your wants, appeal to the humanitarian ideals of France. . . . You will receive satisfaction after you ask for justice." [23] Another Annamite intellectual, Nguyen-Tinh, maintained that the current political unrest in the colony was in a sense a tribute to France, since it was a direct result of the attempts of the native leaders to "indoctrinate the masses with French democratic ideas." [24] Like his countryman Nguyen-van-Pho, Tinh was very positive about the role that France was to play in the future of Indochina: "All of today's Gallicized Annamites and enlightened scholars conversant with European ideas want Annam to become Europeanized and to evolve under

French sovereignty toward the constitutional form and political liberty of modern nations."

In the summer of 1925, then, France was still very much admired in Indochina. Most of the native leaders *wanted* French citizenship for their people, French schools for their children, representation in the French Chamber of Deputies, and an Indochinese political and legal system organized after French models. Although they desired independence, they definitely did not envision a return to the government and institutions of their own past. Politically, one could perhaps best characterize this movement as a kind of Gallicized nationalism. The Franco-Annamite reconciliation advocated by the editors of *Indochine* clearly reflected this disposition, and the newspaper obviously sought to encourage further evolution in the same direction.

Malraux's first two major articles, the imaginary letters to Cognacq that appeared on June 18 and 25, had been slashing attacks on the Governor for interfering illegally and forcibly in the political life of the country. His first serious effort to treat the political situation in the colony did not appear until July 4. This was his third editorial, entitled "Upon What Hard Facts Should an Annamite Effort Be Based?" Malraux noted that for weeks he had been receiving letters from young intellectuals in all areas of Cochinchina. These ardent Indochinese youths, shaped by French culture and imbued with its ideals, fully realized the injustice of the conditions under which they were forced to live. In Malraux's view, they were becoming increasingly angry at "the impossibility of giving a direction and a purpose to their energy." From all sides they asked the same question: What could they do to help liberate their country and themselves from Cognacq's authoritarian regime?

Malraux minced no words in his reply. He realistically argued that "in order to make Annam a free nation where two peoples live on a footing of equality—as in French India, as in the Antilles —it is indispensable that the first part of your life be sacrificed. You can set up a real Annam, but it is your children who will enjoy it." Malraux contended that the first and most necessary step toward improving the political situation in Annam was for the *colons* to admit, honestly and openly, that they had come to the peninsula primarily to make money. It was pointless "propaganda by bluff" to try to dissimulate the underlying financial motivation for what was pompously called "the French presence in Asia." Moreover, there was nothing shameful in the profit motive,

Malraux wrote, as long as Frenchmen earned their profit legitimately *by their labors*. Flagrant abuses and "special arrangements" motivated by greed had grown up in the colony, and these must be abolished. But the Annamites must not fail to acknowledge that the French had acquired *by their labors* legitimate rights in the country. These must be protected.

Most of the Annamites who wrote to *Indochine* regarded action through political channels, especially the Chamber of Deputies in Paris, as the most efficacious way of making their grievances known and of obtaining their "rights." However, Malraux was frank to characterize this belief as one based on an idealization of Western political processes. Democratic governments change often; requests based on so abstract a principle as one's "rights" are soon forgotten by politicians faced with more urgent and concrete problems. Fortunately, a much more satisfactory way of bettering conditions in Indochina was available. First of all, noted Malraux, a radical change must take place in the thinking and in the traditional values of the Annamites. They must cease looking to the safety and prestige of minor jobs in the government, virtually the only civil-service posts open to them, and seek *technical* training: "Let each family realize that to be any kind of technician is much better than to be a clerk in the Administration. There are no Annamite technicians. They must be numerous in twenty years. Make engineers of your sons, construction foremen, doctors. Make of them, above all, agronomists. For that purpose, send them to France. If they try to keep you from doing so, leave it to us." Thus, with remarkable foresight, Malraux put his finger on the fundamental problem that has plagued all the colonial areas of the world, particularly since the end of World War II: the terrible shortage of technically trained personnel, and the inbred prejudice of the educated elements of the population against doing any work except bureaucratic administration.

After returning from France with a professional or technical education, Malraux wrote, young Annamites should organize themselves into "professional organizations," led by active and aggressive officers. Backed by a united membership, these leaders could force a recalcitrant Administration to listen to their grievances. Even more important—and powerful—would be unions of workers, especially those in agriculture. As Malraux foresaw it, the chief of a rice growers' union, for example, could say to the government:

If the voice of liberal Frenchmen is systematically stifled; if our demands that Parliament deigns to hear are postponed indefinitely because of certain influential persons; if we do not get more schools; if we do not have separation of administrative and judicial powers; if the system of bureaucratic coercion under which we suffer continues to operate; if we cannot go to France freely—within a week, all agricultural activities in Indochina will cease.

This method of bringing about reforms would be slow to initiate; it would require a a long period of training and of organization. However, in Malraux's opinion, it was by far the best method for two reasons. First, it was nonviolent persuasion, much like the Hartal, or peaceful work stoppage, practiced in India by Gandhi's followers. Even more important, it was a fundamentally honest means of obtaining redress because it was based *on the labors* of the petitioners. As such, it would be supported by free Frenchmen everywhere. But Malraux was sadly aware that many young Annamites were impatient with a reasonable approach; they would be happier, he said, "if I spoke of quick and impractical solutions and pointed out visions of great castles in the sky, full of wonders."

On Thursday, July 16, eight issues later, Malraux published a second serious political editorial, "Concerning the Role of the Administration," which further developed his ideas on the problems facing the colony. Like the article of July 4, it was written in reply to a letter from an Annamite reader. The subscriber had gratefully acknowledged the important role that *Indochine* was playing in helping to focus the acute but somewhat unorganized discontent of the native population and had praised the editors for their courage in attacking, virtually alone, the corrupt French Administration. Yet, he had observed, many Annamites felt the newspaper was too preoccupied with attacks against particular persons, and they were reluctant to support its programs until the editors gave a more extensive exposition of their underlying general principles.

Malraux first explained that *Indochine* was attacking certain officials not as individuals but rather as representatives of an authoritarian mentality that was jeopardizing the economic future of the colony: "Our attacks . . . are directed against the slow evolution by which the force that—right from the period of conquest —came to replace military force has continued to apply its laws *and to manifest its spirit,* when nothing could be more detrimental to the economic development of the country than that spirit." As

Malraux saw it, the merchants who came to Indochina at the time of the conquest and immediately thereafter had largely resisted the demands of an aggressive and authoritarian Administration. They had succeeded in this because they were imbued with the very same "decisive and forceful spirit" that motivated the admirals and other officers who were governing the peninsula. Unfortunately, subsequent businessmen were not so vigorous; they offered less and less resistance to the usurpation of power by the Administration. The most obvious result of this situation was the discouragement of large-scale commerce and industry. To be sure, Malraux conceded, there were a few big businesses in Indochina, but their annual income was but a small fraction of what it would have been if the economy had been allowed to develop in the preceding twenty years without the increasingly tight control of the government bureaucracy.

Even more pernicious, in Malraux's eyes, was the mental outlook that an excessively aggressive Administration fostered among members of the business community. The basis for authorizing any undertaking—especially in public works—was not its probable contribution to the economic life of the colony, or even the competence and bid of the entrepreneur. The contract was awarded to the man who had supported the right candidate in the previous election or who put forward the most ingenious and lucrative arrangement for draining large sums from the project. Understandably, the more desirable types of businessmen, "those who—by genuine labor—create something," became discouraged at finding themselves constantly faced with "official or semi-official monopolies, arrangements, and deals." Someday, concluded Malraux hopefully, perhaps one of these exasperated, honest men will finally lose patience and bluntly tell the authoritarian bureaucrats, *"the Administration is supposed to serve the country, not the country to serve the Administration."*

These two brief editorials revealed something of the tenor of Malraux's thinking on economics and politics during this time. In both areas, he was essentially conservative, apparently convinced of the virtues of capitalism, private enterprise, and competition. He frankly admitted that the profit motive underlay the French presence in Indochina but felt that this was not injurious provided that profits accrued from honest, productive labor. Moreover, he insisted that the private property and legitimate financial interests of French businessmen in the colony be safeguarded. Although he believed in strong workers' unions, he did not share the Marxian view of capitalist society as being the battleground for a struggle to the death between different economic classes. Personal initiative remained the essential element in a dynamic economy and society. He believed that the government should interfere as little as possible in economic and political life; such intervention not only stifled business and gave rise to corruption, but inevitably led to the suppression of fundamental individual political liberties and to the establishment of a dictatorial state.

On social questions, young Malraux was much more liberal. His attacks against the colonial system, particularly as practiced in Cochinchina, stemmed in part from his conviction that it was politically and economically unsound, but even more from his fundamental humanism. He wanted the French and the Annamites to live together not as masters and slaves, exploiters and exploited, conquerors and conquered, but as equals, because as men they *were* equals. The Annamites had a right to the same educational and economic opportunities, to the same justice and personal freedoms, as the French. To deny them these things, to treat them as unworthy inferiors, was a betrayal of some of the fundamental tenets of France's liberal intellectual tradition, represented by such outstanding contemporary figures as Paul Painlevé, Marius Moutet, Henri Simon, and Ferdinand Buisson. This aspect of the colonial problem seems to have been especially disturbing to Malraux. To a certain extent, it reflects an appealing idealism, but it also indicates the high regard that the future author of *Man's Fate* and *Man's Hope* already had for man, whether European or Asian.

VII

The "Bolshevik" Ghost

Although Malraux and others like him had great respect for the indigenous people and civilization of the Indochina peninsula, many Indochinese did not share this opinion. Like other non-Westerners who had been subjugated by the superior technical achievements and wealth of the European nations, some Annamites had lost pride and confidence in their own traditions, had turned their backs on their cultural past. As one of them put it, "Conquered, we lost both our national honor and our dignity as men." [1] This inferiority complex was intensified by the conservative *colons* who ruled the colony. These Frenchmen were sincerely convinced of their superiority, and their attitude, tragically, had infected some of the native population. However, many leaders of the new nationalist movement saw that the situation had to be corrected, and they undertook vigorous efforts to give their countrymen a new pride in their cultural heritage. *Indochine* strongly encouraged this movement, causing Chavigny and his friends to redouble their cries of "Traitors!," "Anti-French!," and "Bolsheviks!"

A number of examples could be cited as evidence of the "national rehabilitation" program, which was actively supported by the Malraux-Monin paper. The Annamite language, for instance, had been the vehicle of a long and rich cultural tradition and could be a source of national pride. Because it had been supplanted by French in all branches of the Administration and at most levels of the educational system, however, it was falling rapidly into disuse, especially among the younger generation. Annamite was taught as a second language in the secondary

127

schools, along with English, but even this minimal instruction had been effectively sabotaged. As Annamite scholars demonstrated, the *quoc ngu* texts issued by the Colonial Ministry of Education were virtually parodies of the native tongue; they abounded in misprints, grammatical errors, and barbarisms of all kinds. *Indochine* joined the scholars in demanding that this shameful situation be corrected.[2] To stimulate interest in the native literary heritage, the editors began to print French translations of traditional Annamite stories and folk tales in their paper.[3]

Physical fitness for the natives was another goal of the reformers. Like most Asians, the Indochinese felt somewhat inadequate when confronted by superior physical strength and vigor in the Europeans. The new leaders therefore exhorted their countrymen to improve their diets and to observe elementary rules of hygiene. These measures would cut down the staggering rate of infant mortality and invigorate the Annamite race.[4] One article in *Indochine* urged the setting up of an extensive program of physical education in all native schools so that the upcoming generation of Indochinese would be stronger and healthier than its parents.[5] All the nationalists were emphatic in their demands for suppression of the opium traffic, houses of prostitution, gambling dens, and the alcohol monopoly.[6] They saw that these legal and semi-legal institutions were encouraging the weaknesses of the mass of the population and draining their meager physical and financial reserves.

Unity was another potential source of strength. The Chinese minority in Indochina exerted a great deal of influence through its closely knit societies and organizations. A number of Annamite leaders had begun to realize that this was virtually the only way in which individuals could be effective in working toward a particular goal, whether it was to restore personal liberties, to save money, or to boycott foreign-made goods. They pressed their people to form similar groups, but it was difficult to do any organizing among the natives. Not only was the Administration opposed to it, but the Indochinese seemed to find it hard to work with one another without bickering. Nevertheless, as one writer declared in a "Forum" article, at this critical moment in the national history, it was essential for each Annamite to "make a supreme effort to forget the personal hatreds and ambitions that vitiate good will, industry, and energy." [7]

Of all the programs initiated by the nationalists, the colonials

most feared their efforts to re-integrate Indochina with the rest of
the Far East, to make Annamites once again proud to be Asians,
rather than ashamed that they were not Europeans. In 1925 Asia
was a continent in travail; India and China, the two giants, were in
full revolt against the domination of the European powers. Most
conservatives regarded the nonviolent program of Gandhi and the
struggles of the long-suffering Chinese laborers in Hong Kong as
fruits of an identical "Bolshevik" agitation. Cognacq and others
like him were anxious to prevent the spread of this revolutionary
infection to Indochina. Malraux and Monin, on the contrary, were
among those who saw that an enlightened French Far Eastern policy could not be "pointed in any other direction except toward a
close reconciliation . . . with the India of Gandhi and with
China," [8] and their newspaper gave extensive coverage to events in
these two countries.

Most of *Indochine*'s reportage on India concerned the activities
of Gandhi, now one of the most influential figures in all Asia.
Most *colons* genuinely disapproved of the Indian leader. Moreover, they felt that many of the dangerous movements in Indochina—such as demands for wider use of the native language,
for revival of native industries, and for a return to the national cultural past—had been inspired by Gandhi's programs in India. In
order to lessen this supposed influence, the conservative press
made deliberate efforts to denigrate him. On several occasions
L'Impartial featured the anti-Gandhi comments of Cochinchina's
Deputy, Ernest Outrey, including the familiar accusation that he
was a Bolshevik.[9] In Tonkin the editor of the French-language
L'Eclaireur wrote that he regretted seeing the wide propagation of
a new and dangerous "Gospel according to Saint-Gandhi." [10] Dr.
Trinh entered the fray with a particularly vicious article in his
Progrès Annamite.[11] After the curious assertion that Gandhi was
little more than a "clever charlatan pursuing a definite goal which,
however, one would have great difficulty in pinpointing," Trinh
stated that in a 1922 crisis the Indian leader had "addressed a
kind of ultimatum to the Viceroy of India, warning him that he
would decree general civil war if the English Government per-
severed in its actions."

The editors of *Indochine* vigorously countered this propaganda
with the declaration that Gandhi could never have advocated
violence: "It is contrary to the fundamental principles of his
doctrine of patience, gentleness, and universal brotherhood." [12]

They praised him for having created a great moral force that was sweeping across the Far East. His example had deeply impressed all other Asian leaders; they drew constant inspiration from his struggle to obtain—by *peaceful* means—a minimum of rights for the 300 million people of the subcontinent. Moreover, the allegation that Gandhi was the direct instigator of the Annamite agitation for political reform was palpably false. The movement had begun spontaneously, long before Indochinese intellectuals had had any extensive knowledge of the Mahatma's program. In any case, noted *Indochine*, there was a difference in attitude between Indian and Annamite nationalism. Gandhi was arriving at a policy of noncooperation with India's colonial rulers. In 1925 most of the Indochinese leaders still believed that they could achieve their ends by *using* French institutions rather than by subverting them.

Great barriers of distance and language kept the struggle in India from exerting much direct influence in Indochina, but this was not at all the case with China. Not only was it nearer, but a long political and cultural tradition linked it closely with Annam. Also, there were large numbers of Chinese living in cities all over the peninsula. Although many had been in Indochina for generations, they still considered themselves Chinese and maintained close contact with their families at home. Most important, however, the Celestial Kingdom was in the throes of a revolution that held out new hope to all the conquered peoples of Asia. As the French-trained doctor of laws Phan-van-Truong pointed out in *Indochine*, China had only recently been a defeated nation. Like Annam, she had suffered all kinds of humiliations at the hands of European conquerors. Now at last, she had "again become aware of her strength and dignity." Overnight she had become a figure on the international stage, "a power with whom the world must reckon. One can no longer speak to her as before, with loud voice and menacing gesture." Truong urged his countrymen to look to China: "Let us follow events in China attentively. They will have world-wide consequences. As for us, let us never forget that our destiny is intimately linked with that of the whole Far East." [13]

Cognacq was aware that so proximate and successful an agitation for national independence was dangerous to his regime, and he made repeated efforts to restrict news of what was happening.[14] Malraux and Monin set out to counter this. Events in China were moving with great rapidity in the late spring of 1925.

On May 20, a clash had broken out between students and British police in Shanghai, and a dozen Chinese had been killed. This had set off a wave of strikes and other demonstrations all across the country. Inevitably, other incidents of violence occurred, further arousing the anger of the native population against the colonial powers, especially England.[15] The first issue of *Indochine*, on June 17, carried an official dispatch, datelined Peking the day before, which reported: "A procession of 10,000 representatives of the craft and trade unions staged an anti-English demonstration. The Chinese businessmen burned their stocks of English goods. . . . A strike of houseboys employed by the English is imminent; it will lead to a sympathy strike among all servants employed by foreigners. . . . The deep agitation among Chinese groups is causing apprehension in foreign circles." On the back page of the paper appeared a picture of the Hong Kong orphanage "where numerous Chinese fleeing the civil war have just taken refuge," and several photographs of areas in Canton where "struggles continued all during last week."

These items were evidently obtained from the official sources that furnished information to all the other newspapers of the peninsula. However, in the third issue, *Indochine* began a new front-page feature: "Dispatches from Our Special Correspondents." These stories clearly came from independent sources not available to the other newspapers. The first column, in the June 19 issue, carried a further item about the situation in China: "CHINA: ARREST OF A BOLSHEVIK GENERAL. Police and volunteers from Shanghai yesterday made numerous searches, arresting many suspects and confiscating an impressive quantity of Bolshevik propaganda pamphlets. The Soviet General Alexander Guschen was arrested at the Astor Hotel. The official report states that the general had brought some $2 million into the country to use for Bolshevik propaganda." A headline the next day noted that "WAR BETWEEN ENGLAND AND CHINA IS IMMINENT." It was followed by bulletins from the two centers of the struggle:

Canton. The heads of the Chinese Government consider war against England imminent. This news—as soon as it became known —aroused extraordinary enthusiasm in all of Kwangtung Province. The Chinese hope that the terrible danger represented by the English threat will permit the rebuilding of Chinese unity. The various governments are said to be ready to unite against the foreigners. [A Chinese source.]

Hong Kong. The gravity of the situation is extraordinary. However, it is hoped that an armed intervention may still be avoided, but England is ready to act if satisfaction is not given her. [An English source.]

On the afternoon of June 18, a momentous event had occurred in the Hong Kong–Canton area. The Kuomintang leaders in control of the Canton government had ordered all Chinese crews on British ships to walk off their jobs. *Indochine* made space for this last-minute bulletin on the sixth page of its June 20 issue: *"From our special correspondent.* Latest bulletin. Happenings in China. All English boats stopped. Yesterday at two o'clock a general strike was declared by the crews of all the English ships. Shipping is completely stopped. The consul is expected to intervene momentarily." In contrast, the day's news bulletins from the ARIP, printed in the other Saigon newspapers reported that there had been "no new incident" in China. It was several days later before this official source gave any information on the new turn of events. At that time, the editors of *Indochine* gleefully announced that this information had already been published in detail "by us ALONE, AS EARLY AS THREE DAYS AGO." [16]

During the next three weeks, the situation in China steadily worsened. On June 21 the seamen were joined in their strike by most of the other Chinese employees of foreign firms in Hong Kong and in the foreign concession of nearby Canton, called Shameen. Two days later, during a demonstration near the bridges leading to Shameen Island, more than 150 Chinese were killed or wounded by machine-gun fire from European troops. The Canton government immediately declared a general strike and boycott, and the Europeans in Shameen and Hong Kong were almost completely cut off from the outside world.

None of the other Saigon newspapers had any up-to-date China news during this period, but the front-page dispatches in *Indochine* closely followed the rapidly changing situation. These newspaper reports are the materials around which Malraux organized the opening section of his first novel, *The Conquerors.* In fact, the young author went so far as to incorporate some of them almost verbatim into the text of his book.[17] Among the items carried by *Indochine* during the week of June 23–30 were the following: [18]

June 23. China. Latest. In the English banks, Chinese drafts are no longer accepted. . . . Chinese ships sail directly to Canton. The Canton government has ordered Chinese vessels to no longer enter the port of Hong Kong. . . . The English government of Hong Kong has decided—in case of a declaration of war—to give the Chinese 24 hours in which to leave the territory. All the coolies have already left. Only the rich Chinese remain.

June 24. Will war be declared? In London the situation is considered to be very serious. But in Hong Kong reliable financial authorities claim that this opinion is erroneous and that the situation will work itself out satisfactorily with time. In Hong Kong . . . all the banks are closed as a result of excessively large withdrawals. . . . The officers of the Cantonese troops have signed a directive declaring their wholehearted support for a war with England.

June 25. Street fighting is beginning in Canton. We have just this moment received this telegram without any commentary. The closing of the Shameen telegraph office obliges us to wait until new dispatches reach us through another office. . . . Some English ships are said to have sailed upstream as far as Shameen. Received without comment. . . . The Eastern Company informs us of the closing of the post office of the foreign concession on Shameen. . . . Xenophobic disturbances are spreading through all the provinces. Foreigners, particularly the English and Japanese, are being attacked in most of the provinces. . . . The postmaster general of Hong Kong states that until further notice, telegrams written in code will not be accepted unless the code used is indicated on the telegrams.

June 26. Canton under a state of siege. The Europeans, after the departure of the women and children, have fortified themselves in Shameen. All communications with the Chinese city have been cut . . . . The Chinese newspapers are leaving Canton. Since the closing of the office on Shameen, the Chinese newspapers that had moved their offices from Hong Kong to Canton have transferred them elsewhere.

June 27. Change in tactics. After the events of these last few days, the Chinese have decided to attempt a complete general strike of all the workers in contact with foreigners.

June 29. Canton. China is preparing herself for a new effort. It is reported that today's relative calm is due to preparations for a sweeping action by the Chinese. The disagreement reported in Canton between various elements [in the Kuomintang] is said to be a mistake. The strike is still spreading.

June 30. All China against England? The rival generals are reaching an agreement. . . . In Canton the agitation is continuing.

The Chinese papers are portraying the defense of the Shameen bridges as a massacre and are loudly shouting for war. With great reservations. Without comment. The English troops defending Shameen concessions are said to have been taken prisoner by the Cantonese army????

Obviously the editors of *Indochine* had very close links with sources in China, probably Chinese newspapermen. There may even have been someone at Kuomintang headquarters who telegraphed news to them. From time to time, this communication link was interrupted. A notice in the July 15 issue states that "not a bit of genuine news from China has reached us between the 12th and 15th. The telegrams that we received by a roundabout way arrived scrambled." Two days later, an item notes that although all communications with Hong Kong have been cut, *Indochine* has obtained "by a roundabout way, some telegraphic information. We shall publish it tomorrow." Under the blaring headline "ONLY NEWS FROM HONG KONG PUBLISHED IN INDOCHINA," the following issue, of July 18, presented a series of bulletins on the effects of the work stoppage by nearly 500,000 men: the population of the Crown Colony was reduced by one third; most of the newspapers were shut down; the English had to do all household chores themselves; all Chinese businesses and many English firms were closed due to the lack of native help. The strike was unbelievably successful, and one of the bulletins tersely reveals the reason: "The strikers have obtained their results by taking measures against the members of the families of those who refuse to go out on strike."

Toward the end of the month, news from various points in China indicated that the initial wave of xenophobia was dying down. Although the Hong Kong–Canton struggle still occasionally occupied a major part of a foreign dispatch column, the situation was no longer so tense. An August 3 bulletin from Hong Kong made this clear:

China. News from Hong Kong. They are beginning to demobilize the volunteers, who are gradually returning to their usual occupations: they are turning in their arms and equipment to the quartermaster and are becoming civilians again. The demobilization is beginning with the reserve corps, and it is believed that soon there will be no need to retain anyone except for those in units detailed to special duties. The market place is beginning to be well stocked with fruit, fish, and vegetables.

Indochine's bulletins hinted at a struggle going on among the Chinese factions for control of the forces fighting for liberation. One telegram, published on July 31, noted that an army of supporters of the Kuomintang government of Canton had defeated a rival Chinese army from Yunnan that was trying to take control of the area. The bulletin stated that the Kuomintang troops were commanded by "Chinese cadets and Russian officers." Another item published in the same column three days later gave a further glimpse behind the scenes: "*Canton.* The struggle is beginning between the Communist Party and the first section of the Kuomintang. The latter is said to be already affiliated with the Pan-Asiatic Federation being organized in Japan." [19] The relationship between Chinese nationalism and the Communist Party was crucial in determining the direction of the revolution, and Malraux examines the problem in detail in *The Conquerors.* However, no further discussion of it appeared in the pages of *Indochine.*

The struggle in China was very important because it proved that Asians could—if they wished—muster physical forces that could successfully challenge the power of a great European nation like England. It was even more significant from another point of view. It proved that the new native republican government of China had great *moral* strength. According to *Indochine,* this moral force had been "born of the principle, consecrated by the unanimous agreement of the so-called civilized nations, that peoples have the right of self-determination, born also of the spreading among the masses of certain republican ideas that France was the first to propagate throughout the world." [20]

Naturally, most French *colons* rejected this enlightened view. They were convinced that the Kuomintang had engineered the Canton–Hong Kong disturbances primarily to further the worldwide Communist revolution. Malraux and Monin tried to counter this erroneous impression with a number of highly informative articles and editorials. Among these was a long interview with one of the Kuomintang leaders, Sun Fo, son of Sun Yat-sen, founder of the Chinese nationalist movement.[21] Sun Fo carefully underlined that the Kuomintang was a republican party and not a Communist organization. It had one primary political aim: "Chinese

liberty." It was true that in order to achieve this end it had accepted into its ranks anyone who was willing to help, including
avowed Communists. But this did not indicate any alteration in its
basic political philosophy. Any allegations that it had changed,
affirmed Sun Fo, were ridiculous, a desperate last-ditch propaganda
effort by colonialists fearful of losing their privileges in the Far
East.

Another Kuomintang leader, Doctor of Laws You Wen Chew,
vigorously seconded this view.[22] In a subsequent interview, he attacked the illegal and oppressive measures of Governor Cognacq,
especially the restriction of news from China, as prejudicial to
the future of the French colony. The outcome of the Canton–
Hong Kong affair had shown that the Chinese republican government was a force to be reckoned with. Not only had it won a
moral victory over England, but it reportedly had under its command an army of some 250,000 men, 300 cannon, and 60 aircraft.
Since Cognacq's injustices affected large numbers of Chinese living in Cochinchina, as well as the Annamites, it was to be expected that sooner or later the new government of China would
consider intervention on their behalf, using force if necessary.

Indochine's warm espousal of the ideals of the Chinese nationalist movement as represented by the Kuomintang was further revealed by Monin's first editorial, in the third issue of the newspaper. The article was prompted by a letter sent to the French
Consul in Canton by Wu Tchao Tsu, Minister of Foreign Affairs
for the Chinese Republican Government, and originally printed in
a Chinese-language paper in Hong Kong. Wu's letter protested
the French sale of guns to marauding southern war lords whom
the Canton government was trying to pacify. Monin translated the
letter and included it in his editorial because he shared Wu's opinion that such activities by European powers contributed materially
toward prolonging the civil war in China. He asserted that the
essential motivation for the European presence in China was
greed; the country had become little more than "an immense battlefield where the appetites of all the great powers confront one
another." However, in the South, under the leadership of the government of Canton, "direct heir and champion of the republican
ideal," the unification and pacification of China had begun at last.
The triumph of the Kuomintang was the "victory . . . of a
democratic and indigenous government" over the rapacious war
lords and foreign commercial interests. Monin recognized that this

turn of events had provoked a deliberate campaign in Indochina to
discredit the new republican government of Asia, and he promised
that *Indochine* would do everything possible to counteract such
propaganda.[23]

One of *Indochine*'s Annamite collaborators, Phan-van-Truong,
best summed up the newspaper's fundamental position.[24] He saw
events in China as a lesson for the future rather than a threat of
an immediate Communist revolution: "Let us hope that the European and United States governments will draw from present
events the lessons necessary to modify their attitude toward the
Asian world and eventually to arrive at a sincere and lasting reconciliation of two races that, although they are so different in color,
nevertheless constitute the most advanced elements of mankind."
Another Annamite warned that if this lesson was not heeded and
reforms were not forthcoming, then "the legend of Communism
in Indochina propagated by people like Outrey could become . . .
a reality. Certain exasperated Annamites, unable to wait any
longer for the fulfillment of official promises, would move—not
toward Communism—but toward Communists. And the Communists, here as in many other countries of Asia, would be welcomed
—thanks to their promises to respect the rights of oppressed
peoples—as saviors." [25] Once this happened, only violence could
determine the future of the Annamite nation.

The conservatives in the colony were outraged. Not only had
Indochine dared to castigate the policies of the French Administration and expose the corruption of its officers, urging the
Annamites to demand reforms, but it had gone so far as to espouse
and publicize the revolutionary cause of the Chinese republicans!
To Cognacq and his band, these articles were a clear indication
that Malraux and Monin could be considered agents of the "Communist" Kuomintang. Early in July, the Governor decided to pursue this line of attack energetically. He was forced to take this step
because his other efforts to silence or discredit the newspaper had
proved ineffective. The two editors were immediately alerted to
this forthcoming campaign by sympathetic Annamite employees
on Chavigny's *L'Impartial*. And so a headline in the July 11 issue
of *Indochine* proclaimed: "We warn our readers that next week
L'Impartial is going to pull the 'Bolshevik gambit' on us. Saigon
has never laughed so hard."

Militant anti-Bolshevism was nothing new for Chavigny. His
1919 and 1924 election campaigns on behalf of Outrey had been

based almost exclusively on the latter's anti-Communist position, and his newspaper continued to feature articles on the "Bolshevik danger." These items became increasingly frenetic during the early summer of 1925, as the unrest in China grew more widespread. They were an appropriate prelude to the attack against *Indochine* unleashed on July 17. Under a headline that screamed "Documents! Proof! Paul Monin has sold out to the Chinese Bolsheviks!" Chavigny resurrected the Huynh-vi-Khanh affair to "prove" that Monin was a Communist with "one admitted aim . . . to drive France from the Far East by bringing about the union of the Chinese people and the people of Indochina."

Huynh-vi-Khanh was a Kuomintang member who had been taken into custody by Cognacq's Sûreté several months earlier. Monin had taken charge of his case and had quickly obtained his release. In gratitude, local Kuomintang leaders had organized a dinner for Monin at a Cholon restaurant, where they had given him a check for the sizable sum of 5,000 piasters ($10,000), a small part of which was in payment for his legal services, the remainder a retainer fee to assure his services in the event that other party members had any difficulties with the Administration. In return, Monin had given his hosts an autographed photograph of himself. This photograph was published a short time later, on May 27, 1925, in the Hong Kong paper of the Kuomintang, the Chinese-language *China News*. It was accompanied by a letter, written in Chinese, in which the members of the Cochinchina group expressed their gratitude to Monin. They also announced: "Today the party—in conformity with the view of the Central Committee—requests Counselor Monin to be its legal adviser." [26]

Now, almost four months later, Chavigny was putting this event to use. In Chavigny's article, Monin had been paid the money to become a *director* of the Kuomintang party; he had been "bought" by the Chinese Communists! As proof, *L'Impartial* reprinted both Monin's photograph and the letter that had accompanied it in the *China News*. A misleading translation of the text concluded with the sentence: "Today the Cochinchinese section of the Kuomintang party has decided . . . *to name M. Monin as a councilor of the party*." Chavigny declared triumphantly, "That's the political role he wants to play in this country: *To drive France from Indochina and turn it over to the Chinese*."

This thrust by the Administration was parried even as it was made. Forewarned of the attack, Malraux prepared a rebuttal. It was carried on the back page of *Indochine* on the very day that the *Impartial* attack began. Beneath a photograph of the items from the *China News* was Malraux's preliminary explanation of Chavigny's maneuver:

> It escaped no one that the little *Impartial* campaign was predestined to end with the affirmation that *Indochine* is a Russo-Sino-Bolshevik newspaper, etc. . . . Since M. de la Chevrotière intends to publish the above paragraph . . . followed by a falsified translation of the Chinese characters that accompany it, we are publishing it . . . to clearly show everyone how much we 'fear' revelations, publication of documents, and other nonsense.

The accompanying French translation of the Chinese text made it clear that Monin had been named a "legal counselor," not a "party councilor," as Chavigny suggested.

The next day, *Indochine* carried the long "Second Letter to M. Henry Chavigny Forward-to-the-Rear," in which Malraux gave further details about Chavigny's deliberate deception:

> Thinking that no one among your readers was acquainted with ideographs, you pulled the "translation trick." A mistake, sir, a mistake. Falsified translation is a badly timeworn deception. . . .
>
> The four characters above the dot, on the far left of the photograph, which we have translated as "legal counselor" in order to follow the Chinese text as closely as possible, would normally be translated into French as "lawyer-consultant." We request anyone who is curious about your recklessness to look up in the public library the third and fourth ideographs below the dot, on the left, in the Sino-French dictionary. If they do not mean "law, legislation," I will give the cost of 1,800 secret subscriptions to *L'Impartial* to the distinguished Sinologist who will give me their meaning. Next time, don't have your texts faked in the offices of the government or, as your friends have promised, have me knocked out first. For as you were good enough to tell me, I could establish an archaeological review, which would be bothersome to people who want to play at revised and corrected translations.[27]

Chavigny was taken completely unawares. Confronted by the proof of his bad faith, he pretended that Malraux's demonstration was utterly unconvincing, the "pointless show" of a criminal caught redhanded. After dropping some dark hints about forthcoming revelations, he asked his readers to be patient: "If we do not continue . . . our bill of indictment today, it is because it pleases us to wait to observe the reactions of the accused. Thus proceeds the public prosecutor who, having struck a telling blow in the course of a summation, stops a few seconds, swallows a drink of water while observing the physiognomy of the criminal. We are observing this evening the contractions on the faces of those we accused, their muscles taut with anxiety." [28]

During the next ten days, the editor of *L'Impartial* made several other attacks on Malraux and Monin. In one article, he suggested that the Kuomintang's gift of money was a bribe that had enabled Monin to establish *Indochine*.[29] Malraux retorted heatedly that "*Indochine* was founded with my personal funds and with Annamite money," in Paris and some four months before the Huynh-vi-Khanh affair; he published texts and photographs of letters that proved that this was true.[30] Chavigny replied that such an affirmation was unbelievable because, after all, "a millionaire certainly doesn't take up the profession of burglar of bas-reliefs or pillager of ruins." [31]

In any case, Chavigny continued, *Indochine* was not a bona fide newspaper but a propaganda organ financed by malcontents in the colonies and the coffers of the Kuomintang:

> By flattering the nationalist sentiments of certain Annamites, it is possible to unloosen their purse strings; ancient money chests open up when promises are made to combat French influence, and that is where funds are drawn from. Then there is the Kuomintang, a Bolshevik group that, like Moscow, has at its disposal a sizable propaganda fund. Thus, nothing is easier—when you are not at all hampered by scruples—than to establish a newspaper. However . . . one sells one's pen to the adversaries of France!

The only cause that *Indochine* defended with conviction was that of the "Chinese Bolsheviks, of those Chinese who would quickly become masters of Indochina the day we abandon it." It was essential, he concluded, that "the healthy press of this country unite in order to banish such individuals from its midst. One cannot have too much contempt for people like Malraux and Monin."

A lead story in the July 22 *Impartial* about "Communists and Morocco" provided Chavigny with an opportunity to make a brief reference to the links between world Communism and "the Monin-Malraux pair," a theme that he developed at length in his

July 24 editorial, "The Bolshevik Movement—the Organization of the Class Struggle." He said that there was little nationalist sentiment among the Annamites on which to base an anti-French movement—"because French activity in this country is a humanitarian work, benevolent and fruitful"—and accused Monin of following "the directives of the Moscow Communists to the letter" and wanting to instigate "the class struggle" in Indochina. Although it was against the law, this Bolshevik had set up a number of unions among the skilled workers in the Chinese city of Cholon. At a signal from him, Chavigny warned, they would strike and disrupt the economic life of the entire community.

As proof of the power held by union organizer Monin, Chavigny offered two incidents. On July 3, a group of eleven waiters had decided to leave the employ of a restaurant owner in Cholon. As their representative, Monin had written the owner a letter informing him of their decision and requesting him not to "use intimidation toward your employees" in order to get them to stay. According to Chavigny, this move was part of a scheme to eliminate competition for one of Monin's Chinese friends who owned a restaurant across the street! Such actions would be "repeated tomorrow against others," Chavigny said, if the Vietnamese and Chinese "well-to-do classes" did not unite with the French to throw such agitators out of the colony. When the workers at the Saigon arsenal went out on strike a few days later to protest the intransigent nature and arbitrary acts of a newly appointed director, Chavigny announced that Malraux and Monin were behind the move. Presenting this work stoppage as an outstanding example of the tremendous potential threat to the colony represented by their political agitation, he tried to arouse other *colons* to the danger: "Do you know what Communism is, what Bolshevism is? Why, very simply, it is expropriation established as a principle; it is your possessions, your money, your wives even, shared by everyone else. It is the confiscation and distribution of your fortunes. It is anarchy and organized piracy. That's where Monin and the Kuomintang are leading you." [32]

Since Malraux and Monin constantly exploded these allegations by printing the truth, Chavigny undertook one final effort to discredit their paper. He wrote an editorial on the newsgathering "Frauds of the Malraux-Monin Pair" that was obviously calculated to cast doubt on *everything* printed in *Indochine*.[33] His basic contention was that the newspaper "doesn't receive a single special

bulletin; it manufactures them out of nothing" in order to "pre-
dispose people's minds in favor of China, Bolshevism, and the
Kuomintang." This propaganda aim had been apparent from the
beginning in articles like the one praising Das, "the revolutionary
Indian Communist" and the interview in which Sun Fo had predicted the eventual alliance of all the Asian peoples of the Far
East. However, it was most evident in the news items under the
heading "Dispatches From Our Special Correspondents." Chavigny cited several recent ones about India, and proved that they
were not from a special correspondent; they had simply been translated from the usual English news sources.

Was this not proof, he asked rather illogically, that "their
vaunted bulletins from China, defeatist bulletins, are pure inven-
tion and have been dreamed up for the requirements of an unsavory cause?" On June 20, for example, *Indochine* had published
a report that English soldiers guarding the foreign concession at
Shameen were rumored to have been taken prisoner. This, according to Chavigny, was a bit of fiction calculated to exaggerate the
power of the native Chinese forces and make the French in Indochina fearful for the possible fate of their compatriots. An *Indochine* column on July 17 noted that a group of nationalist Koreans
was said to have poisoned the water supply of Seoul to protest the
occupation of their country by foreign troops. Chavigny characterized this as another obvious attempt by the editors of *Indochine* to
"suggest criminal ideas to the native populations" and to incite
them to violence in accordance with accepted Bolshevik technique.

These charges were patently ridiculous, and Malraux needed
only half a column to demolish them.[34] He commented that the
editor of *L'Impartial* should decide which of his two allegations
was true: either the dispatches were lifted from other newspapers
or they were written in Moscow. Then he admitted that *Indochine's*
only exclusive news sources were in Japan and China and said that
their truth could be judged from the fact that "they are found the
following day and sometimes the day after that, in the official
communiqué from the French ARIP agency." As for any "defeatist" items, concluded Malraux in a pointed reference to Chavigny's avoidance of war service, they came exclusively from a
Colombo correspondent!

L'Impartial's violent two week anti-Communist campaign had
been undertaken in part to discredit *Indochine's* incriminating

Camau exposé and to silence its other criticisms of Cognacq's regime. But another factor was the imminent visit to Saigon of Monguillot, Acting Governor General of Indochina, and his Attorney General, Colonna. By having Chavigny create a furor over Malraux and Monin, Cognacq hoped to divert the visitors' attention from the scandals in his Administration. Perhaps he also hoped to induce these officials from Hanoi to take positive steps to protect the colony from such pro-Chinese, Communist revolutionaries.

To this end, an "anti-Bolshevik" committee was organized, composed of Chavigny, de la Pommeraye, and others among the Governor's friends. This group called upon Monguillot shortly after his arrival in Saigon. Malraux caricatured this meeting in an editorial:

> They were seen, clinging to one another, presenting themselves before the Governor General. They were leaders, and their touching faces expressed the ultimate in heroic feelings. That is why Chavigny, who had been chosen spokesman, pricked up his ears, and after uttering a few joyous hee-haws, began:
> "We have come, Monsieur the Governor General, in the name of our past, to ask your support for the *patriotic* league that we are going to found in order to fight against the disturbing advances of Bolshevism in this country." Choked, overwhelmed, dazzled by such genius, the Governor General let out a howl of joy, a laugh such as the gods of Cochinchina had never heard. He leapt, danced, cried out. He twisted himself into spirals, disappeared beneath the table, tried to fly off, caught up in convulsions of boisterous laughter. The pitiful delegation collapsed. De la Pommeraye, in a last effort, raised a finger. But upon a severe glance from the Governor (who could not calm himself), he precipitously crammed it into his nose.
> That was the end of it.[35]

The Attorney General was no more receptive than Monguillot. In spite of numerous reports from the Sûreté purporting to prove that Monin and Malraux were dangerous, he was unconvinced. Cognacq himself intervened, declaring that Monin should be imprisoned as a seditious Bolshevik, but Colonna steadfastly refused, in the absence of concrete evidence, to take any action. Malraux praised this forthright position in his August 3 editorial, "Open Letter to M. Colonna, Attorney General." It was well known, he said, that the angry Cognacq and his acolyte Chavigny had recently begun to take singing lessons: "They are memorizing—for you, sir—the song 'Invitation to Travel.'" Colonna's presence, Malraux wrote, had become intolerable to them because he was an honorable man:

> You believe that the Law is not at the disposition of Saigonese philanthropists and that the orders of Father Ubu cannot suffice to have people imprisoned. You will be punished for this some day.
>
> In spite of insinuations, allusions, propositions, and other solicitations, you refuse to place the Bolshevik Monin under arrest. This arrest has been often demanded of you, however. Some valid reasons for it have been given you: the aforesaid Bolshevik possesses as many as three perfume-shooting revolvers, and he communicates with the ghosts of Lenin and Sun Yat-sen by means of a ouija board. You don't believe that is enough to put people in prison? You are a bad magistrate, belonging to the particularly hateful species of judges who try to find out if the accused are guilty. You destroy order, you downgrade the family, you overturn the State . . .
>
> Oh, Mr. Attorney General, why don't you go away! The Dalat resort is a pleasant spot. . . . You would be replaced quickly, believe me. And on your return, you would find the Bolshevik Monin correctly imprisoned, condemned—already—to write ballades to Cognacq! Unless the prison air, which is unhealthy and conducive to sadness, should cause him to waste away rapidly. In two or three days, say.
>
> For we must have done with Communism!

Needless to say, this taunting revelation of the failure of the anti-Bolshevik campaign against Monin and Malraux did little to endear them to the Administration!

VIII

Indochine's Death and Resurrection

Cognacq undertook the Communist smear campaign against
Malraux and Monin because he feared for his regime. Whether he
actually believed Malraux to be a Communist is immaterial. The
point is that he feared everyone who was not dedicated to maintaining the status quo, whether Communist, socialist, nationalist,
or even enlightened conservative. When it became obvious that
Chavigny's anti-Bolshevik campaign was proving to be ineffective,
the Governor of Cochinchina turned again to his two most powerful weapons, the vast government bureaucracy and the political
police.

As administrative head of Cochinchina, Cognacq was in absolute control of a far-reaching bureaucratic network. *Indochine* had
been harassed by this ponderous machine from the moment it
began publication. Although it was a flagrant violation of French
law to intimidate government employees because they read a liberal newspaper, Malraux and Monin came into possession of some
documents that proved conclusively that Cognacq had done just
that. These were cited in several of Malraux's editorials on freedom of the press.[1] The earliest and most damning document was a
"confidential and urgent order" dated June 17, which had been
sent "in accordance with Urgent Directive No. 12 from Administration headquarters" by a provincial administrator to the head of
a village under his authority:

The Mayor of the village of Phung-Hiep is ordered to inform himself discreetly as to whether some Frenchmen or natives have come into his village in order to make propaganda to sell some newspapers. One of these papers appeared just a few days ago. If the affirmative, record the names of the subscribers carefully, the number of subscriptions, the cost of each subscription, and whether payment has been made. And have your report forwarded to me secretly about 5 o'clock in the afternoon of June 18, 1925.

The editors of *Indochine* soon learned of this measure, as well as of other coercive acts. On June 20 they sent a letter of protest directly to the Governor General in Hanoi, then printed its text on the front page of the next issue for all Saigon to see:

Sir:

We have the honor to inform you that—just as we had anticipated —an official propaganda campaign directed against our newspaper has begun in certain provinces.

The Administrator of Travinh has called in some Annamites guilty of having subscribed to *Indochine* and has heatedly reproached them for this action—not neglecting to slander us personally. He forced his native subordinates to act likewise.

Firmly resolved to defend ourselves against such maneuvers and even to go so far as to protest to the Chamber, we are however taking it upon ourselves to inform you of these facts, which we want to document for you with the testimony of our subscribers as soon as you return.

A number of protesting letters were subsequently published in *Indochine* as further evidence that provincial administrators were threatening to imprison any of their subordinates who read the Malraux-Monin newspaper. When Cognacq learned that the two young editors had actually obtained Administration memos prohibiting the reading of their paper, he issued a garbled statement of explanation through the *Courrier Saigonnais*. According to the Governor, it was not his orders but rather the "illegal maneuvers" of Monin and Malraux that had *"led certain administrators to take action* by warning their subordinates that they were probably being confronted by swindlers." [2]

Somewhat later, a letter to Malraux from a provincial subscriber indicated that a new technique of harassment had been devised by the Administration: "Don't be surprised if one of our subscribers from Gocong today returns to you the latest number of *Indochine* that was sent to him. He has the impression that a French official comes to the local post office each morning (and this has been going on for several days) on behalf of the Administrator-in-Chief of the province, to be present at the sorting of the mail coming from Saigon and to find out the addresses to which your newspaper is being sent." [3] At the same time, one of *Indochine*'s provincial reporters informed the Saigon office of the newspaper that "militiamen from the local civil guards are prowling around Annamite houses . . . for the sole purpose of catching—from a distance, of course—those who have subscribed or plan to subscribe to this independent newspaper." [4] Anyone who came to collect subscription money was closely followed by agents of the Sûreté, further alarming the local Annamite readers.[5] In the face of such acts, wrote Malraux heatedly, was it any wonder that Indochinese and Frenchmen alike were "thoroughly disgusted"? [6]

Police harassment was nothing new for Malraux and Monin. Ever since their newspaper had first appeared, the Sûreté had maintained close surveillance over them and their collaborators. Voluminous reports, which Monin called "monographs," about their "subversive" activities were regularly submitted to the Governor. In a sarcastic front-page article on June 29, Monin observed that since these reports contained more fiction than fact, they were really creative literature. He then offered his services, as a modest *littérateur*, to help M. André, Chief of the Sûreté, write better Bolshevik fiction. These and other gibes had little effect; Malraux and Monin continued to be closely watched. Indeed, as the tempo of their attacks against the Administration increased, police surveillance intensified, in an obvious attempt at intimidation. At the height of the Camau furor, this facetious but revealing comment appeared on the front page of the July 22 *Indochine*: "The Sûreté has been good enough to station two of its men, one before the entrance of our office, the other in front of our printshop. They are very ugly. Can't they be changed?"

The Sûreté was apparently prepared to use physical violence on the two editors. A note near the masthead of the July 15 issue revealed that they had received information of a police plot "to have us beaten up before the 17th with weighted canes, under some kind of pretext. We warn them that we shall continue to go for a stroll in the evening as usual, alone and without arms. If we are attacked, the public will be the judge." This warning was apparently enough to keep the police from using their usual weapons on

Malraux and Monin. A sarcastic front-page notice three days later read: "As of today, the 18th, we haven't been attacked. It is true that the Governor General [Monguillot] isn't arriving until the 24th. You see, you see, one should never pay in advance."

The most overt act was an attempt to silence Monin, considered by the Administration to be the more dangerous of the two editors. The incident, which is very reminiscent of the opening scene in Malraux's novel, *Man's Fate*, was recounted by Monin for *Indochine Enchaînée*: "I awaken one fine night at the precise second when a gentleman, in whom I recognize one of the benevolent guardians who surround my home with vigilance, had just finished opening the mosquito netting at the height of my neck, naked to the razor. Don't you understand that I committed suicide? Good riddance!" [7]

These allegations are not hard to believe; three widely reported murder trials during 1925 give ample evidence that certain members of the colonial Sûreté were without scruples and quite capable of murder for money.[8]

Malraux and Monin had long been aware that their mail was carefully scrutinized by the police, and they made several references to this practice in their editorials. Toward the end of July, Cognacq evidently issued a new and more radical order to the head postal official in Saigon. All but a few of the copies of *Indochine* sent through the mails to provincial subscribers were to be "lost." When the editors learned of this, Monin immediately went to register an energetic protest, but the postal official refused to receive him. Monin thereupon wrote him an angry open letter, published on the front page of the July 27 issue of *Indochine*. It read in part:

> Each day I entrust to the department of which you are the responsible head a definite number of newspapers, addressed to provincial subscribers. Your service consents to send off a few of them; the others disappear and nothing more is heard of them except in the protests of their disappointed subscribers. The detailed information that I possess . . . does not permit me to believe there has been any negligence; it is a matter of carrying out an order.

Monin concluded with the promise that he would take every possible step "so that my newspapers will no longer be stolen." After the end of July, distribution of the newspaper to provincial subscribers was probably undertaken by Annamite and Chinese political organizations, such as Young Annam and the Cochinchina section of the Kuomintang. This ensured *Indochine* of an even wider circulation.

Malraux and Monin were enjoying ever-increasing respect among members of the native community because of their energetic support of the Annamite cause. Since its founding in mid-June, *Indochine* had become more and more embarrassing to Cognacq, both personally and politically. The wide publicity that the newspaper gave to his financial schemes and to the despotic means by which his Administration restricted the freedom of the Indochinese, added to the Governor's largely unsuccessful attempt to label the nationalist reform program as Communist, had caused liberals everywhere in Cochinchina to second *Indochine*'s demands. At the very end of July, this whole situation suddenly became critical.

On Wednesday, July 29, the government in Paris issued a bulletin that was immediately flashed to the Far Eastern colonies. Cognacq and his friends were stunned. A new Governor General for Indochina had been appointed—from the ranks of the *socialist* party! He was Alexandre Varenne, a widely known liberal lawyer and journalist, the founder of the socialist provincial newspaper *La Montagne*. First elected a deputy from Puy-de-Dôme in 1896, he had quickly established a political reputation as an eloquent speaker and a tireless worker, notably as a member of the Commission for Universal Suffrage and the Budget Committee for Education. Before being named to the post in Indochina, he had been Vice President of the French Chamber of Deputies.[9]

The governor generalship had been vacant since early in 1925, when the incumbent, Martial Merlin, had been recalled because of his apparent inability to cope with the worsening political situation.[10] Maurice Monguillot, who was filling in as Governor General, was a man of integrity, but his temporary status made him reluctant to engage in any power struggle over abuses in the Administration of Cochinchina, and he had adopted a policy of nonintervention. Cognacq had no reason to expect a similarly tolerant attitude by the new Governor General.[11]

The newspapers of Indochina reflected the reactions of the colonials to the new appointment. In Tonkin, the conservative *France-Indochine* regretted that Monguillot had not been given the post and hoped that Varenne could do as good a job as the man he was replacing.[12] Chavigny's *Impartial* recounted the new Governor General's career in an article that was almost comic in its lack of enthusiasm. It was noted without comment that Varenne had been known "primarily as a militant socialist" and that his writings appeared regularly "in the leftist press." [13] But an outspoken editorial in the *Courrier de Haiphong* best summed up the position of the conservative majority on the peninsula: "This appointment cannot but seem surprising because nothing, so it would appear, destined M. Varenne for the task that falls upon him today and for which his political life has scarcely prepared him. . . . He will have much to learn on arriving in this country . . . He will have to serve an apprenticeship." [14]

The reaction among liberals was very favorable. In Paris *Jeune République* published a long interview with Duong-van-Giao, President of the Association of Indochinese Intellectuals. He hailed the appointment as the beginning of a new era in French colonial history: "Today the government of the Republic at last seems to consent to shine a little light into the darkness long gathered over Indochina by an outmoded colonialism. This appointment is thus received by us with satisfaction. For us, as Annamites, it is a happy event." [15] Malraux and Monin were no less enthusiastic. Their announcement of Varenne's appointment appeared in banner letters across the bottom of the front page of the July 30 issue of *Indochine*. Next day appeared a laudatory editorial that began: "It is with real pleasure that we have just learned of the appointment of M. Varenne as Governor General of Indochina. . . . For twenty years, M. Varenne has constantly shown himself to be the friend of liberty, the adversary . . . of despotism. We feel we may hope that his coming to Indochina will be marked by numerous and salutary reforms in this country."

In Paris, Varenne was immediately pressed by newspapers and political figures to make some statement regarding his plans for Indochina. He bluntly declined, saying that he had not had time to inform himself of the situation in the colony. However, he reaffirmed that his opinions were "republican, in the broad sense of the word, and socialist," and said that he had informed Painlevé of his intention to undertake all "necessary reforms" after he had gathered some on-the-spot information. Above all, he said, his regime would be characterized by justice.[16] These remarks were very disturbing to Cognacq and his friends and strengthened their determination to silence the stridently critical voice of *Indo-*

chine. Now they had a deadline to work against. The new Governor General was scheduled to arrive in Saigon early in the autumn.

The pages of the early August issues of the Malraux-Monin paper made it clear that relations between the two editors and Cognacq's Administration were steadily worsening. On Tuesday, August 11, there appeared Malraux's long and carefully documented exposé of Chavigny's early career as an *indicateur*, or paid informer, for the Sûreté. Precise details were printed from the official records of his trial before a military court. An inside page of the same issue carried more revelations of the Governor's illegal political manipulations, followed on Wednesday and Thursday by additional information on this sensitive subject. Also featured in these issues were accounts of the trial of a policeman who had brutally murdered several Annamites, and letters from provincial farmers about a new land fraud at Baclieu, similar to the one at Camau.

The final issue for the week came out on Friday, August 14, because the following day was the Feast of the Assumption, a holiday observed throughout the colony. On the front page appeared a long and brilliant editorial by Malraux. It was to be "the first of a long series, in which we will examine our colonization, its virtues and its faults, the hopes to which it gave birth, and which will propose a few avenues of conciliation." The article, entitled "Selection of Energies," is by far the most eloquent of the three serious political pieces he contributed to *Indochine*. In style and in certain ideas, it is a clear presage of the great novelist to come.

Malraux began by attacking the shortsighted Administration policy of permitting only the most servile Annamites to go to France to study. Since freedom of movement—especially for educational purposes—was guaranteed to France's colonial peoples, both by custom and by legislation, the government of Cochinchina was deliberately thwarting the intent of the law by the special procedures that made it almost impossible for an Annamite to leave the country unless the Administration felt that he showed unmistakable evidence of strong loyalty to his French masters. As Malraux ironically commented, if an Annamite could produce such evidences of loyalty, they simply proved that he was a traitor, at least from the Indochinese point of view. The whole selection process thereby entered "the serenest regions of happy stupidity."

Met with a refusal, the young Annamite could meekly accept it—in which case it would clearly be "safe" to send him to France anyway—or he could circumvent it. According to Malraux's figures, since January 1, 1924, no fewer than 400 Indochinese had surreptitiously left the colony to study abroad. Some had fraudulently obtained temporary seamen's papers and shipped out on vessels going to China, England, or the United States. Others had assumed an appropriately pious mien and gone to certain American Protestant missionary groups in Central Annam; within a fortnight they were on their way to San Francisco and an education in the United States. Understandably, these young men returned to Annam with strong feelings against the French.

In a vehement paragraph, Malraux protested that he was not necessarily attacking a specific administrator but rather the myopic political attitude that assumed that all energetic and independent-minded Annamites would automatically become social agitators, "Bolsheviks," if they were permitted to study in France. This attitude angered Malraux, because it not only was "so stupid as to make one weep with rage, but it will also bring about—in a very short time—the most dangerous assault that our colonization here could experience." By deliberately thwarting the strongest and most dynamic of the Indochinese youths, the potential leaders of the country, the shortsighted colonial government was paving the way for a revolt that would drive France from the peninsula.

In a moving, lyrical passage that reveals both his affinity for Nietzsche and the wellsprings of his own personality, the twenty-three-year old Malraux speaks of force, power, and revolution:

> Every power that feels within itself a will to expand and the controlled violence that makes certain people colonizers sets itself as a first task the seeking out of strength. Those whom Rome sent to the marches of the Empire, those whom Tai-Tsong sent into the depths of the Gobi, those whom our Kings sent to Louisiana, applied themselves above all to ferreting out, among the scattered forces that were opposing them, what elements of resistance, vigor, and energy lay hidden, in order to bind them to their cause by granting them, unmistakably and without contest, the prerogatives of masters. Never did a great king, never did a great statesman forget to seek out this characteristic of quickly provoked independence and honor by which the strong are recognizable.
>
> Our policy in Cochinchina and in Annam at the present time is very simple: it affirms that the Annamites have no reason whatsoever for coming to France, and it immediately creates *against us* a coalition of the noblest characters and the most tenacious energies

of Annam. It appears that politically motivated and financially greedy idiots are applying themselves with rare perseverance to destroying what we have been able to create, and to awakening in this old land—sown with great memories—the sleeping echoes of more than six hundred revolts.

Whatever cultured Annamites here may say, the history of the Chinese domination in Annam, in spite of all the reservations that must be made, took place beneath a banner of blood. I remember the ancient streets of Florence, near the Arno: on each tawny or golden palace, an inscription recalls a murder committed by some great family in order to obtain the domination of the city. The hell of the *Divine Comedy* is written in its entirety on the walls of the old princely residences, but today the glory of the city towers alone above the tumult of those stilled battles. Annam, when one crosses it from the mouths of the Red River to the Mekong Delta, leaves a single impression: the name of every illustrious city there is the name of a revolt; the most stirring of its plains bear the names of battles. The tomb of Le-Loi is in ruins, but the songs that exalt the somber grandeur of his life of courage and adventure are still on the lips of all women and in the memories of all fishermen. In Quang-Ngai, in Thanh-Hoa, in Vinh, the stores of energy of which we have so great a need in the Far East wait to see the realization of the collaboration that we have promised. . . . [Let us show] that we know how to do something besides direct against ourselves— thanks to an ingenious system—one of the finest, one of the purest, one of the most perfect streams of energy that a great colonial power could turn upon itself.

This prophetic article was a swan song. Some days earlier, Cognacq—realizing that his previous efforts against the editors and distributors of the newspaper had been fruitless—turned his attention to those who actually produced it—the independent printer Louis Minh and the typesetters who worked for him. Special agents from the Sûreté called on the native typographers to forcefully remind them how dangerous it was to remain associated with a Bolshevik newspaper like *Indochine*. The Annamites felt a deep gratitude to the two young editors who had so vigorously taken up their cause, and for a time they courageously resisted. However, when the police threatened prison for them and destitution for their families, they were forced to agree to a work stoppage, to be disguised as a strike against Minh.[17]

Next the police went to see Minh. All previous attempts to coerce him had been unsuccessful; for nearly two months he had refused to break his original agreement with Malraux and Monin. Now, however, confronted with new threats and an impending typographers' strike that would cost him all his other printing business, he weakened. Cognacq, sensing victory, sent Chavigny around with a lucrative offer to buy the entire Minh establishment for *L'Impartial*.[18] The weary printer finally accepted this thinly disguised bribe. After the August 14 issue of *Indochine* had gone to press, he regretfully informed Malraux and Monin that he could no longer print their paper.

The two men were greatly dismayed by Cognacq's success, but they had absolutely no intention of giving up without a struggle. They immediately began to canvass other private printers in Saigon. Anticipating this, however, the Governor had simply repeated an earlier threat that any firm that accepted a contract from *Indochine* would immediately lose all government-connected business. Since such work constituted the bulk of the printing done by these small shops, its loss would have meant certain bankruptcy. Moreover, it was no secret to anyone in Saigon that the difficulties Minh had had with his typographers and with the Sûreté were entirely due to his connection with the Malraux-Monin paper. After ten days of intense effort, the editors had not found anyone who would agree to help them resume publication.

On learning this, the government-supported newspapers, sure of their victory at last, began to publish joyful obituaries of their late rival. Chavigny, using his pen name, Rictus, led the chorus with a front-page article in the August 25 issue of *L'Impartial*. Entitled "Migratory Birds," it contained an incredibly gross misrepresentation of the facts of *Indochine*'s demise, liberally sprinkled with Chavigny's elephantine humor. His basic contention was that Malraux and Monin had organized their paper only to swindle money from an unsuspecting public. Although they were penniless, they had succeeded in obtaining large sums in advance from "naïve and credulous subscribers . . . by promising them decorations, honorific titles, supposedly powerful friends." All of this money had gone into their own pockets. No capital outlay whatsoever had been necessary because they had been able to hire Minh to print their paper.

Chavigny charged that the anti-government and obstructionist position taken by *Indochine* had been carefully calculated to win additional support and financial assistance from groups of malcontents and "dupes" in the colony. Everyone was invited to help the new venture by taking out a subscription: "One collects one-year subscriptions in the largest number possible, one comes out some-how or other for a month or two, enough time to take in the cash. Then the keys are put under the door mat, and the game is over. A few thousand dollars have been extorted and a few people vic-timized." Thus, according to this government version, the disap-pearance of *Indochine* was the logical, deliberately induced termi-nation of a fraud.

About a month later, the hand of the conservatives was further strengthened; the full text of the Court of Cassation judgment in the Malraux-Chevasson case was received in Saigon. Chavigny published it on the front page of his September 26 *Impartial* "as a public service." The "decree of nullification," it turned out, was based on an error made in the transcription of the Saigon proceed-ings. As the judges in Paris were careful to point out, this error made it unnecessary for them to "rule on the other points in the appeal." Chavigny maliciously insisted in his accompanying edi-torial remarks that

> as our readers can see, there is no question of untranslated docu-ments, or of secret items in a dossier, as the party concerned claimed. The decree was set aside because of a simple flaw in its drafting . . . Thus Malraux will have to appear once again before the Court of Appeals in Saigon, which will once again consider his case, and this time there will certainly be no flaw in the drafting, which means that the conviction will be definitive.

Malraux and Monin fought back against the conservative coali-tion as best they could by speaking out at public meetings and rallies.[19] They were incensed at the lies being circulated about the closing of *Indochine*, and they wrote indignant letters to the vari-ous newspapers that were slandering them. Only one such letter, addressed to the Tonkin paper *Courrier d'Haiphong*, was ever published. It was an energetic protest against a disparaging *Cour-rier* article announcing the disappearence of *Indochine*: "It is completely misleading to entitle 'Falling Leaves' the news item in which you note that, as of twelve days ago, we are no longer being published, when everyone in Saigon knows that suspension is due to certain odious machinations on the part of the Government of Cochinchina." [20]

It was painfully evident that without a newspaper, the reform

movement was seriously crippled. There was only one way out of
the impasse engineered by Cognacq: the two editors would have
to print their paper themselves. But, on contacting a number of
Saigon shops in an effort to buy the necessary equipment, they
found that the Sûreté had foresightedly issued strict orders that no
such materials were to be sold to them. Undaunted, Malraux and
Monin sought the help of several sympathetic Annamites who
worked in the big printing plants of the city. Using discarded
pieces of machinery, makeshift parts, and great ingenuity, they secretly managed to put together a printing press. Malraux described
it as "a clown's equipment," "without forms, almost without
anything"—but it worked! [21]

There was still one more obstacle: they had a press, but no type.
Through various intermediaries, they tried to purchase some in
Saigon, again without success; the Sûreté had intimidated every-
one. Malraux subsequently wrote a parody on one of these efforts:

> *The scene takes place in one of the big French printing houses in*
> *Saigon. Enter a young Annamite (seventeen years old).*
>   Sir, I would like to buy some type.
>   Isn't it for *Indochine?*
>   No, it's for a newspaper that I am going to establish.
>   What is it to be called?
>   *The Bomb!*
>   But . . . but . . . that's a revolutionary newspaper!
>   Certainly.
>   Just a moment.
> *The worthy director mobilizes three of his employees, who seize*
> *the young Annamite* (Above all, don't let him go!) *and bring him*
> *to the police station, which is perfectly illegal.*
>   Soon I shall send that printer another one of my Annamite
> friends, who had also decided to found a Bolshevik newspaper. He
> is two and a half years old, and the breeze wafts pleasantly through
> his downy locks.[22]

Realizing that the situation in Saigon was impossible, Malraux
sought help in Hong Kong. It was near the end of August, and the
great city was still caught in the throes of the crippling strike.
Nearly 100,000 Chinese laborers had left the crown colony and
gone to Canton. Those who remained behind refused to work,
subsisting on the strike dole paid by the Kuomintang government
of Canton from its meager resources. All foreign commercial and

industrial activity had ceased, and shipping was at a virtual stand-still. The only vessels that moved in or out of the harbor were for-eign warships and passenger ships manned by non-Chinese crews. Because there were no coolies on the docks, travelers had to han-dle their own baggage.[23]

Malraux probably arrived in Hong Kong aboard one of the French ships that had begun to transport Annamite workers into the English colony in a last-ditch effort by Europeans to break the strike.[24] As head of Young Annam and a friend of the Chinese na-tionalists in Cochinchina, he was doubtless welcomed and aided by Kuomintang agents in Hong Kong. In any event, he quickly located and purchased the needed type. Before returning to Indo-china, he made a brief visit to Canton, the headquarters of the new Nationalist Government of China. He must have sailed up the Pearl River from Hong Kong aboard one of the English river-boats that still kept the Europeans, isolated at Shameen, in contact with the outside world. During this visit he probably met and talked with Borodin and the other organizers of the strike. This brief firsthand contact contributed significantly to his vivid re-creation of the historical moment in *The Conquerors*.

When he returned to Hong Kong, he experienced no difficulty in having his crates of type loaded aboard a vessel leaving for In-dochina; the local Kuomintang was in firm control of the striking dock workers. However, Cognacq had learned of the success of Malraux's trip and had ordered the port police in Saigon to have the shipment impounded. According to law, such property was re-deemable, and the young editor made immediate efforts to re-possess it, only to be met with flat refusals. As he sarcastically re-lated the incident later: "I bring printing type back from Hong Kong. As if by chance, this type—seized by customs—is sur-rendered by the captain, to whom it does not belong, on orders of the Customs Administration. In an unprecedented development, this surrendered type—as if by chance—is not put up for sale." [25]

There was only one thing to do. Malraux hurriedly informed his contacts in Hong Kong of the situation, and a second shipment of type arrived in Saigon on Monday, October 26. The commissioner of the Port Police, M. Monnier, again telephoned the chief of cus-toms and ordered him to impound the merchandise in accordance with Cognacq's instructions. But this time customs refused to act, and Malraux and Monin quickly removed their crates from the dock.[26] Their elation soon dissolved: the new type had been de-

signed for the English language and contained none of the accents
required to print French. Fortunately, as soon as their native
friends learned of the situation, help was forthcoming. One afternoon an Annamite worker from a government printing plant
walked into the *Indochine* office and spilled a number of printing
characters onto the table before the astonished editors. Malraux's
emotional response to this spontaneous gesture of solidarity is still
evident in his account of the incident, written nearly a decade
later:

> I remember you. When you sought me out, the action of the
> government had finally silenced the only revolutionary newspaper
> in Indochina, and the farmers of Baclieu were being robbed in a
> great tranquil silence. . . . From your pocket you drew a hand-
> kerchief knotted into a bundle, with its corners erect like a rabbit's
> ears. "It's only acute *e*'s . . . There are acute, grave, and circumflex
> accents. As for the diaeresis *i*'s they will be more difficult; but per-
> haps you can get along without them. Tomorrow many workers
> will do as I have done; and we are going to bring all the accents
> we can." You opened the handkerchief, emptied the letters of
> type, entangled like jackstraws, onto a press stone, and you aligned
> them with the tip of your printer's finger, without saying a word.
> You had taken them from the printshops of the government's news-
> papers, and you knew that if you were caught you would be con-
> victed, not as a revolutionary, but as a thief. When they were all
> lined up flat, like the markers of a game, you merely added: "If
> I am convicted, tell people in Europe that we did this. So that
> they will know what is happening out here." [27]

Thus it was that *Indochine* finally reappeared early in November, 1925, some two and a half months after Cognacq had closed it
down. Most of the issues in this new series are undated, apparently
because the equipment was so makeshift that the editors were not
sure how regularly they could put out the newspaper, now a semiweekly; by omitting the date, they could make any gaps in publication less obvious. Internal evidence indicates that the first number
probably came out on Wednesday, November 4,[28] and the impro-
vised presses held up well; it was not until early January, some
eighteen issues later, that they finally broke down. Publication was
interrupted from January 2 to February 2, then after five more
issues appeared, dated February 2, 6, 10, 20, and 24,[29] finally
ceased altogether.

The new paper was christened *Indochine Enchaînée* (*Indochina in Chains*). A note on the first page—beneath a huge caricature of Cognacq—indicated that it was a "temporary edition of *Indochine,* appearing on Wednesdays and Saturdays, until the day—certainly distant—when the Administration will consent to return the printing type that belongs to us but that it has seen fit to take into its own custody." The newspaper was changed in more than name. In size and format, it resembled an octavo magazine or review. The colored cover was of slightly heavier stock and bore only the title and the number of the issue within a small woodcut device. The usual printing was 2,000 copies, later 2,500— just about half that of *Indochine.*

Numerous technical difficulties plagued the newspaper and caused it to have a somewhat unprofessional look. Since the editors lacked the metal frames required to hold the lines of characters firmly in place during the printing, the articles in *Indochine Enchaînée* sometimes contained transposed letters and letters turned on one side or upside down. Because there were not enough l's, capital I's were used as substitutes. The French-accented letters—notably the ê and û—that had been surreptitiously acquired from various Saigon printshops were of different type styles and added to the uneven appearance of the lines of text. The type from Hong Kong contained both upper- and lower-case letters, but they were all the same size. To print the banner headings of the regular columns and features, such as "Saigon Chronicle," "Annamite Topics," and Claude Farrère's serial "A Hundred Million in Gold," Malraux used a number of specially cut wooden blocks. As he proudly pointed out in one of the first issues, the new newspaper was utilizing "wooden type, as in the sixteenth century." [30] Wooden blocks were also used to print various typographic symbols and an occasional illustration.

In many other respects, however, the new paper was a continuation of the earlier *Indochine.* The inside pages carried a number of literary selections from *Candide,* including some short stories and serialized books. Notable among the latter was Léon Werth's *Notes from Indochina,* a violent attack against the shortsighted and reactionary Colonial Administration.[31] Various aspects of the Parisian scene were reported by G. de Pawlowsky, Sacha Guitry, and Léo Larguier. Foreign political news included interviews with such figures as Lloyd George and C. K. Edwards, as well as articles on the situation in Morocco, Syria, and Iran. Dispatches from

Havas and wire reports from the "special correspondents" of *Indochine* appeared regularly. The discussion of financial matters, including the re-evaluation of the piaster and the problems of commerce in Asia, continued as before. A few cartoons and an occasional page of women's fashions were included for less intellectual readers.

There was, however, one very noteworthy change in the contents of *Indochine Enchaînée*. Local political news was accorded more space, giving the publication a somewhat different tone. This modification was understandable. Forced to reduce their publication from a daily eight-page in-folio newspaper to an octavo semiweekly magazine, Malraux and Monin cut down on those items that did not directly serve their reform cause. The proportion of such political material increased as time went on, but because space was at such a premium, there was also less sarcastic diatribe than before. On the whole, *Indochine Enchaînée* was a more serious publication than its predecessor.

The first few numbers of the new paper did not specify who the editors were, but beginning with the fifth issue, Malraux and Monin are listed as "Directeurs," with offices at 12 Rue Taberd. When Malraux decided to leave for France at the end of the year, Lê-the-Vinh, one of his associates in young Annam, became co-editor with Dejean de la Batie.[32] Dejean had earlier been "manager" of the paper, but Malraux took on this job for issues Eight through Fifteen. One of the Annamite printers signed in his place during December 9–16 when he went to Pnom Penh.

Malraux wrote a larger proportion of *Indochine Enchaînée* than he had of *Indochine*. He contributed two or three items in almost every one of the first fifteen issues, and two of his satires were published after he left for France.[33] Of the more than thirty pieces that can be positively assigned to him, about one-third were "Saigon Chronicles," written jointly with Monin and signed with the initial amalgam A.P.M. Another ten were short editorials on a variety of subjects that appeared on inside pages, and eleven were lead editorials, two signed jointly with Monin.

The honor of flinging the gauntlet in Cognacq's face after the long period of enforced silence fell to Malraux. The first article in the first issue was his editorial "Reopening," which appeared alongside the familiar caricature of Cognacq's rotund features. Comparing him to a jealous husband who ensures his wife's fidelity by keeping her locked up, Malraux wrote that Cognacq had long tried to keep the truth about Cochinchina in chains. It was especially important that the facts be hidden during the Saigon visit of the new Governor General, Alexandre Varenne, because he was sure to ask embarrassing questions. When he does, wrote Malraux helpfully,

> You will tell him, for instance, that French laws are improved by being applied in Indochina according to the spirit of the Aztec code; that freedom of the press consists in having newspapers stolen or boycotted by the postal service; in having typesetters terrorized by agents of the Sûreté; that the best way to have Annamites clear virgin land is to give away what they have already cleared to cronies; that threats made against the families of young Annamites who find that your native policy is not exactly gentle give French prestige an incontestable sway; that prohibition of newspapers like *L'Oeuvre* in the library is equitable and normal; that the transfer of officials who read the said newspapers at home is essential; that it is good to give the Chavignys and the Outreys a subsidy of a million a year, a subsidy carried in the budget under the heading: "Charity: Deaf-Mutes."

Malraux was well aware that Cognacq could command several powerful allies in his campaign to deceive Varenne. Because of restriction and bribery, the press of Cochinchina had become his mouthpiece, a "fountain of governmental naïveté." His faithful acolyte, Dr. Trinh, sang the praises of the Administration in the name of the native population whenever called upon. He would assure the Governor General that the Annamites were altogether satisfied with the state of things. Most important of all, Cognacq felt sure of his control over the three major consultative bodies in the colony—the Chamber of Commerce, the Chamber of Agriculture, and the Colonial Council. He was counting on them to join at the appropriate moment in acclaiming him "the most brilliant Governor that Indochina has ever known."

To discredit this chorus of praise, Malraux could produce some 200 affidavits and letters of protest, documentary proof that the Governor had been flagrantly violating the laws that France had established for her overseas territories. As he pointed out, all these injustices, all these oppressions, all these maneuvers that transformed the provinces into personal fiefs had their origin in Cognacq's rapacious philosophy of government:

Certain financial and commercial cliques in Indochina have become more powerful than the local government. The latter, instead of being a mediator between these groups and the populace, sides with the former. Their policy is very simple: Make the most money possible in the shortest time; and they would reply to whoever attacks them that they are there to carry on their business and not to take care of that of the State or to lighten the burdens of the men who make it up.

At the end of this editorial, Malraux made Cognacq a promise: "This article will have a sequel, my good doctor, like an ordinary serial novel." He and Monin were determined to defeat the Governor's shortsighted, corrupt, and brutal policies. Their efforts during the next three weeks were specifically directed to arousing public opinion in preparation for the impending arrival of the new Governor General. For the editors, "the arrival of M. Varenne, of the socialist Varenne, ought not only to mark the end of the period of Administration crimes but also to toll the inescapable, necessary hour of retribution." [34]

IX

Varenne: Socialist or Conservative?

On November 18, 1925, the long-awaited Alexandre Varenne arrived in Saigon aboard the *Paul Lecat*. To the great astonishment of Cognacq and other functionaries awaiting him on the pier, the new Governor General of Indochina came down the gangway dressed in a plain dark suit instead of the usual elaborate gold-braided uniform of a colonial Governor. His explanation was simple: "It's the Annamites who have to pay for all that embroidery." [1] Such a debut augured well for his stewardship of the colony.

Although the editors of *Indochine Enchaînée* were naturally not on the reception committee, they were determined to be heard. It was essential that the carefully orchestrated official paean for Cognacq and his "rosy Cochinchina" should not go unchallenged. To this end, they prepared an especially informative issue of their paper and distributed it on the day of Varenne's arrival. [2] The featured item was a very long editorial entitled "Open Letter to M. Alexandre Varenne, Governor General." Although this article was signed "The Editors," its general style and certain specific references indicate that Malraux was the author.

He first informed Varenne that he intended to establish three fundamental points:

> The elected bodies [of Cochinchina] . . . have been formed under conditions of flagrant illegality; their leaders, whom the Governor holds by the hand like children, are without authority.

163

> The press is dominated by the same Governor in the same way. If Indochina is—according to M. Daladier's expression—a "private preserve," then Cochinchina is one for the Governor himself and for his friends, contrary to all law.

He charged that although the Governor was supposed to be exclusively an administrator, "he has never ceased to interfere forcefully in all the elections and in those activities of public life where impartiality should have been his duty." This, of course, was essential to the maintenance of his power. Two recent frauds involving elections for the Chamber of Agriculture and the Colonial Council were striking illustrations of his methods, and Malraux gave ample details in his open letter editorial.

The expected reorganization of all the chambers of agriculture of the peninsula had finally been decreed by a proclamation of July 10, 1925, and the election of new members was scheduled for September 30.[3] However, as the deadline for filing approached, the conservative roster, headed by Labaste, was still one name short. The group apparently had considerable difficulty in finding candidates. Knowledge of Cognacq's interference in the activities of the Chamber was widespread, and many reputable men had no desire to serve. Only at the last minute did Labaste remedy the situation. He added the name of a respected planter, Mézin-Guétan, to his ticket. His action was quite illegal; the reorganization directive had specified that all candidates must file a signed and notarized declaration before they could be nominated. Mézin-Guétan could not possibly have done this since he had been on vacation in France for some time. Nevertheless, the Administration condoned the move, and even publicly expressed a preference for the Labaste slate, another illegal act.

A preliminary tabulation made immediately after the election gave Cognacq a shock. Although most of the other Frenchmen on his endorsed ticket had won, Labaste had been defeated. The Governor was well aware that this upset would seriously weaken his control over the colony, and he immediately took energetic countermeasures. The election commission, composed of four officials whom he had appointed, was very cooperative. First, contrary to the regulations, they added to the tally for Labaste some twenty-five unsigned ballots that had come through the mails and whose envelopes in several cases showed signs of having been tampered with. The editors of *Indochine* had had ample evidence of the strange things that happened in the postal service of Cochinchina, and they were probably correct in suggesting that some of the ballots had been altered.

Also, a number of votes for Labaste were counted even though they were received *after* the close of voting or were submitted to a provincial administration center rather than to the official voting place at Saigon. When even these steps failed to give him a plurality, a post-election "adjustment" was made to shorten the list of eligible voters. After a number of names had been removed, Labaste had the required majority. His election was then declared official, and Cognacq saw to it that he was reappointed both the President of the Chamber of Agriculture and its representative on the Colonial Council. Thus, commented Malraux bitterly in his letter to Varenne, "if it was written that God created man in his image to love him and serve him, it is likewise written that Cognacq twice created Labaste in his image, to render him the same adoration . . . and especially the same duty of proclaiming it."

Although Cognacq had returned Labaste and other amenable *colons* to the Chamber, the conservative Annamite candidates whom he supported were roundly defeated. *Indochine Enchaînée* revealed some of the difficulties that one victor, Nguyen-tan-Duoc, encountered in his campaign.[4] They were typical. Shortly before the election, a number of local administrators in his province arranged meetings with the Annamite voters and ordered them to vote for the "approved," pro-Cognacq ticket. Duoc quickly learned of this action, but it was only after a long argument with postal officials that he finally succeeded in sending a telegram of protest to the authorities in Saigon. He experienced similar problems in securing certification of proxies to be present on his behalf to observe the voting in the remote districts. On election day, these representatives reported numerous irregularities to him, including overt intimidation of voters by local police, and administrative sanctions against "uncooperative" municipal employees. In spite of all these measures, Duoc was elected. This was a resounding defeat for the Governor, "a masterful spanking, well-deserved by the disgusting baboon who comes poking his dirty paws into the white linen of the family wardrobe," as *Indochine Enchaînée* noted rather inelegantly.[5]

The most important and recalcitrant of the three "elected" bodies of the colony was the Colonial Council. To strengthen his

control over that body, Cognacq had decided early in the autumn
to unseat Monin, the councilor who always led the opposition to
his schemes. Accordingly, on October 13, just before the initial
meeting of the new session of the Council, a writ of bankruptcy
was issued against the young lawyer by the Court of Commerce,
an organ of the Chamber of Commerce presided over by de la
Pommeraye. Not unexpectedly, Chavigny broke the news in a
front-page story in the October 13 issue of *L'Impartial*. Three days
later in another article, he urged creditors to begin suit immediately before the bankrupt's assets were entirely committed. As
Monin angrily pointed out to Varenne, a Saigon court had already
cleared him of these very charges some months earlier. The whole
thing was another blatantly political maneuver by the Governor:
"Bankruptcy—by reason of the rapid and considerable advantages
that it offers: immediate seizure of all the property of the bankrupt, the affixing of seals on all his papers, the forfeiting of all his
civil and political rights—was not destined to remain excluded
from the governmental arsenal." [6] After a hearing on the writ,
Monin was acquitted once again, and the decision was issued during the week Varenne was in Saigon.

Although Cognacq failed to unseat Monin, he was more successful in another effort to weaken the Council. Malraux's open
letter provided Varenne with some interesting details on this
move. For several years the Administration had controlled a solid
majority bloc of votes among the some twenty-one members of the
group. Cognacq had hand-picked the two Vice Presidents, his
close associates Chavigny and Dr. Trinh, but the President of the
Council, a moderate independent named Fays, sometimes voted
against the majority. In the face of increasing unrest in the colony,
the Governor decided that it would be prudent to replace this man
with a more reliable individual, the incumbent Vice President,
Henry Chavigny.

The first meeting of the 1925–26 session of the Council took
place in mid-September. The election of new officers was the first
order of business, and it soon became clear that the Administration was seeking to award the Presidency to Chavigny. Such a possibility was incredible to many of the members; his checkered past,
especially his activities as a police informer and his malingering
during the war, were well known in Saigon. Indeed, it had only
been due to his friendship with the Governor that he had been
elected Vice President in the first place. The incumbent President

Fays was particularly angry at this unwarranted interference in the proceedings of the Council and protested vigorously, but to no avail. Thereupon, as a gesture of disapprobation, he withdrew his name as a candidate for re-election. As was to be expected under the circumstances, Chavigny won the post. He was put into office, as Malraux put it "by people who despise him but who don't dare tell him so." When he took his place on the podium, several of the Councillors left the room in disgust. Significantly, one of these was M. Dusson, the judge who had presided at his wartime trial for blackmail. Later, another of the Council members was heard to admit that he had only voted for Chavigny because "it made the Governor happy."

The Chamber of Commerce, the third elected body of Cochinchina, was presided over by an equally unworthy individual. Malraux put it bluntly in his editorial: "Concerning M. de la Pommeraye, President of the Chamber of Commerce, for the time being we will say only one thing: his fortune was built in its entirety on the subsidies which were granted to him by the Governor. . . . Let us not dwell on the freedom that a man in this position may have in respect to the Governor." To illustrate for Varenne how the Administration controlled both de la Pommeraye and the Chamber that he headed, the young editor wrote an imaginary "Interview with M. . . , President of the Chamber of Commerce." [7] This short satire is reminiscent of the Coignard letters he had published in the first issues of *Indochine*, nearly six months earlier. Subtitled "Good Institutions and How to Use Them," it suggested how French democratic institutions and practices could degenerate in the climate of Indochina.

Malraux, the interviewer, began his chat with the fat President —obviously a caricature of de la Pommeraye—in a rather cavalier manner:

It is certainly not the interest that we take in your person, sir, which leads us to make known to the public your opinion on a few subjects that are not entirely without importance. No. But it seemed appropriate to us to show the Annamites the effects of tropical heat on French institutions. . . . Under the influence of heat, bodies expand. With regret, M. President, I note that this is not the case with liberty. . . . The climate of Indochina is unfavorable to it. Under its influence, it diminishes until it becomes imperceptible.

He asked the President—who looked at him "with a haggard eye"—to explain the purpose and function of the democratic institution over which he presided. When the President proved incapable of even understanding the question, the interviewer undertook to do so.

He noted first that the Chamber of Commerce was supposed to be a *representative* body; the decree of organization stipulated that its members were to be *elected* by the small businessmen of Saigon. This seemed to the interviewer somewhat of a paradox, because the Administration—in opposing Annamite self-government —obviously took the position that these "good people [were] . . . much too stupid to elect a deputy who would be the only one with influence enough to have their decisions carried out—if they took it into their heads to make some." To be sure, the authorities were forced to permit a few elections, but they interfered in them constantly, using "intimidation and a few piasters" in order to get the Annamites to "vote right." Although the Chamber thus elected was a parody of a representative institution and the whole process a perversion of democracy, this was of little concern to Cognacq and his friends.

The imaginary de la Pommeraye now began to doze off, but the interviewer continued. The essential role of the Chamber of Commerce, like that of the other "elected" bodies in the colony, should be to curb aggressive and acquisitive administrators, to "remind them that they are to obey the laws." Its members were supposed to "defend French and native interests in the colony," and "not at all to deliver tradesmen and merchants into the clutches of the Administration." Under the leadership of its corpulent President, the Chamber had become increasingly neglectful of this fundamental duty. The major foreign firms in Saigon, those "who have friends in France," were not particularly disturbed by this situation because it did not affect them. However, continued the interviewer, becoming more excited, "this is not at all the case with the small businessmen, above all the native ones. . . . They see those whose mission it is to defend them on the side of those who attack them. They are astonished and inquire if elected bodies have really been instituted to act as they do in Indochina."

The sharp tone of this sudden angry statement woke the napping President with a start. After a moment, he abruptly terminated the interview by intoning a formula he had evidently used many times before: "The duty of the President of the Hunting Clubs is to protect the interests of the hunters, who are constantly threatened by the ferocious rabbits."

In his open letter to the newly arrived Varenne, Malraux declared—as he had done many times before—that one man stood behind all the intrigue and political manipulation which had turned the colony into an authoritarian state and filled its native inhabitants with a growing hatred for their foreign rulers. That man was Maurice Cognacq: "Governor Cognacq, we repeat, has done as much harm to this country as a war. The hostility which his violence and brutality have provoked among the natives is beginning to affect all Frenchmen." Yet, his perversion of the political institutions of the colony to serve his own selfish ends was only one aspect of his destructive influence. In order for him to "govern" as he chose, "it was essential that no public protest whatsoever should rise against him. He was therefore obliged to suppress freedom of the press in fact, since it was not in his power to abrogate the laws which permitted it." Malraux then detailed the system of "Administrative" subscriptions by which Cognacq bribed the Saigon papers and the coercive methods that he had used in order to silence *Indochine*. The young editor emphasized to Varenne that these charges were not empty diatribe and slander: "We affirm that we have more than sixty proofs of all that we have just said. A number of them have already been published. We are keeping them, Monsieur the Governor General, at your disposal."

Perhaps the worst of Cognacq's crimes was his crude exploitation of the very Annamites whom he had been appointed to protect. The latest such instance had been the land swindle at Camau, which was "even more odious" than anything that had preceded it. Malraux devoted several paragraphs of his editorial to a succinct exposition of the case, adding that he had prepared for Varenne's examination a number of documents and "more than fifty formal, detailed, signed complaints" in connection with the incident.

Malraux also wrote a grotesque psychological portrait of Cognacq in his brilliant, accurate, and delightfully sarcastic "Interview with the Governor of Chynoiserie." [8] The Governor modestly denied that he had brought anything new into the Government of Chynoiserie:

Strictly speaking, I didn't invent anything. I merely gave a few innovations attributable to the ingenuity of various parliamentarians, governors, and other culture bearers an intensity, a perfection that they had hitherto not attained. If I were presumptuous, I would say that I refined them.

It was not I who invented the giving of State monies to companies that have considerable funds at their disposal—which permits them to issue founders' shares—and the refusal of all aid to those whom little sums could save. It wasn't I who discovered the absolute necessity of judging men's acts in relation to their votes, in the name of the well-known axioms: every engineer who does not vote for Outrey makes poor roads (in particular the one that leads to perdition); every official who voted for Digoutey [Disgusting] will have the right to a twenty-four-hour siesta per day, because he sleeps the sleep of the just.

Impressed by such modesty, the interviewer pressed the Governor to reveal the principles that underlay his actions, to outline his concept of colonialism. The Governor's answer was very much to the point:

Colonization, as you know, may employ two auxiliaries: texts inspired by a desire for justice on the one hand; the club, on the other. But all this is rather old hat. My modernism led me to the following principle: Before using the club, it is appropriate to wrap it carefully in legal texts. Thus it is the law that strikes the natives, and our well-known liberality entitles us to plenty of decorations.

The Governor explained that in order for his Administration to function well, it was necessary "to make the good French public simultaneously believe that the red dragons of Communism are going to devour Chynoiserie, and that the state of mind in the colony has never been better." He found the assistance of his eminent friend Chattigny de la Souricière of great help because, as President of the elected Council, he could refuse "to put to a vote those questions that seem a little embarrassing to me" and that might contradict the impression he wished to give.

In an expansive mood, the Governor further confessed his hope that a few malcontents, "ten or twelve . . . half of them agents of the Sûreté," would create a slight agitation in the colony. This would enable him to take a number of salutary measures: "to request troops, to speak about the necessity of order and of strength, the ingratitude of the natives, and once the real rebels have been executed, to be certain to see postponed *sine die* those demands which so bother my cronies."

The interviewer was uneasy about the effects of such a policy on the future of Chynoiserie. Was the Governor unaware that there was considerable unrest in the colony and that certain of the educated native elite were giving "a form to this discontent"? The Governor replied that in the event of trouble he would simply request troop reinforcements from France. The interviewer persisted: "What do you think about the several hundreds (at least) of soldiers who will die, not only from the battles, but above all from the countryside itself, in order to permit your respectable friends to continue to pay sixty francs in taxes while earning 50,000 piasters, an excellent way to help France?" The Governor looked at his questioner for a long time in silence, "an expression of friendly disdain animating his likable countenance. Then a hearty laugh uncovers his white teeth: 'What the hell do I care about that!' And he cordially pats me on the stomach."

Could the gross financial appetite of the Governor and his cronies have been portrayed more graphically than in these few lines?

Cognacq's regime had seriously compromised the French position everywhere in Cochinchina, Malraux warned in his editorial to Varenne, but nowhere more than among educated Annamites. For Varenne's benefit, Malraux reiterated his conviction that—

> It is by means of this university elite, and by it alone, that France may form a stable government in Indochina at a time when difficulties are beginning. The passive masses are not yet stirring, but they detest us as foreigners. It is the orientation that they are given by those who have diplomas and are naturalized—the logical intermediaries—that will cause them either to remain passive or to rise up against us.

It was not yet too late. If most of the educated Annamites had greeted the appointment of a new socialist Governor General with passionate enthusiasm, it was primarily because they saw in him the man who would at last do something positive about the potentially explosive situation. Malraux concluded by frankly admitting that he had written this editorial to give Varenne an idea of the true character of Cognacq and his oppressive regime: "Today, since all the leaders of a reception ceremony that was organized by threats are going to sing its praises, we want one voice at least to speak the truth to you, Monsieur Governor General, you who have assumed the noble and sad role of showing France her task—so as not to have, soon, nothing to show her but a vast expanse of ruins."

This open letter and other articles in the Malraux-Monin paper made it impossible for Varenne to remain ignorant of the accusations against the Governor of Cochinchina, but because of the repeated denials of the Administration lackeys who constantly surrounded him, he probably gave little credence to the charges. However, the revelations made by one of the most respected Annamite councilors at a stormy meeting of the Colonial Council shortly after his arrival in Saigon should have removed all doubts that Varenne might have had about the Malraux-Monin accusations. The Council had been called simply to give rubber-stamp approval to the annual budget.[9] Cognacq, believing himself securely in control of the body, evidently had not anticipated the slightest difficulty. He could not have been more wrong.

At the previous meeting of the Council, its first, an important event had taken place.[10] As was customary following the election of Council officers, the new President invited the Governor into the chamber to present the Livre Vert, or Green Book, the Administration's yearly report on affairs in the colony. Because of the imminent arrival of Varenne, Cognacq had taken great pains in preparing this 500-page compilation of facts, figures, and comments. Everything in it was calculated to depict him and his regime in a very favorable light. It was not just a report by the Governor; it was an apotheosis of the Governor. As Malraux wrote in his long editorial "Reflections on the Green Book," "it is there that we can read—with the marveling admiration which all his actions inspire in us when he himself explains their lofty value—the complete list of his benevolences, the profundity of his thought, the grandeur of his justice." [11]

Almost all of Cognacq's remarks were untruthful, but his comments on the political situation in Cochinchina most flagrantly so. He asserted that the opposition press was not taken seriously at all, and that certain recent attacks against his Administration "have not been able to infect the healthy portion, that is to say the totality of the population." He explained that the colony was prosperous because the majority of its people were basically indifferent to the political controversies that certain traitorous Annamites, Chinese, and Frenchmen were trying to spread. Furthermore, as Governor he had seen to it that special measures were taken to help the population protect itself from "the contagion of unhealthy ideas . . . of unsettling doctrines . . . the ideas of propagandists of revolt and violence." He concluded his report to the Councilors with a glowing appraisal of the political accomplishments of his regime:

> The policy of the Government of Cochinchina during the year that has just ended has remained the same as the one followed during the three years preceding. Characterized by benevolence, it has aimed at the maintenance of order, which is the essential factor for the peace and prosperity of a country, but a prudent maintenance, obtained by conviction rather than by constraint.

This blatant distortion of the truth provoked Malraux to write a bitter editorial of rebuttal, in which he suggested that the Governor had highly personal definitions of the terms used in his panegyric. In Cognacq's eyes, it was "disorder" when peasants protested against corrupt administrators, or when newspapers exposed a scheme to permit the wholesale confiscation—for the profit of a few high officials—of rich farm lands in Camau. "Benevolence" was the awarding of honors, medals, and money to those who collaborated with him in his various schemes. Benevolence had led him to make the Sûreté the major arm of his government, and terrorism the primary characteristic of his Administration. In essence, wrote Malraux, Cognacq's regime was organized like that of a dictatorship: a central wielder of power had grouped around himself "the elements of his personal power" and thus had created a network of forces that supported the whole system. Once this was done, the area controlled could be treated like the personal property of a small clique of leaders and drained of its wealth.

Any citizens daring to protest this exploitation are called political agitators by those in power, continued Malraux, but "they are, much more simply, just people seeking justice." In his view,

> the policy from which we are all suffering, the odious and ridiculous policy that is creating a visible discontent in Cochinchina at the present time and that, if we are not careful, will one day bring about tragic results, was brought here by neither the Annamites, nor

the Chinese nor the French. It was Governor Cognacq who, having admired it in the Antilles, found it so worthy of a Governor that he hastened to institute it here as soon as he could.

Only an independent newspaper like *Indochine Enchaînée* could reveal the whole Green Book for the parody of truth it was. Malraux concluded his long editorial by rephrasing Cognacq's summation in the words of a certain Governor Ubu:

> After benevolently trying by all possible means to disqualify those who do not approve of us, we have brought them to the conviction that they themselves ought to request their death. Spurred on by some evil spirit, they have opposed this. We have therefore pronounced their sentence ourselves, with all the solicitude of which we are capable, and have had them benevolently executed. The excellent sources of information that we have at our disposal and that we censor ourselves permit us to affirm that they repented after their death and today admire us without reservations.

A majority of the French members of the Colonial Council were provincial planters whose lives were rather restricted. Since they had little firsthand knowledge of many of the subjects covered in the Green Book, they were predisposed to accept the rosy account that the Governor presented to them at their first meeting. The native-born Vice President, Dr. Trinh, further reassured them about the contentment of the Annamites. Reports to the contrary were obviously the work of malcontents or revolutionaries. When the first meeting was adjourned, most of the Councilors were convinced that all was well in Cochinchina and that the new Governor General would find nothing to criticize.

The second meeting of the Council was called to order by the President, Chavigny, at 4:00 P.M., Tuesday, November 24. Malraux was seated among the spectators to provide a firsthand description of the session for *Indochine Enchaînée*.[12] Twenty-one Councilors were in attendance; among these were Paul Monin, who had just been exonerated of the bankruptcy charge; another Saigon lawyer, named Gallet; and Nguyen-tan-Duoc, the delegate from Sadec whose election to the Chamber of Agriculture had been so vigorously opposed by Cognacq. Also present was the Government Commissioner, M. de Taste, who represented the Administration. His role was to explain any items in the budget that were not clear to the Councilors and to answer their questions on related matters. The Council was forbidden by Article 30 of its Charter from discussing purely political matters, and de Taste was supposed to see that this restriction was observed.

Shortly after the session opened, Duoc, one of the most respected and moderate of the group, requested the floor in order to comment from an Annamite point of view on the Governor's report. He was recognized. Then, to the great discomfiture of the President, he bluntly declared that the Green Book was "categorically inaccurate" and embarked on a lengthy and detailed correction of it. When the burden of his speech became evident, several of Cognacq's closest allies found it prudent to leave the Chamber temporarily. However, overwhelming approval was evident among the remaining spectators, who frequently broke into applause.

Duoc centered his comments on the major abuses and misrepresentations by Cognacq and his government, the very issues that Malraux and Monin had so often taken up in their editorials. The Councilor also pointed to the corruption and incapacity of many local Annamite administrators, who were more interested in pleasing their French masters and in becoming rich than in serving their people; the injustice of a fiscal organization that gave huge loans at low rates to French planters and businessmen while the most productive members of the economy—the Annamite farmers —were forced to go to Chinese usurers for help; the constant and illegal interference in elections by the Administration and the frequent suppression of the basic civil liberties of the Annamites; the deliberate Administration efforts to minimize educational programs for the native population; and the inequity of demanding four *years* of military service from Annamites and only eighteen months from French citizens, a particularly flagrant injustice in that Indochinese troops were being used by France to suppress rebellions among the "Colonial" peoples of Syria and North Africa.

The most telling of Duoc's remarks were directed at Cognacq's assertion that the colony was tranquil and its citizens were contented. The Councilor found this statement difficult to reconcile with the large increase requested in the budget for the Sûreté. The Sûreté was only one of several law-enforcement agencies in the country; there were also local and provincial police forces and a national militia. The money to support these groups had to be diverted from projects of greater value to the Annamites, such as the school-building program and the provincial medical service. If the country were as tranquil as the Governor claimed, asked Duoc, why were so many policemen required? "Is one to believe . . . the gossips who, for their part, affirm that the government maintains—at great expense—a political police for the purpose of shadowing and hunting down people whose only crime consists in proclaiming ideas that, rightly or wrongly, are considered subversive and in not being entirely devoted to those presently in power?"

Duoc voiced the hope that the numerous inaccuracies in the Governor's report would be rectified, and he resumed his seat amid what Malraux termed "vigorous applause."

Councilor Gallet got the floor next. After impassioned praise for the courage and integrity of Duoc, he turned to the Governor's representative, M. de Taste, and called upon him to explain to the Council how two such contradictory versions of the situation in Indochina could both be true. The Government Commissioner refused to reply to the question, saying that these were political matters and therefore outside the competence of the Council by virtue of Article 30.

Monin immediately rose to argue that these questions were not political but administrative in nature, and therefore quite within the jurisdiction of the body. Moreover, they were extremely pertinent since they concerned points that the Governor himself had raised before the Council in his annual address. De Taste continued to invoke Article 30 and refused to reply. An Annamite member, Truong-van-Ben, was recognized. He was particularly distressed that Annamite soldiers were being used in French "wars of conquest" in the Middle East, and he introduced a motion requesting the Governor to demand their immediate recall. His proposal was quickly seconded by Monin, amid vigorous applause by several members of the Council and a large group of spectators led by Malraux. Chavigny ordered Malraux removed from the Chamber,[18] then completely ignored all that had occurred during the meeting and called for a vote on the budget submitted by the Governor. As a gesture of protest, the only one open to them, a third of the Council members voted against the budget; it passed by a two-thirds majority.

The following day a few government newspapers mentioned the meeting, but none made even a passing reference to Duoc's speech, since it would have been imprudent to do so with Varenne still in the capital. Typically, Chavigny's account of the session was a half truth. Beneath a headline that trumpeted A BOLSHEVIK MOTION IN THE COLONIAL COUNCIL, he ridiculed Truong-van-Ben's request that the Indochinese troops be recalled and their four-year draft service reduced. He commented that Monin's support of the motion was very revealing: "It was a repetition of the Communist motions that Doriot was accustomed to making in the French Chamber of Deputies." [14]

The following morning, *Indochine Enchaînée* was the only newspaper that gave precise details of the meeting.[15] In a front-page editorial, "Appeal to French Public Opinion," Malraux quoted de Taste's sole reply to all the charges leveled against the government—"Those who have grievances need only complain to the Administration or to the courts"—and observed that the idea of asking an Administration to correct its own abuses was ingenious and admirable in its stupidity. In the present instance, recourse to the courts was equally useless. As everyone well knew, the judiciary in Indochina was so closely bound to the executive branch of government that it could render independent decisions only with the greatest difficulty. What, then, could be done? he asked. Was there no recourse for those Annamites who were determined to correct the abuses of the corrupt colonial Administration under which they were obliged to live? Malraux tersely answered his own question: "If there remains no way for them to obtain justice in their own country, perhaps one still does exist elsewhere: an appeal to French public opinion."

Malraux's suggestion that the reform battle might ultimately have to be fought in France indicates his suspicion that the Cognacq Administration might succeed in concealing the movement of protest in the colony from the new Governor General. His fears proved to be well founded. Varenne spent only a week and a half in Saigon. The first several days were a whirl of official meetings, receptions, and tours of Administrative offices. Then the pace slowed appreciably, and he made several speeches giving the general direction his Administration would take. Liberals in the colony were stunned to hear him declare that "Annamite reforms" would have to be postponed until later in his term of office. His immediate concern was "primarily to have social legislation enforced." He indicated that he did not intend to take any positive steps toward restoring the personal and civil liberties that Cognacq had taken from the Indochinese. He also refused to take a stand on the problem of citizenship and higher education for the

Annamites. In short, on most questions he seemed to echo the ultraconservative sentiments of Cognacq and his cronies. As for the various abuses, thefts, and malfeasances of which the Administration of Cochinchina had been guilty, he urged all concerned to "forget the past." [16]

This was a severe blow to the reform group in the colony. As *Indochine Enchaînée* pointed out with the bitterness born of great disappointment, this position was particularly incongruous for Varenne: "Yesterday a socialist, today an outstanding conservative among prominent conservatives; another conversion under the sign of the piaster." [17] The two liberal Annamite newspapers of Saigon, *L'Echo Annamite* and the newly reorganized *Cloche Fêlée*, expressed a similar "disappointment" at the attitude of the new Governor General and their deep "regret to see that liberty and equality were not export items."

Aware that his frustrated countrymen were becoming desperate, the greatly respected Nguyen-phan-Long, a Municipal Councilor from Saigon and a member of the Colonial Council, undertook one final effort to impress Varenne with the seriousness of the situation.[18] After considerable difficulty with the Administration, he finally managed to schedule a public discussion with the Governor General for Friday, November 27, the day before Varenne was to leave Saigon for Hué and Hanoi. News of this traveled like lightning. When Varenne arrived for the meeting, he was greeted by more than 600 Annamite leaders and dignitaries who had streamed in from all over the countryside. They hoped that their presence would give greater weight to the protests that Long was to make in their name. As Malraux pointed out, they were perfectly aware that the Administration would subsequently find ways to punish them for daring to try to "obtain a little freedom."

In his presentation to the Governor General, Long recited once more his people's lengthy and familiar litany of grievances against Cognacq's regime. He was eloquent and sincere, and he was warmly supported by the anxious crowd of Annamites. Varenne could not ignore such a forceful demonstration of the discontent of the native population; he responded with a promise to investigate the situation and correct any abuses and illegalities he found. However, he underscored his lack of sympathy for any Annamite requests for reform that implied a new and dangerous philosophy of colonialism. He cited the example of increased freedom for publishing newspapers in the native language. He declared: "If that freedom which is so close to the hearts of Annamites were granted them immediately, and if Annamite newsmen, as yet ill prepared to use it wisely, were to abuse it and spread unrest in the country by an extremist statement of their ideas, there would soon be a wave of reaction that would sweep everything away."

This justification for one of Cognacq's most repressive policies was bitterly attacked by Malraux. How was it possible, he inquired, for Annamites to prepare for the responsibilities of a free press if they were never given a chance to experience freedom? As for the Governor General's suggestion that they might encourage violence and spread dangerous ideas if they were permitted to write in their native tongue, Malraux said:

> The journalists whose influence would be great in a free press in *quoc-ngu* are the very ones who have been able to make themselves heard when writing in French. . . . There is no basis for thinking that men who express their ideas calmly in French will express them violently in Annamite; and if some new Annamite writers did show some violence, it would mean one of two things: either the land is calm, and all this is unimportant; or it is *not* so, and the best way of pacifying it is not to silence those who, for good reason, are discontented but rather to give them satisfaction.[19]

Malraux expressed the hope that the Governor General would keep his promise to investigate censorship. But he was well aware that this would not be enough. Any Hanoi directives ordering a liberalization of Cognacq's policy would remain a dead letter for the simple reason that

> *This censorship will never have any occasion to be applied.* The newspapers written in the Annamite language cannot be published until their director has obtained preliminary authorization from the government. Now, this authorization is given only to the Governor's friends. And the censor doesn't have to suppress any of their texts, since those texts don't say anything. . . If freedom of the press is not granted to the Annamites, if censorship is maintained, one reform at least is essential: the elimination of the preliminary authorization, the possibility for Annamites to see their ideas expressed by those whom they respect, rather than the ideas of M. Cognacq expressed by those whom they despise.

Varenne departed for Hué the morning after his meeting with Councilor Long and the 600 Annamite leaders. In the group that saw him off, there was only one Indochinese, Cognacq's supporter, Dr. Trinh. Only ten days before, crowds of natives had warmly welcomed the new Governor General because he was a socialist with a long record of concern for securing justice and social rights for the oppressed. He left the city in dishonor. *Indochine Enchaînée* noted bitterly: "This is the first time that a Governor General has taken so little time to lose public esteem." [20] In their impatience, the reformers did not realize that what appeared to them to be a betrayal was actually the wait-and-see attitude of an honest public official who wanted to study the whole situation firsthand before making any major decisions. Indeed, Varenne proved to be so enlightened that he caused uneasiness in the Colonial Office in Paris and was eventually recalled.[21]

However, Malraux and Monin had expected immediate changes. When these were not forthcoming, they turned again to their newspaper with the conviction that it was the only hope left to the reform movement in the colony.

X

The Malraux-Monin Legacy

Although Varenne's apparent acquiescence to the worst of French colonialism was a severe blow to Malraux and Monin, it ultimately served a good purpose. It brought home to them the shortsightedness of pinning their hopes for reform on any individual or any reshuffling at the top of the administrative hierarchy. The system itself had to be changed. The most important thing was not the removal of Cognacq and his cronies, but the complete reformulation of the fundamental principles of colonialism. To this end, most of the articles in *Indochine Enchaînée* were discussions of general abuses in the Administration rather than exposés of the personal corruption of the men who headed it.

To be sure, whenever an appropriate opportunity presented itself, Malraux did not hesitate to renew his sarcastic personal attacks. He launched several vigorous assaults against Cognacq over various misrepresentations in the Green Book.[1] He often ridiculed Chavigny for his greed and pomposity.[2] One particularly caustic account recounted how the editor of *L'Impartial* had had a violent disagreement with several colleagues over the naming of an honorary president of a local press club. Malraux was sure the altercation would not last long: "Powerful gods, those who control Administrative subscriptions, will calm this storm with a few bits of paper. And the return of the prodigal children will be celebrated." [3] Ernest Outrey, returning from Paris, elicited similar sarcasm: "M. Outrey is coming back . . . to us, his arms loaded with gifts. He brings us peace, won from Bolshevik troops, and a study plan that is clever, ingenious, serious, complete, and intended to procure happiness for everyone in Indochina." [4] Outrey's idea was to

181

permit only those with perfect records of conservative voting to have any role whatsoever in the political and economic life of the country. In his view, only such men were worthy and capable of being leaders. Malraux observed with heavy irony that it was precisely this kind of "street-corner Nietzscheism" that had brought about the revolts against the French administrations in Syria and Morocco.

The young editor had begun a really serious examination of the theory and practice of French colonialism in his last two articles for *Indochine*. The first issue of *Indochine Enchaînée* made it clear that he intended to examine this problem further; his discussion of "Government by Traitors" [5] is a continuation of the August 14 editorial "Selection of Energies." It deals with what he considered to be a fundamental issue of the colonial question: "Among all our associates, which ones will we choose to make into leaders?" In other words, to what sort of Indochinese did the colonial bureaucracy entrust the delicate task of bridging the gap between conquerors and conquered, between European and Asian?

Conservatives like Cognacq were clearly not interested in having energetic and intelligent young Annamites assume this role. Any such natives who tried to obtain an education, the prerequisite for responsible government service, were thwarted. Then just where did the Administration recruit its native functionaries? According to Malraux's analysis, Annamite bureaucrats were chosen almost exclusively from two groups: the descendants of the old ruling mandarin families, and the "newcomers" from the lower classes of society. The former were desirable in the government because they still enjoyed a certain deference and respect, born of centuries of tradition. The "newcomers" were valuable because they were still close to their peers and could exert a powerful influence over them.

Frenchmen occupied all the top civil-service posts, but the mandarins constituted most of the second echelon. Malraux argued that a number of these officials were honorable and conscientious men. Properly consulted, they could be extremely helpful in governing the colony. Unfortunately, the French conservative mentality was not very receptive to such assistance. Even the most patriotic of the mandarins quickly realized that it was imprudent to offer suggestions or criticisms that went counter to what the

French wanted to hear. Rarely indeed would a high Annamite official or administrator speak up on behalf of his people.

On the whole, native bureaucrats from the lower social groups closely followed the mandarins' example. Those few who dared to protest injustices perpetrated against their countrymen were usually silenced by threats, and, if intimidation failed, the government simply arranged for "loyal" natives to issue denials and contradictions. This created doubt and confusion in the minds of the Annamites, making it even more difficult for them to act effectively. Native officials who collaborated with the Administration were rewarded with money and honors, and so their interests soon became identical with those of the foreign rulers. In a very real sense, they shared in the French exploitation of their countrymen.

In Malraux's view, the *colons* were encouraging the least desirable element of the native population to join them in protecting their unfair financial advantages. Under this sytem, blackmailers, traitors, and opportunists of all kinds became local leaders. Was it any wonder, he concluded, that a great hatred against the French was building up everywhere on the peninsula? "This murmur which is rising from all parts of the land of Annam, this anguish which for several years has been uniting scattered rancors and hatreds may become . . . the song of a terrible harvest . . . I ask those who read me to try and find out what is happening here, and when they have found out, to dare to speak up."

The injustice of French fiscal policy was another aspect of Cognacq's brand of colonialism that increasingly disturbed Malraux. *Indochine* had featured a series of theoretical discussions by economists and bankers; *Indochine Enchaînée* carried a number of articles, written by Malraux himself, which discussed specific cases he had observed. In his eloquent plea "On Behalf of Some Poor Frenchmen," [6] he pointed out that there were nearly 200 Frenchmen in great financial need in Saigon alone. These men wanted to work, but there were no jobs for them. The lower ranks of the Administration were reserved for Indians or Antilleans who worked more cheaply and who could be counted on to vote as directed. Business firms could not hire these Frenchmen for supervisory positions because all such jobs were filled directly from France; they could not afford to employ them in lesser posts because a Frenchman must be paid three times the salary of an Annamite.

These Frenchmen were neither stupid nor inexperienced, Malraux wrote. Would it not be possible to give at least the best and most industrious of them a government loan that would enable them to start small enterprises and thus become self-supporting again? Adequate safeguards could be devised to ensure that the money was not used fraudulently. The official policy of granting loans only to large industrial firms and to men who were already very rich was scandalous; it was particularly infuriating to realize that the 80,000 piasters which de la Pommeraye had stolen with impunity in the theatrical-season swindle would have helped more than 400 Frenchmen to regain their dignity and would have contributed appreciably to the economic life of the community.

In an article on "Infant Mortality and the Assessment of Taxes," Malraux dealt with a similar government mismanagement of funds, but this time from the Annamite point of view.[7] It was generally recognized that the colonial tax structure was extremely inequitable because it placed the heaviest financial burden upon those least able to bear it—the poor rice farmers of the provinces. Even greater injustices were associated with the allocation of tax revenues. On the average, only 30 per cent of this income was used for projects that would benefit the people who paid the bulk of the money. The remainder disappeared in graft or in schemes to bring profits to high government officials. When the Annamites pleaded for more schools for their children and for measures to lower the very high rate of infant mortality, the Administration's invariable reply was that there were no funds.

There would certainly be money available for such projects, suggested Malraux, if M. de la Pommeraye were less eager to get fat and Governor Cognacq less bent on acquiring ricefields. Beneficial results would be immediate if the Administration would load its payroll with teachers and doctors, instead of with Indian clerks whose main duty was to vote as directed. Yet, even with extremely limited resources, a great deal could be accomplished by a government acting in good faith. It would cost very little to carry on a campaign to teach Indochinese women the elements of infant hygiene, for example. Malraux's earlier request for permission to establish a "popular scientific magazine," which would have been useful in this endeavor, had been summarily refused, but there were many other means of propaganda. Frequent articles in Annamite newspapers, accompanied by simple illustrations, would reach a minimum of 5,000 women all over the colony. A number of doctors in Saigon stood ready to give free lectures to any interested groups. All this information could be widely disseminated in a very short time because most Indochinese liked to show off their learning before their friends. A medal could be awarded to the outstanding women in each village. However, concluded Malraux, "I am here only giving a few suggestions. For I know well that it would suffice that the idea be attributed to me for it never to be tried out. It would become Bolshevik and revolutionary. In a way, it really is revolutionary—to want to see the taxes paid by the Annamites contribute first and foremost to the development of Annam."

Beyond these fiscal injustices, however, and even more damaging to French prestige, was the incredible corruption often involved in the collection of taxes. Malraux dealt with one aspect of this in articles appearing in the seventh and eighth issues of *Indochine Enchaînée*. An early decree from the Colonial Office in Paris had made native village officials everywhere in the Overseas Empire personally responsible for any taxes not paid by those under their jurisdiction. Although this edict had been vigorously applied in the colonies during the war years, it generally had not been enforced after 1919. Most administrators, realizing its injustice, had ignored it. However, in the autumn of 1925, a number of complaints from the Cochinchina province of Mytho indicated that local authorities had begun to apply it strictly once more. An Annamite member of the Colonial Council had urgently asked the Government Commissioner for clarification of the matter but had received no answer. Finally, in desperation, the mayor of one of the villages in the area—acting on behalf of his counterparts everywhere in the province—addressed a plea directly to the Governor General. His open letter giving specific details of the situation was reprinted on the front page of *Indochine Enchaînée*, accompanied by a column of comment by Malraux.[8]

On instructions from Saigon, the government of Mytho had recently issued orders that the leaders of the province were to be held liable for all personal taxes in arrears from their villages for 1924 and 1925. The sums due were often in excess of 1,000 piasters—a considerable burden for the village leaders, many of whom were poor men. The law was especially unjust since the taxes were owed by citizens who had moved to other parts of the country but whose names the local Administration refused to remove from the village register. As the mayor pointed out, it was certain that these people had reregistered on the tax rolls of their new villages; otherwise, they could not get their identity cards validated. Thus the treasury would actually be paid the same tax twice. However, the government officials in Mytho refused to consider this. They constantly harassed the village leaders and threatened them with prison if they did not pay the sums demanded.

In commenting on the open letter, Malraux developed two points he had made in connection with other Administration abuses. It was clear, he said, that injustices such as this were hastening the demise of the colonial empire because they were uniting the local Annamite leaders against their French masters. The poorer village leaders, obliged to pay out such sums, could either take them from their own meager savings or extract them from their fellow villagers. In either case they would hate the French authority that had pushed them to such an extremity. The more affluent could furnish the money required without oppressing their countrymen further, but henceforth they would have no faith in French assurances of a just and equitable Administration. Thus, by this one act of greed, Governor Cognacq had aroused a whole province against the nation he represented.

For Malraux, the most culpable thing about the matter was its flagrant betrayal of the very spirit of French rule. In an eloquent paragraph, he expressed his indignation at this heartless exploitation of a poor, defenseless minority:

It is impossible to be clumsier, but it is also impossible to be more stupidly hateful.

For it is a question, we are told, of an Administrative measure to ensure the collection of taxes, and the only one capable of so doing.

This is absolutely false.

If such a measure brings about the collection of the taxes, it is only by virtue of the law that might makes right. . . . But in such a case, let the Administration that so acts no longer speak to us of solidarity, of Franco-Annamite reconciliation, of love of the masses and other tragic nonsense. Let it admit that if this is not a question of simple theft, it is indeed a question of a new means of coercion directed against the poor; let it state that here it represents the desire for conquest and expropriation, and—faced with the desperate ground swell that will rise, thanks to it . . . let it say: "Thanks, all of you who have—by your revolt—at last justified my brutality.

"You who are without food, you who are without shelter, all of you from the realms of misfortune and poverty, contemplate my justice and my serenity, and do not complain at having nothing left at all, because you still have your taxes!"

In spite of the furor created by *Indochine Enchaînée* and several Annamite-edited newspapers, the Administration did not weaken its fiscal demands. The Saigon officials were certain that the agitation would die down when the journalists turned their attention to other matters; without support and faced with jail terms, the Mytho leaders would pay the taxes demanded. In concluding his article, Malraux assured the Annamites that men of conscience in the colony were acting to correct the injustice. Telegrams and letters had been sent to various influential people in France, and a complete dossier was being forwarded to the Minister for Colonies. Malraux was certain this action would bring favorable results, because "it is highly unlikely that the Minister, even if he is informed by M. Outrey . . . will refuse to take into account the discredit that would be cast on the French Government by the imprisonment of respected men, or any other measure of coercion directed against them for the sole purpose of making them pay money that can be demanded from them only in the name of force." [9]

For Malraux, the substitution of expediency (or profit) for justice, the rule of *force* for the rule of *law*, was the most hideous aspect of Cognacq's administration, the one that most grossly violated France's fundamental principles. The despotic government of Cochinchina was possible only because its judicial institutions had been completely perverted. Cognacq, controlling both the police and the courts, ruled as a virtual dictator. During the last six months of 1925, several flagrant instances of collusion between the police and the courts gave Malraux a chance to comment at length on this situation. In August, he criticized the court's finding in the trial of a Sûreté agent accused of torturing an Annamite prisoner to death during an interrogation.[10] The policeman did not deny the charge. However, he affirmed that he could not be held responsible for the murder since he had been carrying out the interrogation under the direction of an Examining Magistrate. This judge could not be called on to corroborate the story because he had returned to France. Nevertheless, the court accepted the defendant's version of the killing and acquitted him of all charges.

Malraux reported a similar incident in an article "In Praise of Torture." [11] A Sûreté agent on special assignment for the Governor had tied an Annamite to a tree and beaten him nearly to death. Later, the officer maintained that he had only been trying to obtain vital information; the victim stated that money had been the sole motive for the brutal assault. Nothing would have come of this incident if the Annamite had not gone to a European physician for medical assistance. The doctor treated the badly injured man and then made an affidavit as to the nature and extent of his injuries. On learning of this, the police agent spread the rumor that the affidavit had been obtained by a bribe, and he produced a notarized document that contradicted it. The doctor, his professional integrity maligned, immediately brought his patient to Saigon and had him examined by three of his most respected colleagues. All three supported his findings. At this point the Governor intervened directly; in one of his famous personal interviews, he ordered the doctor to drop the matter. Unsuccessful in this maneuver, he rewarded the accused with a promotion and an assignment to a post in Saigon. Malraux closed his narrative with the comment that such a "torturer" and "stool pigeon" from the Sûreté was not out of place in Cognacq's suite; he might even hope to be appointed, "at the very next session, to the presidency of the Colonial Council."

The most striking illustration of the extent to which the colonial courts had been corrupted was a trial that took place in mid-December, only a few weeks before Malraux left the peninsula to return to France. The Bardez case, heard before judges in Pnom Penh, Cambodia, made it obvious to everyone that the judiciary in Indochina existed not to dispense justice but rather to carry out the policies of the Administration. This was the final cause in which young Malraux became involved, and it summed up all the injustices against which he had been struggling for nearly two years. In its flagrant disregard for both the spirit and the letter of French law, the Bardez case closely paralleled his own experience in the same courtroom some eighteen months earlier. The memory of what he himself had endured there lent great vividness and force to the four long eyewitness accounts he wrote of the Bardez proceedings.[12]

The taxes imposed in all of France's overseas possessions were heavy, but it was generally admitted that those exacted from the Cambodian peasants were by far the most onerous in the empire.

A 1920 report by the Inspector General, corroborated by the local political affairs officer, had called attention to the fact that these farmers paid nearly twice as much in taxes as their neighbors in Cochinchina. Nevertheless, late in 1923 the High Commissioner at Pnom Penh approved a wholesale revision of the tax base that would raise hundreds of thousands of additional piasters in 1924. The extra money was required to finance a number of Administration projects, primarily a lavish resort hotel to be constructed on the Gulf of Siam for vacationing French civil servants. When still more money was required for these projects, the Cambodian King was prevailed upon to issue a royal decree placing an additional special tax on the 1925 summer rice crop.

The Cambodian farmers were basically a gentle, peaceful people. As Theravada Buddhists, they abhorred all violence, and most especially the taking of human life. Yet even they began to stir at the news of still another tax. During the late winter and early spring of 1925, the unrest of the rural populations grew, especially in certain provinces. The headmen of the villages sent delegation after delegation to the French deputy commissioners in the provincial capitals and to the High Commissioner in Pnom Penh to warn of the widespread discontent among their people, but to no avail. In late March some minor Cambodian officials in the service of the French were roughly treated when they visited several villages in the region of Kompong Chnang. The Administration was well aware of the reason for this unrest. The High Commissioner wrote to a friend that such demonstrations were a "kind of protest against the present demands of the Treasury department." Yet orders were given to proceed with the collections.

One of the men charged with this duty was a provincial commissioner named Bardez. Shortly before mid-April, he decided to visit a number of villages in the troubled area around Kompong Chnang "to establish contact with the community authorities." The Cambodian Governor of the province tried to dissuade him, warning him that his life would be in danger. Bardez realized that this was true, but nevertheless, on April 16, he and two guards from the native militia set out to visit Krang Leou, a hamlet in the region.

The villagers had already shown their angry mood to a Cambodian official who had come on a similar visit a month earlier. On learning of the Frenchman's arrival, they gathered around the porch of the Buddhist temple, their habitual meeting place. News of the presence of a representative of the oppressive central authority spread quickly. During the hours that followed, groups of peasants from neighboring villages joined the crowd around the temple until there were more than 1,000 people present. Bardez had a village official read the Administrative directive aloud, and then he urged the crowd to pay the special tax. There were murmurs of refusal, requests for delay; the Commissioner remained adamant. A Buddhist priest intervened, but he was unsuccessful in arranging a compromise.

Finally losing his patience, Bardez—on his own authority—took a number of the village males to be hostages until the taxes were paid. The money was slowly, grudgingly brought to him, but still he failed to release the men. When an irate woman suddenly moved forward to pull her husband from the group of hostages, the militiaman on guard spontaneously cocked his rifle. That sharp sound triggered the angry, silent crowd. They seized pickets from the fence that surrounded the pagoda and hurled themselves with one accord on Bardez and his two guards. In an instant, the human wave swept by, leaving three lifeless bodies on the steps of the temple. A rage that had smoldered deep in rural Cambodia for decades had at last broken out into fury, and the rebellion spread like wildfire. Within hours, large groups of men, many of them armed, were moving about the countryside. Some even set out for the provincial capital at Kompong Chnang, determined to seek out the authority that had so long oppressed them.

The French Administration quickly learned what had happened at Krang Leou and sent soldiers into the area to make wholesale arrests. Scarcely thirty-six hours after the crime, some 300 Cambodian men, women, and children had been jailed. They came not only from Krang Leou but from many other villages scattered over the district. After being detained for interrogation as long as ten days, all but eighteen were finally released. However, they no longer had any homes or farms to which they could return. As punishment for the revolt, the Cambodian King had placed the area under a royal interdict. For years it would be prohibited to men, slowly reverting to jungle.

The murder of Commissioner Bardez presented the French Administration in Cambodia with a delicate situation. There was widespread interest in the case, not only in Indochina but in France as well.[18] A number of leftist newspapers in Paris had suggested that the crime was part of a widespread "popular movement" against the oppressive practices of the colonial government. To many French intellectuals, the incident was clear proof that the authorities on the peninsula were continuing the outmoded colonial policy of exploitation and domination, rather than the more liberal one of association. In the colony, this political controversy gave rise to the rumor that special observers were on their way from France to cover the trial, and that extensive investigation and revision of the whole administrative organization in Indochina would be undertaken if warranted by the facts of the case.

Local officials were understandably determined to forestall this. To do so, they had to make it appear that the death of Bardez had no connection with politics, that it was simply the work of criminals. As Malraux put it sarcastically, "Perhaps you believe that this business is somehow related to an unfortunate tax levy on rice? How wrong you are! The murder was . . . an accident. Some pirates were passing by." [14] This was the basic contention of the prosecution, and the administration marshaled all its forces to shore it up.

However, as *Indochine Enchaînée* hastened to point out, the "pirate" story was patently false. In the first place, there was no record of even a single European ever being attacked in the entire area. Professional bandits, realizing that a whole army would be sent after them if they dared molest a Caucasian, limited their depredations to fellow Cambodians. Moreover, Bardez had not been robbed of a single thing; all his money and personal possessions had been found on his body. Also, sixteen of the eighteen "pirates" came from the same village, Krang Leou, which made it ridiculous to contend that they were wandering marauders. Finally, the accused men had been arrested along with a number of others; all were part of a single group that, guns in hand, had set off toward Kompong Chnang after the tragedy. The others in the band, mainly well-to-do landowners and town fathers, had quickly been released because their appearance in court would weaken the already shaky pirate hypothesis.

Irregularities characterized the case from the very beginning. The High Commissioner of Cambodia appointed a man named Bonnet as Examining Magistrate to prepare the case for trial. Bonnet was not a judge. He was the chief administrative officer in Kompong Chnang, a colleague of Bardez, and a subordinate of the High Commissioner. His first act was to open the papers of Bardez, sealed at the time of his death, in the presence of attor-

neys for both the defense and the prosecution. He summarily impounded a large number of documents, including the red-covered
personal diary of the murdered man, before the defense lawyers
could even glance at them. Bonnet justified his action on the
ground that confidential political information was involved. Later
it became clear that many of the papers had been confiscated because they contained information that would have been useful to
the defense. During the trial the defense forced the prosecution to
produce a number of them from their place of hiding in Bonnet's
home, and Bardez' highly informative diary was eventually ex-
tracted from the coat pocket of the Examining Magistrate himself,
as he sat in the front row of spectators in the courtroom.

Bonnet prepared a very extensive preliminary dossier and turned
it over in its entirety to the prosecuting attorneys and to the presiding judges. The defense lawyers, however, were given only part
of the material, the least useful part. Thus they were completely
unprepared when certain documents were presented to the court
by the prosecution. Malraux satirized this technique, which had
been used at his trial:

> From time to time, we see . . . unexpected bits of information
> appear. "Where are they coming from?" asks the defense. "They
> aren't in the dossier." "Don't bother your head about *that*," replies
> the prosecution. "We're going to put them there.". . . I propose
> the following: henceforth, reports and important items in trials
> in which politics are involved will be communicated to the defense
> immediately after the condemned men have had their heads cut
> off." [15]

Among the documents in the dossier were "confessions" by the
indicted Cambodians. Under defense questioning, it soon became
clear that not only had the Examining Magistrate been present
when these affidavits were made, but several members of the
Sûreté had used rather vigorous means of persuasion to obtain
them. The prisoners stood mute in court, their eyelids still raw
from the ferocious attacks of red ants; deep scars from burning cig-
arettes and livid wounds from beatings were evident all over their
bodies. However, the presiding judge would not allow the defense
allegation that the confessions had been obtained by torture because it could not be proved that the wounds and scars had been

inflicted on the prisoners *after* their imprisonment. Malraux noted with bitter sarcasm:

> We have learned that it is a good thing to beat up the prisoners before their interrogation. That's an old treatment, fallen into disuse today, but which it would be appropriate to revive. It is excellent for the care of the tongue; it gives it a certain agility. Moreover, a witness full of good sense and kindness [Bonnet] declared at the hearing: "What the devil! Perhaps you think the rubber hose doesn't exist in France?" The presiding judge could have replied that this custom has a few small defects, although it marvelously represents the gentleness natural to civilization. He did nothing of the kind. But the State's attorney made the spectators aware of his special knowledge: "There doesn't exist a Cambodian," he told us, "who doesn't have his body covered with scars." To be sure. . . . Thus, the Cambodian is a striped creature, of the zebra family.[16]

The actual conduct of the proceedings was something out of *Ubu Roi,* one of Malraux's favorite literary allusions. Like Malraux's judge the previous year, the Bardez magistrate showed a marked inclination to ignore the whole defense presentation and to favor the State. As Malraux described it, Judge Mottais did not cease "to second the prosecution; to show the interest he took in it by nodding his head, by short sententious phrases, by round eyes and an open mouth; and to show the defense the scorn he felt by keeping it from intervening in the proceedings, and by manifesting—through enormous sleep-harbingering yawns—the frenzied interest he took in its summation." [17]

The array of prosecution witnesses was formidable. The widow of the dead man would not appear for either side, but Bonnet, the Examining Magistrate, gave lengthy and vehement testimony. His participation in a case he had helped to prepare was highly irregular. Moreover, he developed what defense attorney Gallet termed "tropical amnesia" on a number of important points. Two other prosecution witnesses, the head of the local police and the chief jailor, were also afflicted with this peculiar malady. Their memories were particularly defective about events that had taken place during the first ten days of the villagers' imprisonment, April 18 to 27.

A number of minor provincial government employees testified for the prosecution. These simple Cambodians were terrified to see

their immediate superior, Commissioner Bonnet, seated in the
front row of the courtroom, carefully comparing their oral testimony with their written statements in his hands. He immediately
brought any discrepancies to the attention of the court and demanded retractions. Several village elders from Krang Leou took
the stand. To redeem themselves in the eyes of the Administration
and to divorce themselves completely from the crime in which
they had participated, they did not hesitate to accuse their eighteen fellow villagers.

Political considerations had been introduced into Malraux's trial
on a criminal matter; similarly in the Bardez proceedings, a M.
Chassaing, the Director of Political Affairs for Cambodia, was constantly present in the courtroom, and each time the prosecution
got into difficulty or a witness faltered, "he leaped up like a jack-in-
the-box, intervened with an authoritative voice, settled everything
once and for all." [18] He was finally called as a surprise witness for
the prosecution. His appearance was allowed on the grounds that
his report on the Bardez matter was an important part of the
dossier prepared by Bonnet. This report had not been given to the
defense because it had been classified as an "Administrative"
rather than a "judicial" document, so Gallet and his colleagues
were totally unprepared for it. An angry Malraux, recalling similar
incidents at his own trial, commented on this maneuver:

> Administrative inquiries, hints the Administration, have nothing to
> do with the trial proceedings. Their purpose is different. . . . This
> is so much the case that the testimony of M. Chassaing is considered
> by all the magistrates to be capital and to change the positions
> [previously] established in the affair. Now, this testimony is the
> verbal account of what M. Chassaing knows about the matter. He
> had already made a written account of it in the form of a report.
> By reason of the brilliant principle enunciated above, this report
> had not been communicated to the defense.[19]

The central proposition of the defense was that the Cambodian
farmers were innocent of any crime because they had been provoked beyond endurance by the onerous exactions of a rapacious
Administration. The Bardez affair was really only a small part of a
much wider movement of revolt. As Gallet summed up his position: "It was all Cambodia that committed the crime of Krang
Leou, it is the general discontent that is party to it! . . . It is not
these accused men who should be penalized, it is the mistakes that

have been committed, it is the guilty men and institutions that should be struck down." [20] Gallet's prime witness, the Cambodian driver of Bardez who had seen the crime, had been killed "resisting arrest" shortly before the trial began. However, a number of the murdered man's friends took the stand for the defense. All of them agreed that the countryside had been in a state of great unrest because of the new tax levies. The most telling evidence was given by a man named Maurel. He substantiated his testimony by producing a letter from Bardez, written shortly before the Krang Leou trip. In it, the commissioner stated categorically that the taxes were causing much discontent in the area and that he feared violence might erupt and be directed against him.

Although greatly handicapped in their presentation, Gallet and his associates struggled hard to win the acquittal of their clients. Malraux, still sarcastic, commented:

> One could note on reading the accounts of the proceedings that the defense attorneys—by the inappropriate interest that they take in the accused, by their ridiculous concern to fix responsibility, by their protests, requests for explanations, insubordinations, and other questionings—becloud the minds of listeners of good faith. That cannot be tolerated.[21]

Gallet, in fact, became so intolerable that during the weekend recess a clumsy attempt was made to poison his morning tea. Although he was violently ill for two days, he recovered in time to appear in court on Monday morning. He tried to lodge a motion of protest with the presiding judge. However, as Malraux noted caustically, "since he wasn't even dead, an autopsy couldn't be performed," [22] and the judge refused to entertain the motion.

The prosecution became even more incensed on learning that the defense lawyers had taken the precaution of hiring their own stenographer, Mme. Tourniaire, a secretary on leave from the Saigon Chamber of Commerce. When her daily reports of the proceedings began to appear in Saigon in Dejean de la Batie's *Echo Annamite,* they created consternation in the Administration. Her verbatim accounts contradicted the impression that the government press, led by *L'Impartial,* was trying to convey. Mme. Tourniaire's regular employer, M. de la Pommeraye, hurriedly summoned her back to Saigon and threatened her with dismissal if she returned to Pnom Penh. The defense lawyers energetically protested this overt intervention, but the presiding judge would not even hear their arguments. He ruled that what had happened outside the courtroom was not germane to the matter before him, and warned Gallet and his colleagues that they would be liable to disciplinary action if they did not drop the matter immediately.[23]

In his report on this, Malraux again resorted to the heaviest irony. As before, irony provided an outlet for his anger and frustration at being utterly powerless to take any positive action to correct the injustice he saw before him.

Shorthand is a detestable discovery attributable, without any doubt, to some Bolshevik or other who wants to subvert the various branches of the Indochinese Administration.

What! The words spoken during the course of political trials can be set down? But that would be the end of everything! Then one could no longer rectify offensive remarks, painful allusions, embarrassing testimony and other manifestations of the truth! It is certain that the accounts of trials—as soon as they take place in the presence of stenographers not belonging to the Administration—become rather different from what they might have been. Shall I dare say that they become "romantic"?

One suddenly discovers antitheses. One sees in them—a thing inconceivable in Cambodia, in Cochinchina, and in those blessed spots where right thinking has maintained itself—that the prosecution and the defense are not completely in agreement; that they express different ideas and feelings. A fig for this gloomy disorder! I protest, along with MM. the commissioners and governors, in the name of the classical tradition. Order, gentlemen, agreement! The most noble quality of society is harmony. Just as it is appropriate that every living creature be an expression of the Divinity, it is fitting that each lawyer be an expression of the Administration. Thus he will be similar to the public prosecutors, with whom—until now—he made a contrast that grieved all artistic souls. . . .

The prosecution is guided by the principle that the Administration cannot be involved; to which the defense replies that since, according to its contention, the Administration is the principal culprit, it cannot be kept out of the trial. These two points of view are perfectly irreconcilable; thus there will probably be new difficulties.[24]

The judgment handed down by the Pnom Penh court in the Bardez case was very severe. One Cambodian was sentenced to death, apparently at the insistence of the High Commissioner of the Protectorate, four to life imprisonment, seven to hard labor, and a minor was given a lengthy prison term. Only five were acquitted. The defense lawyers and others in the colony immediately sent a telegram of protest to the Paris headquarters of the League for the Rights of Man, outlining the irregularities and the "scandalous Administrative pressure" that had characterized the whole proceeding. In spite of threatened "reprisals," they later forwarded a complete dossier of the case to Paris for study and action.[25]

Malraux returned to Saigon, angered and disgusted by what he had witnessed in Pnom Penh. He gave vent to his feelings against colonial "justice" in a short, sarcastic paragraph in *Indochine Enchaînée*:

> We cannot repeat it too often; the various codes, before being promulgated in the colonies, should be reworked. For example, I should rather like to see a code that would be based on the following principles:
> 1. Every defendant will have his head cut off.
> 2. Then he will be defended by a lawyer.
> 3. The lawyer will have his head cut off.
> 4. And so on.
> To which could be added:
> 5. Any stenographer employed by a lawyer will see the few possessions she has confiscated, and her contract canceled.
> 6. If she has any children, she will pay over to poor M. de la Pommeraye, as damages and interest, the sum of 1,000 piasters per child.
> 7. Her husband will have his head cut off.
> And we're back to No. 1 (see above).[26]

In returning to Indochina, in founding Young Annam, and in using his newspaper to fight for the rights of the colonial peoples, Malraux had been trying to force reforms by the colony itself. He had had greater confidence in this on-the-scene action than in long-distance intervention from Paris. However, after eighteen months of struggle against the overwhelming power that the Administration was able to marshal against him, his views began to change. In an editorial at the time of the Green Book controversy, he suggested that it might be best to try to arouse public opinion in France against the abuses of the Colonial Administration; in the colony itself, the bureaucracy was so powerful that the mass of the populace was completely cowed. The Bardez trial left no doubts in his mind. When he returned to Saigon, he had already decided that he would carry the fight to Paris.

The sixteenth issue of *Indochine Enchaînée*, which appeared a few days later, made this clear. A notice on the front page announced that M. Malraux was going to "return to France in order to make a series of speeches aimed at provoking a certain number of Frenchmen to intervene in order to obtain from the government the freedom sought by the Annamites." His final editorial, entitled "What We Can Do," followed this announcement. About to leave Indochina, the young editor did not neglect to take his leave of Chavigny and Cognacq. The former, he noted, was particularly worthy to be the "President of the Academy of Moral Sciences," because he was himself so constantly torn by an inner moral conflict: "On the one hand, the urge to keep silent, acquired by long practice of the profession of stool pigeon, torments him; on the other hand, the urge to talk, acquired by long experience in the profession of *provocateur*, tortures him." [27]

As for the Governor of Cochinchina, Malraux compared him to Count Ugolino, the damned soul in Dante's *Inferno* who ate his children in order to stay alive. Cognacq was one of those governors who "eat up their subordinates in order to preserve a protector for them." Unfortunately, "the Annamites—who have a very foul disposition—were lacking in gratitude. They didn't at all admire M. Cognacq, as it would have been fitting. They fell prey to brazen adventurers, to Bolsheviks." They had hoped that with the appointment of Varenne the situation would change, that the promises so often made to colonial peoples in official speeches would at last be carried out. They had been mistaken. What recourse was now left to them?

Malraux replied eloquently:

> We are going to appeal to all of those who, like yourselves, suffer. The people—in France—will not permit the sufferings whose marks you bear to be inflicted in their name. It will suffice for them to know about the Bardez affair . . . all this misery in Annam and Cambodia that the Administration each day seems to make more tragic and more moving. We must appeal to them by speeches, by meetings, by newspapers, by pamphlets. We must have the working masses sign petitions on behalf of the Annamites. Those of our writers—and they are numerous—who still have some generosity must appeal to those who admire them.

The great voice of the people must be raised to ask the leaders for an explanation of all this heavy affliction, of this devastating anguish that hangs oppressively over the plains of Indochina. . . .

Will we obtain freedom? We cannot know yet. At least we shall obtain a *few* freedoms.

This is why I am leaving for France.[28]

A few days later, he was gone from the colony. His Indochina adventure was over.

Epilogue

In spite of his courageous public stand, pessimism eroded Malraux's indomitable spirit during his last two months in Indochina. Weakened by illness, exhausted from the unequal struggle against the ponderous colonial bureaucracy, and somewhat disillusioned by the lack of widespread upper-class Annamite support for his liberal program, he began to feel that effective reforms in the colony could be initiated only in France. In his final editorial, he clearly stated that he was returning to France to arouse French public opinion in support of the Annamite cause "by speeches, meetings, newspapers, pamphlets." What did he actually do to carry out this program after he arrived in Paris? Superficially, it may appear that he promptly forgot the principles for which he had fought so long and so earnestly in Indochina. But this is not the case.

It is difficult to give specific details about what Malraux may have done privately on behalf of the Indochinese during this period. However, he has a well-deserved reputation as a brilliant conversationalist and as a moving public speaker,[1] and it is known that he used these talents on several occasions in an effort to reach a wide audience with his views on the colonial problem. Shortly after his return, he became associated with the Union for Truth (Union pour la vérité), a group of intellectuals founded in 1906 by the philosopher and man of letters Paul Desjardins to encourage discussion of contemporary philosophical, political, and social problems. During the winter months, lectures and public debates were organized in Paris, and Malraux joined in some of these, notably in the round-table meeting with Léon Brunschvicg and Gabriel Marcel concerning his novel *The Conquerors*.[2] For some years,

in the late summer, Desjardins had invited a number of outstanding men of letters from all over Europe to participate in the
"Entretiens de Pontigny," a series of ten-day discussions oriented
on a particular topic held at the Abbey of Pontigny, his summer
home in Burgundy. Malraux attended a number of these sessions,
along with Gide and other friends. It is probable that he enunci-
ated the basic ideas of his essay "Concerning a European Youth"
during the 1926 meeting.[3] A lengthy passage in his novel *The
Walnut Trees of Altenburg* echoes one such meeting where the
participants considered the problem of cultural contacts between
East and West. At such a moment, Malraux—deeply committed
to the cause of oppressed colonial peoples everywhere—must certainly have spoken out with force and eloquence on the situation
in Indochina. Since his audience was the intellectual and artistic
elite of France, his words could not fail to have repercussions.[4]

Malraux's written pleas on behalf of the Annamites are of
course more readily verifiable. But considering the vehemence of
his final statement on leaving Saigon, they are surprisingly rare.
During the decade 1926–35, he spoke out in print on a specific Indochinese question only twice: in 1933 in a newspaper article and
in 1935 in the preface to a friend's book on Indochina.[5] In both
instances, he made a strong attack on the corruption of colonial
courts.

In the years after his return to Paris, the situation in the unhappy colony progressively deteriorated, and French intellectuals
were well aware of what was happening. A steady flow of books,
articles, and newspaper reports by reputable, first-hand observers
documented both the extent of the Colonial Administration's
abuses and the depth of Annamite discontent with its harsh, authoritarian rule. Unfortunately, a vicious circle existed: as the Annamites became increasingly restive, the Administration became
increasingly severe in its efforts to crush any "dangerous" reform
movements. Democratic French institutions were thwarted or
completely perverted, and there was widespread suppression of
even the most fundamental human rights. To liberals, such conduct hardly seemed in keeping with Europe's much-vaunted "civilizing mission" in Asia.

As the decade of the 1930's opened, signs of imminent disaster
in Indochina became more frequent. Native troops, provoked by
the brutality of their French officers, mutinied in several areas.
These revolts were quickly and vigorously put down, but the sol-

diers remained sullen and unreliable. Elements of the civilian population also rebelled, notably destitute farmers and the incredibly wretched urban workers. Everywhere, incidents of robbery and brigandage became more frequent—and more violent—as exorbitant taxes and the rapacious venality of the administrators, both French and Annamite, drove the native population to desperation. The problem was further complicated by the almost complete lack of communication between rulers and ruled and by the blatant ineptitude of most of the administrators—often retired military or naval officers who were psychologically incapable of dealing with the acute human problems confronting them.[6]

In spite of the exhortations of certain farsighted individuals in Paris, French public opinion could not be aroused sufficiently to *demand* the long-overdue reforms that might have ameliorated the situation. As Malraux put it dryly: "Indochina is a long way off; this is an excuse for taking little heed of the cries that are raised there." [7] Gradually, the Annamite leaders were forced to the conclusion that the oft-repeated pledge of "collaboration" emanating from Paris would remain a dead letter in Indochina unless the native peoples themselves took direct action. In this impasse, they turned more and more frequently to the only force that they believed could successfully combat this colonial fascism: Communism. As one native intellectual explained in an unsolicited 1931 report to Paul Reynaud, Minister for Colonies, this step did not really represent a *political* commitment as such; it was simply the only solution left open to his people:

> As soon as the Annamites saw that a policy of honest and loyal collaboration was no longer possible, they had to take the path that seemed best to them, because come what may, they had to live their lives. Under such circumstances, how could they protect themselves against the intense propaganda of agents from Moscow, who made beautiful vistas flash before their eyes—national liberation, the departure of the foreigners, the sweeping away of a rotten society and its replacement with a Communist society where each one has his place and his share of the wealth. It would be done quickly. The country was all the more receptive to this propaganda because floods followed one another without interruption, because a succession of poor harvests increased the misery of the farmers, because young people by the thousands were thrown into the streets in search of nonexistent jobs, because the economic crisis reduced thousands of workers to unemployment. And then the arrests of

suspects, the extortions of the mandarins, denunciations motivated by personal revenge, every kind of difficulty that one encountered in business, all these acted like oil poured on a smoldering fire. *In point of fact, Annamites—even the most educated among them— do not know exactly what Communism is.* On the other hand, the devotees of Lenin don't possess any miraculous formula capable of bewitching the people, either. Their merit consists in knowing how to exploit skillfully a situation that the government has done nothing to avoid. . . . So many different classes being joined together in the same movement of protest clearly proves to us that it certainly has its deepest roots in the dissatisfactions that have been piling up in everyone's heart for many years. It is Communist only in name. In reality we are not confronted by Russians or Chinese or any other foreigner, but rather by Annamites, that is to say by the protégés of the government who, at the end of their rope, dragged into foolhardy adventures by the force of events, desperately offer themselves to airplane bombs and machine-gun bullets to seek a death they no longer fear. How could it be in France's best interest to prolong this situation by the same erroneous policies that have cost us so dearly already? [8]

The only reasonable solution for the colonial situation was a prompt, far-reaching, and honest reform, but such a step was as unthinkable to the retired military men in the Colonial Administration as it was to the *colon* planters and businessmen they served. In keeping with the character of their rule, these men decided to impose a solution on the native peoples by the grossest kind of brute force: the army. Since the Annamite troops in the country were not entirely reliable, especially in situations where they might be obliged to fire on their own people, units of the French Foreign Legion were summoned to the peninsula to "restore order."

These mercenaries were immediately given carte blanche by the local civil authorities. When the situation continued to worsen, they were told to use the harshest measures imaginable in dealing with the native population. For example, it was indicated that out of every group of ten native prisoners rounded up, only one need be kept alive for interrogation; the other nine could be executed as conspirators. Any Annamite suspected of being Communist, or who was participating in anti-government "demonstrations," or who carried arms, or whose "tax card" was not in order was to be shot on discovery—or denunciation—at the discretion of the Legionnaires involved.[9] As Malraux subsequently wrote:

When one has seen, as I have seen, one half a village accuse the other half either of Communism or of making liquor (depending on the law in vogue) because of a field in dispute for 120 years, one can imagine what the government of 20 million men will be like, guided by the acumen of legionnaires in a country where, in addition, they don't know the language.[10]

One horrified colonial, an eyewitness, described the resulting situation graphically:

The conduct of the soldiers—and of the Legion in particular—is viciously brutal. An unleashed soldiery, given over to all its instincts, escaping almost entirely from the control of its leaders, now terrorizes the entire country. They steal, rape, condemn to death, and execute willy-nilly. Legionnaires enter homes, take what catches their fancy, indulge in outrages against women and young girls. For trifles, without proof, men and youths are arrested and shot in cold blood, without trial. A veritable band of pirates in uniform is unleashed over all the land. Denunciation rages, and the region lives under a real reign of military terror. . . . If it is with such methods that we intend to pacify the country, we are gravely mistaken. The most evident result of all this is further to inflame passions and to stir up the most peaceful of the Annamites against us. . . . If this is what we want to accomplish, we won't have long to wait! And there the Communists have a gold mine to use against us.[11]

According to Malraux, such a regime of terror was possible only because the courts, the citizens' fundamental safeguard against the power of the State, had been completely subverted. This unfortunate situation was brought forcefully to the attention of Frenchmen late in the spring of 1933. At that time, Paris received news of two similar and particularly flagrant travesties of justice committed by the courts in Hanoi and Saigon, and Malraux wholeheartedly joined in the wide and heated discussion that ensued. The uproar eventually became so great that the French Government could not afford to ignore it. A commission of inquiry headed by Paul Reynaud was created to look into the matter at first hand.[12] Among those in the official party that sailed for Indochina early in September, 1933, was the brilliant newspaperwoman Andrée Viollis, the wife of D'Ardenne de Tizac, curator of Oriental art at the Musée Cernuschi and a friend of Malraux's.[13]

The Reynaud group was supposed to be a mission of inspection, but elaborate measures taken by local colonial officials made

certain that the visitors saw only what it was appropriate for them
to see. Fortunately, Mme. Viollis made frequent clandestine contacts with representatives of the long-suffering Annamites. She was
horrified at what she learned, and to gather further information
she remained in Indochina a month longer than the rest of the
official party. Upon her return to France, excerpts from her detailed journal were published in the newly founded liberal Catho-
lic review *Esprit*.[14] These articles added considerably to the information available about the Saigon-Hanoi trials, and some time
during the following year, Gallimard decided to issue her complete
notes in book form. Malraux, then an important member of the
firm, doubtless had a hand in this decision. For unknown reasons,
publication was delayed, and *Indochine S.O.S.* did not appear
until early in the autumn of 1935.[15] The volume included the
Viollis diary, together with some 120 pages of supporting documents that she had collected: extracts from court records, eyewitness newspaper accounts, detailed reports submitted to Reynaud
by responsible Annamites but never made public, and letters of
protest from all over the colony.

Malraux wrote a brief but eloquent preface to this highly incriminating indictment of the Colonial Administration in Indochina. To make it clear that his commendation of the book was
based on firsthand knowledge, he made a rare personal reference
to his Far Eastern experience, recalling the incident when the
young Annamite printer had brought him the government type,
stolen for *Indochine Enchaînée*, "so that people will know what is
going on here." It was for this very reason that Mme. Viollis had
compiled her book several years later. Unfortunately, noted Malraux sadly, "since it was written, the dance of death that it depicts
has little changed—except for its cadence." [16]

In *Indochine* and *Indochine Enchaînée*, Malraux had particularly attacked the Colonial Administration for the aggressive authoritarianism it concealed by a mask of benevolent paternalism.
He returned to this point in his succinct Viollis preface. He evidently believed that some kind of guidance was necessary in colonial areas. As he put it, "the effective authority of France out
there, as with any democracy, lies in her power to control." [17]

But for him the only "control" appropriate to a democracy was
the power of example. On a personal level, the unselfish humanitarian achievement of a private organization like the Pasteur Institute was eloquent testimony of the principles for which French-

men stood; it could not but nurture a similar spirit in the hearts of
the Annamites it served. In the political realm, the example of
French tradition and practice would not only ensure a larger
measure of self-government for the native peoples of the peninsula, but would also instill in them that sense of collective responsibility necessary to the proper functioning of democratic institutions.

As one step in this direction, Malraux had suggested (in 1925)
the establishment of a Supreme Court for Annam, to be located in
Paris and independent of the "guidance" of the Colonial Ministry.[18] Such an institution would have concretely represented the
emergence of the Annamites into responsible adulthood. This suggestion had met with a violent negative reaction. The vast majority
of the shortsighted administrators and *colons* felt that political democracy was neither prudent nor efficacious in the colonies; the
natives had to be "guided" by an external authoritarian force. A
more liberal system would paralyze the Administration, and the
economy. As for an independent court, it was unthinkable. Native
peoples should not be given the right to judge their protectors, any
more than a son should have the right to judge his father. As duti-
ful children, they should meekly accept whatever restrictions,
whatever humiliations the colonial government saw fit to place
upon them. As Malraux summed it up, this false paternalism was
just a very thin concealment for gross coercion: "The tactic of the
colonial financiers—and of the Administration they dominate—is
to demand the absolute control over the natives that the state is
supposed to exercise over their own activities—and that is precisely
what they refuse to allow." [19]

This unhappy situation had at last begun to change, he continued. Although most enlightened Indochinese were well aware that
they still urgently needed help and guidance from the West, they
were becoming increasingly determined that accepting such assistance should not involve a surrender of their *political* autonomy:
"when Frenchmen build roads or bridges in Indochina, let them
be paid, as is done when they direct undertakings in Siam or in
Persia; and let them then spend the money they have earned as
they choose. For if those who work ought to receive *political*
power—in addition to their salaries—then soviets should be organized in France, from the specialist to the worker." [20]

Malraux's preface for Mme. Viollis' book was primarily a reiteration of his long-standing belief that authoritarian colonialism was an inherently evil system and doomed to failure. Although it might briefly be profitable to a favored economic group, in the long run it would collapse. This end was inevitable because as a philosophy, it was predicated on the ridiculous assumption that the human spirit could be controlled by external physical force. As he succinctly put it, "It is all too evident that in the area of freedom, there can be no colonization at all; and that in the area of fact, the colonial problem is not a problem of force, but a problem of exchange." [21]

Early in October, 1933, while the Reynaud-Viollis inspection party was still in the Far East, the legal dossiers of the Hanoi-Saigon trials of the preceding spring reached the Court of Cassation in Paris. The horrors they revealed provoked Malraux into writing his only other journalistic piece directly related to Indochina. A long article entitled "S.O.S." took up most of the third page of the October 11, 1933, issue of the liberal Parisian daily *Marianne*. He stated at the outset that his facts were drawn from firsthand sources, including official records and descriptive accounts that had appeared in Indochinese newspapers at the time of the trials. (Most of these documents were subsequently published in full in the appendix to the Viollis book.) Apparently the substantial files of the Committee for the Amnesty of the Indochinese Political Prisoners, headed by Francis Jourdain, and of the League for the Rights of Man were also opened to him.

Central Annam during the spring monsoon of 1931 was oppressed by an atmosphere of hatred and violence. Two thousand Annamite prisoners had just been summarily executed, without trial, and ominously the central provinces watched in hatred over "their corpses bathed and rebathed by the rain." Passing through a village in rural Annam, a Sergeant Perrier of the French Foreign Legion heard a group of Annamites having a violent argument in a native open-air market. Leaving his bicycle by the roadside, he entered the area and attempted to restore order with vigorous blows of his quirt. At first the excited Annamites fell back. Then, a moment later, with the fury of long pent-up rage, they suddenly turned on this representative of the hated foreign oppressors and killed him. Terrified by what had been done, everyone fled, leaving the horribly mutilated body lying on the ground where it had fallen. It was the first link in a long chain of violence.

A few hours later, news of the death of Perrier reached two of his fellow Legionnaires at a small nearby post. As Malraux described it:

> It's the little tropical station, always the same, with its projecting roof, its heat, its rain, and its tall palm trees like wolf-heads. However, to the isolated tree planted like a flagpole across from the installation, a living Annamite is tied, the severed head of a friend in his hands. He had been arrested in the morning, hours before Perrier's murder; he had been leading some taxpayers who had unsuccessfully attacked the local militia on a tax-collecting mission. Communists, obviously. The two Legionnaires question him. Visualize that interrogation of a bound man, a severed head tightly held in his hands, by two Legionnaires, one of whom will admit at the trial that he was completely drunk, in the center of shuttered native huts, where eyes are glued to every crack. . . . He doesn't reply. So he's cut down—with one or two bullets in the skull—and the head that he was holding goes bouncing a little way off. Although it appears that they were within the law in killing this recalcitrant prisoner, the prudent Legionnaires untie the body, not forgetting the severed head on the ground—a taste for neatness—and throw both of them into a nearby river.[22]

The two men then drove to a Legion station close by to take the news to their half-dozen comrades billeted there. In the stockade of the post were eight Annamites falsely accused of being Communists. They had been taken into custody three days previously when they had come to sell food to the native cook. The half-drunk soldiers decided to avenge Perrier's death on these innocent men. They beat them with whips and pick handles, mutilated one with a pair of scissors and a saw, and several different times shot blindly into the bloody, terrified huddle of human beings. When a hapless villager stumbled onto the bacchanal, he was bayoneted and then bludgeoned to death with empty wine bottles to ensure his silence. Finally, the wounded prisoners were thrown into the back of a Legion truck for a wild ride through the jungle. From time to time, the vehicle stopped, a shot rang out, and a body was left to rot in the tropical underbrush. Even after being shot through the head at point-blank range, one man miraculously lived. His revelations prompted the investigation that terminated in the trial of the soldiers before the Hanoi court.

In Malraux's view, these legal proceedings were even grislier than the crimes because they clearly revealed, for all to see, the incredible violence and brutality to which the Colonial Administration had descended. As the testimony progressed, it became evident—as he put it—that "now it is no longer . . . a question of one atrocity among others; it is a question of organized repression." In open court, Legionnaires admitted decapitating Annamites with saws or ordinary knives, and executing on the spot natives whose tax cards were not in order or who were participating in a protest meeting. The invariable justification of the Legionnaires was that they were simply following the example and orders of their superiors.

Called to give testimony on this point, the commanding officer of the Legion pointed out dryly that the civil authorities had certainly not brought his soldiers into Annam to establish convents, and he confirmed that he had indeed been directed to use some of the extreme measures mentioned by the Legionnaires on trial. Unfortunately it was impossible to fix any precise responsibility in the matter because all such orders had been given to him orally and he had passed them on to those under him in the same manner. He was evidently somewhat annoyed at the hypocrisy of the Colonial Administration because he concluded his statement to the Court with this pointed comment: "It may be that certain representatives of the civil authorities have lodged complaints against the perpetrators of these acts. However, it is *they* who issued the order to kill the prisoners. The responsibility devolves upon the civil authorities, who seem to be in hiding today." [23]

In spite of the overwhelming evidence of their guilt, the trial ended in acquittals for the soldiers and—by implication—for the civil authorities to whom they were ultimately responsible. This was not exactly unexpected, noted Malraux bitterly: "Only the dead are not acquitted."

Equally indicative of the bankruptcy of French colonialism was the treatment Annamites accused of minor offenses received in the same courts that refused to convict Frenchmen of murder. For example, in five days in May of 1933, a Saigon court in a burst of energy had judged some 120 natives involved in six different and unrelated semi-political "crimes." The punishments meted out to 80 of them ranged from death, to life imprisonment at hard labor, to ordinary prison sentences totaling nearly 1,000 years. There were glaring inconsistencies. One Annamite was sentenced to fifteen years in prison for belonging to an anti-government political group;

a companion who had taken part in foraging raids and had been directly involved in a political murder was inexplicably acquitted. A village father was given a death sentence for being a member of the "revolutionary" tribunal that had condemned a corrupt local mandarin to be executed; a companion on the very same tribunal was acquitted.[24]

Malraux pointed out that such severity was in striking contrast to the benevolence shown the French Legionnaires who had murdered nearly a dozen innocent Annamite prisoners. To be sure, there was an explanation for this apparent inconsistency. To discourage any political activity in the colony, the government had decided to take "vigorous action." This meant very harsh treatment for "revolutionaries" and leniency for any Frenchmen who became overzealous in suppressing rebellion. Of course, putting this program into operation required certain modifications of traditional French legal procedures: the pretrial inquiry was to be carried out not by an impartial Examining Magistrate but by the police; torture was permitted to encourage the tongues of recalcitrant witnesses; and the verdicts handed down after any such hearings were to be based not on the guilt or innocence of the accused, but rather—as in the Bardez affair and in his own Pnom Penh trial—on the requirements of the political situation.

After this angry recital of the facts contained in the Hanoi-Saigon dossiers, Malraux devoted the remainder of his *Marianne* article to a revealing general discussion of the principles of colonialism as practiced in Indochina. His blunt opening statement reveals how deeply involved he was: "To avoid any misunderstanding, let this be clearly understood: personally, having lived in Indochina, I cannot conceive that a courageous Annamite could be anything other than a revolutionary." Many of his references clearly recall his personal experiences in Cochinchina and echo positions he took in his *Indochine* editorials.

As Malraux saw it, there were three possible attitudes that the Colonial Administration could adopt toward the native peoples entrusted to its care. First was "the democratic attitude," the one it pretended to have adopted. The fundamental tenet of such a political regime, heir to the traditions of the French Revolution, was that the people living under its authority had a right to participate in its decisions. Therefore, the logical thing for such a government to do would be "to grant the natives citizenship en masse" so that they could express their opinions and desires through the ballot box. This certainly had not been done in Indo-china:

> Not only do the Annamites not vote, but those whom they see voting under their noses for the government of their country are— in as large a number as Frenchmen—Indians and blacks from Africa. . . . The cultured Annamite, who bitterly accepts the vote of the white man as the right of the conqueror, doesn't at all accept that of his Indian milkman, transformed into a French citizen for the occasion because he was born in a colony joined to France before the Revolution.

To call so unrepresentative a regime democratic was obviously fla-grant hypocrisy.

The second possible solution for the colonial problem, in Mal-raux's view, was "the continuation of the civil system, overseen by French control commissions and by a native representation in Par-liament." Such direct participation would help alleviate a major cause of unrest among cultured Annamites—a sense of humilia-tion at not having any voice in the government of their own coun-try. Conservative Frenchmen insisted that such a program would be a disaster. Yet, remarked Malraux, the responsible conduct of native parliamentarians from the French possessions in Africa and the Antilles was a certain indication that the colonial peoples would not rush forward to destroy the French Constitution. After all, they were only too well aware that it was the very instrument that had given them their rights in the first place.

The third possibility in Indochina was what Malraux termed "the fascist attitude." This could take two forms: "Either it is the present attitude—and the coalition of the classes in Indochina against France will be effected within ten years—or it is the natu-ralization (in one form or another) of the Annamite bourgeoisie, its alliance with the Colonial Administration against the peas-ants." Both eventualities were equally dangerous because the fail-ure of either of them would drive the farmers—95 per cent of the population—into the Communist camp within ten years. He noted prophetically, "Every fascism that fails summons its Com-munism."

Although he was strongly opposed to any such authoritarian phi-losophy, Malraux admitted that it was at least "a conceivable atti-tude," "a position that one approves or disputes." However, what was guiding the present colonial regime of Indochina was not even a doctrine; it was simply a monumental and unbelievable stupidity. That Administration was not a government; it was "a madman who fires on passers-by while shouting 'I am Order.'" To justify any harsh measures taken to preserve the sacrosanct and profitable bourgeois value called "order," the Administration conjured up a Communist ghost. As Viollis had reported:

> In Indochina they indiscriminately label as 'Communists' not only nationalists who want to see the democratic principles they have learned from us applied to their country, but also the destitute, who plead for someone to come and help them, and all those who—for one reason or another—don't have the talent of pleasing the administration or the police. These people accept that epithet and take pride in it.[25]

In concluding his *Marianne* article, Malraux vehemently insisted that in the long run violent reprisals and wholesale executions would do nothing except drive the hard-core Communists underground. There, in secret, they would continue to organize their revolt, "because cutting off people's heads is not a permanent way of keeping them from using them. Even with a saw." When the inevitable war in Europe broke out, this group would rush from hiding to overturn the French supporters of "order" and drive them—and their bourgeois Annamite acolytes—from the peninsula. Malraux closed with this prophetic plea to the youth of France:

> You young people, men of less than forty, you know that war is here. Today's Europe bears it within herself, just as every living body carries death: perhaps you will die for having waged it, [but] you will not die without having waged it. No matter how hard you shut your eyes, the whole world shouts it into your ears. You who know—from having heard it howled or groaned beside you all during your adolescence—how difficult it is to kill and to die, even in accord with conscience, at the hour when—in whatever ranks you may be—the very meaning of your life will be at stake in France, it is perhaps these very men [Annamites] whom you will be sent to fight. You in whose shadow wars prowl like crouched witches to say to you: "You will die," another Riff war is being made ready for you.
> For—nationalists, Communists, liberals—there is one thing you

all know: that a people will become tired of anything, eventually—even of being murdered for nothing.

Had Malraux's enlightened message been heeded, France might have been able to work out a solution to the colonial problem and have avoided the horrors of the long wars in Indochina and in Algeria. Unfortunately his exhortations—and those of others like him—fell on deaf ears.

The *Marianne* article and the Viollis preface are eloquent witnesses to the depth of Malraux's involvement in the Annamite cause. Yet these two pieces are apparently the only ones he ever wrote that relate to it directly. What can be the reasons for this surprising silence?

Perhaps part of the explanation lies in his personal modesty. Although Malraux has repeatedly shown himself to be cooperative in answering questions about his writings and ideas, he has always been reluctant to furnish even the most elementary information about what he considers to be his "private life." Thus, much of his biography is literally myth. This personal reticence is not restricted to strangers. As one of his close friends, Mme. Théo van Rysselberghe (M. Saint-Clair), points out, even in private conversations "his intimate personality is always pushed into the background." [26] For someone as reserved as Malraux, it would doubtless be psychologically painful to make a public show of so private an experience as his Indochina adventure.

His almost complete silence on the *specifics* of the Indochina situation is also probably related to another of his personality traits. In her literary portrait of him, Saint-Clair notes that Malraux's intellectuality is always strikingly evident: "It takes a long time to know anything of Malraux except his intelligence, which overshadows everything else." Moreover, she continues, the powers of this extraordinary intellect are constantly marshaled to examine a wide range of ideas and experiences, each one of which is "right away considered in all its ramifications, all its consequences, all its impossibilities," and then incorporated into a certain "broad view of the world, the one that is obsessing him for the moment." [27] She feels that Malraux has a deep-seated need to abstract his personal experience of reality and then to integrate it into a coherent world. He must first transform experience into knowledge, and then use it to create a personal, meaningful whole.

Intellectually, a major part of Malraux's interest in Indochina was related to the general subject of the cultural differences between East and West, a question that had fascinated him before he had actually gone to the Far East. Not unexpectedly, several of the works he published shortly after his return to France present an abstract discussion of this subject rather than a specific account of his grievances against the Colonial Administration. Even though he was dealing in abstractions, he was still trying to serve the Annamite cause. By revealing in a new light the fundamental characteristics of the two civilizations, he doubtless hoped to make his countrymen more aware of the fundamental East-West problem. With his writings, he hoped to lead his readers to a new understanding of the over-all situation in Indochina. This might eventually move them to demand action on the abuses that other authors—like Viollis—were revealing in concrete detail. Such was the plan he evidently had in mind when he wrote in his final *Indochine Enchaînée* editorial: "Those of our writers—and they are numerous—who still have some generosity must appeal to those who admire them. The great voice of the people must be raised to ask the leaders for an explanation of all this heavy affliction, of this devastating anguish that hangs oppressively over the plains of Indochina."

Malraux's *Temptation of the West* appeared in June, 1926, a few months after his return from Asia. This book, which he himself has characterized as "a rather special work touching on metaphysics," [28] is a somewhat lyrical presentation of certain basic differences between Eastern and Western civilizations. In form, it is simply a collection of letters exchanged between a Chinese youth and a Frenchman. Although the book is interesting, it lacks focus and clarity, possibly because it was written in spurts over a rather extended period (1921–25).[29] When it appeared, Malraux wrote a special column for the literary periodical *Les Nouvelles Littéraires* to present the essentials of his position to prospective readers. This important but neglected article not only suggests some of the motives that led him to Asia in the first place but also clearly reveals that the incidents and details of his personal experience in Indochina had already been abstracted to buttress a broad intellectual position.[30] Already he had begun to fight for the Annamites in generalities, rather than in specifics. He was trying to destroy the basic mental attitudes that made colonialism possible.

The essay begins with a succinct and rather unflattering characterization of Western civilization: "The fundamental characteristic of our civilization is that it is *closed*. It is without spiritual objective; it forces us to action. Its values are founded on the world that depends on fact. . . . Each of our victories, of our actions, summons other ones, and not repose. The circle is closed." In contrast to the aggressive, self-centered materialism of the West, the civilizations of Asia exude a kind of passivity; they represent stability and order. Such differences of course imply somewhat contradictory views of the essential nature of Man himself. In the Christian West, notes Malraux, "the notion of man . . . was based on the exalted awareness of our fundamental lack of harmony; such a lack of harmony does not exist for the Oriental, for whom man is a locus rather than a means of action."

We Westerners become aware of the frantic rhythm, the closed circle of our culture, only when we leave it. Looking back upon it from Asia, we see clearly that "it has no purpose other than its material development; it offers us only the most base reasons for existence." However, the reason for going to Asia, for immersing oneself in a totally different milieu, is not to pass judgment, to praise or condemn. In one sense, we *cannot* denigrate our civilization because it is truly the product of our deepest needs, whether they are ignoble or not. Such a cultural exile is rather to heighten our awareness of the characteristics of our own viewpoint, to clarify and intensify its problems by contrasting it with a totally different one. Such a concrete experience of the relativity of our values destroys the idea that there is only *one* reality, *one* way of looking at the world. This is truly a liberation. As Malraux wrote, "What the confrontation of two opposing civilizations causes to arise within us is a kind of reappraisal, due to the discovery of the arbitrariness of both of them. To experience the feeling that our world *could* be otherwise, that the modes of our thinking *could* not be those with which we are familiar, gives a freedom whose importance may become extraordinary."

From his vantage point outside Western civilization, Malraux had seen that the youthful generation of which he was a part was moving toward an emphatic affirmation "*of the bankruptcy of individualism, of all the attitudes, of all the doctrines that justify themselves by the exaltation of the Self.*" He realized that the youth of all Europe was in search of a new vision of Man to replace the narrow, selfish, outmoded nineteenth-century concept. Indeed, it was on just such a quest that he had gone to Asia. Yet, as he stressed at the end of his article, Asia itself was in the throes of a revolution and could not furnish the new ideas required; it could only provoke a struggle, an examination, a temptation. Hopefully, since "one of the strongest laws of our spirit is that vanquished temptations are there transformed into knowledge," such a confrontation would eventually lead Westerners to a fruitful understanding of what they—and their civilization—are really like. Such knowledge was the essential first step in finding an answer to the needs of troubled twentieth-century Man.

The second important "Asian" piece Malraux published after his return from Indochina was another philosophical essay, the short but brilliant "Concerning a European Youth," [31] originally called "Characteristics of a French Youth." [32] In this article he pursued the question of intercultural contact further and in a more organized manner. To focus the discussion, he prefaced it with a quotation from his *Temptation of the West*. In it, Ling— the young Chinese—remarked that in the eyes of most Asians, "the highest aim of a refined civilization is a studied non-cultivation of the Self." For Malraux, such a neglect of the self was clearly in direct contrast to the aggressive egocentricity that had long characterized European civilizations and that had attained a particularly extreme form—philosophically, economically, and politically—at the end of the nineteenth century.

To be sure, this self-centeredness, in one form or another, had been one of the prime forces shaping the civilization of the West. In the early period of European history, Christianity had given an explanation, a character, a Reality, to man and his world; it had been the lens through which man viewed the vastness of creation and the deep complexities of his own life. It was a Christian God who presided over all the universe and guaranteed man his exalted place in it. It was the Christian church that emphasized the personal responsibility of the individual believer as he chose between good and evil.

When this religion began to decline, it was replaced by a new one: Science. Man then came to believe that with the help of his rational intelligence he was ultimately capable of truly knowing reality and of shaping it to his will. Such a self-exaltation led to "a kind of passion for Man, who takes within himself the place he used to give to God." During this period Western thinkers were increasingly "obliged to base their notion of Man on the awareness that each individual has of himself." It was a natural transition, as

Malraux pointed out, to move from the proposition "Man is the only object worthy of our passion" to the self-centered affirmation "I am the only object worthy of impassioning myself." [33] Collectively, this philosophical position was reflected in the laissez-faire capitalism that soon became the dominant European political credo.

However, paradoxically, in the years immediately following the victories of World War I, it had become evident that this "triumphant individualism" no longer commanded the loyalty of the youth. At the very heart of a civilization "whose strength came from the most gross individualism," a new movement—intellectual, artistic, and political—was taking shape. As Malraux put it, the more enlightened among the young people of the West at last wanted to "free themselves from their civilization, as others wanted to free themselves from the divine." [34] They wished to seek new goals, to formulate the universe and their own condition in new and more meaningful terms.

Since this movement was only beginning, it had so far manifested itself primarily as an effort to sweep away old institutions, to destroy outmoded concepts and ways of thought. Yet it was already clear that it was essentially idealistic in tenor. In Malraux's words, "the young people of Europe are more concerned about what the world might be than by what it is." As their eyes opened, they were overwhelmed—as he had been in Asia—by "the infinity of possibles" that constituted the reality of the world around them. The late nineteenth century had viewed reality as an ordered, stable, and fixed system; the young postwar generations had a very different apprehension of it, one that transcended the limits of the traditional structures of art, politics, and philosophy. For them, "the world reduces itself to an immense interaction of relationships that no intelligence any longer seeks to fix, since it is in their very nature to change, to incessantly renew themselves." It was, in short, a Bergsonian world in which change was stability, revolution an order, and metamorphosis life itself. Moreover, because this "violent youth" had at last freed itself from selfish withdrawal, from "the base vanity of characterizing as greatness the disdain for a life to which it does not know how to commit itself," it was a world that was founded on real *fact*, not on empty philosophical syllogism. [35]

Malraux, seeking to formulate the character of this new reality into which he had gained such insight from his two years' experi-

ence in Asia, singled out one man as his opponent: Henri Massis.
This articulate neo-Thomist was an outstanding example of the
efforts that traditionalist philosophers were making to resurrect a
cultural corpse, and Malraux had long considered him as being at
the antipode of his own position. As early as the autumn of 1925,
he wrote to his publisher, Grasset, concerning his own forthcoming book:

> Since the definitive title of the work is *The Temptation of the
> West*, perhaps it would be well to announce it immediately, if
> only to take a position in opposition to Massis. . . . If you make
> the publicity effort you spoke to me about, I believe that it will be
> possible to pull off one of the literary coups of the year by the
> almost simultaneous publication of this volume and the one by
> Massis—to which the rightist critics are certainly going to give
> a great deal of attention.[36]

It was both to counterbalance the unanimous applause from the
conservative critics and to further expose his own opposing viewpoint that Malraux wrote the lengthy and highly illuminating review of Massis' *Defense of the West*, which was published in *La
Nouvelle Revue Française*.[37]

Massis had stated his anti-Asian position in the opening pages of
his book:

> Under the pretext of bringing to the soul of the West what it needs,
> it is to the definitive dispersion of the heritage of our culture, of
> all that still enables Western man to remain *on his feet*, that a
> certain Asiaticism enjoins us. Personality, unity, stability, authority,
> continuity, those are the root ideas of the West. They are to be
> dissolved in favor of a dubious asceticism in which the forces
> of the human personality are dissipated and return to nothingness.[38]

To be sure, Western civilization, the epitome of bourgeois conservatism as thus defined by Massis, had long been under attack.
Certain Europeans—like Renan and Gide—represented an indigenous form of the same nefarious "spirit of disintegration." However, in Massis' view, the newly aggressive, nationalistic countries
of Asia now represented a much greater danger because they
embodied both a revolutionary idea and a revolutionary *force*.

In his lucid review, Malraux argued that if such a danger from the East existed, the West itself was ultimately responsible for it. After all, the European colonialist powers had forcibly introduced their civilization with its aggressiveness, its self-centeredness, its materialism, and its nationalism into the essentially passive and nonmaterialist Asian cultures. He went on:

> That certain peoples of Asia have inherited nationalism from Europe along with the way of utilizing it is not very surprising, but the consequences of such a legacy are inescapable, and it is we who have determined them. The great European rashness is in the help that we have never ceased to give to the destruction of traditional authority that, in all the countries of Asia, was linked with culture. The substitution of values of persevering energy for spiritual values is the very mark of modern times. By destroying these spiritual values, we have prepared—in our own country and afar—the reign of force and particularly of the strongest kind, that which lasts.[39]

Of course, Massis did not share this view. In his opinion, the archvillains were not the Western capitalistic colonialists but rather the Soviet Communists. They were seeking, by means of the Third International, to organize and direct the forces of all Asia against the West. Malraux replied that this position was untenable. Not only was Russian Communism as an ideology in retreat everywhere in the Far East, but on a practical level, revolutionary leaders in Asia found themselves unable to form any really cohesive movement of revolt. From his personal observation, such a stubborn diversity seemed to be due to the influence of the West: "Our civilization brings its individualism along with its might; it organizes Asia, to be sure, but into factions opposing one another; this is very perceptible in the revolutionary circles of the Far East." [40]

Essentially, Massis feared that the young generations of Europe would learn a *new* concept of the human personality—and indeed of reality itself—from the "dangerous" Orient. In a certain sense, this fear was fully justified, wrote Malraux, because Asia helps Westerners

> lose certain notions (in particular that of the personality such as M. Massis presents it) which to us seem false, unacceptable, which run counter to all the movements of our thought; and the Orient helps us to free ourselves from a certain academicism of the spirit, just as the paintings gathered together in the Louvre by Napoleon

helped French painters—at a particular period—to free themselves from a plastic academicism." [41]

In short, he reiterated his belief that Asia could not only help modern Europe to better understand itself, but it could also give it a new freedom to *act* in the light of that understanding.

Both ultraconservatives like Massis and young liberals like Malraux agreed that a crisis indeed existed in the West. This was a fact that had to be faced. But how was the danger to be met? What was the answer to the personal and cultural "disintegration" that threatened them? According to Massis, salvation lay in a return to Roman Catholicism, to the shelter of the fixed, stable world of academic neo-Thomism. Malraux observed that such a comforting "architectural philosophy" had nothing whatever to offer those who did not already adhere to it by an act of faith. Moreover, since it was only an abstract intellectual system, it could not fill the inner emptiness of twentieth-century man, that "absence of soul" that afflicted the modern Western world "like a cancer." [42]

For Malraux, the answer to the Asian "danger" lay—in part, at least—in the hope that some day a sweeping force, some "collective appeal of the soul," would catch Western men up in its passion and restore meaning to their lives. That day was unfortunately far off; the majority of those holding power in the West were little concerned with seeking out the purpose of Man's existence, and "those who are seeking the meaning of destinies are precisely those who do not direct them." Malraux was reluctantly forced to conclude that

> the two needs that govern men are—for long years to come—those of the spirit and the passions: knowledge and money; the latter, with its train of dramas, the former, with its unique drama against which every proposition is vain: the persistent struggle between the absolute and the human, when the idea of the absolute has become powerless, and when the passion for Man has died without finding a new object of love.[43]

Although Western man had not yet found a passion to replace dead nineteenth-century egoism, there was at least a path he could set out upon: he could still seek to understand the world that was being born around him. The solution for the Asian problem was not to deny its existence, as many conservatives had done, but rather to seek to *possess* it, to experience it, to permit the "temptation" of its reality to become a fruitful "knowledge" for the future. As Malraux wrote in his critique of Massis's book:

> A new world, suddenly proposed to the men of an epoch by an aggregation of historical causes, is not resolved either by a choice or by an affirmation or by the label *dangerous*. It is resolved, so to speak, by the knowledge of its algebra. In the domain of the spirit, European thought always expressed itself through the creation of symbols, that is to say, of allegories, of coherent myths. Today it is struggling to construct a new one.[44]

To explain this new world to himself and his generation, to conquer it, to make his knowledge of Asia and the forces at work there into a "coherent myth" for all to see, was certainly a major reason young Malraux turned to the novel to state his "Asian" message.

Several additional considerations drew him to this literary form. First, he believed that the historical development of Western civilization had created a wide gulf between the world as we were forced to perceive it by our minds and the world as it actually was. As he put it in his essay "Concerning a European Youth," a major weakness of the West "comes from the necessity we have of gaining knowledge of the world by means of a Christian 'grille', we who are no longer Christian." [45] Most Westerners were encumbered with traditional concepts that no longer had any meaning for modern man nor accurately represented the reality of the twentieth-century world. In a novel, however, the writer could force the reader to accept—however reluctantly—a new framework of concepts, to see reality—however briefly—through a new "grille." Hopefully, such a participation, such a "temptation of the possible," would be transformed into knowledge.

Of course the essential terms of such a novel would have to be true, objectively speaking. As he notes in his Viollis preface, a characteristic of modern artists in all media was a certain "will to truth." [46] This impelled them to use the real world in their creations rather than to seek escape from reality in inventions of pure fantasy. If many contemporary novelists have—as he put it— "prowled around newspaper reports collected into volumes," it is because they sensed that a new vitality, a new validity, was to be found there. The power of such "real" novels, as had been the case with those of Tolstoi, lay "in the possession of the real by the intellect and the feelings, and not in the creation of an imaginary universe." [47] However, for such a novel to become something more than mere reporting, it must have a lens. It must be guided by a "will" or purpose; it must have a commitment. A narration of facts, however accurate and detailed, could never have the force of a deliberately created fictional universe in which the same facts had a meaningful life. In the case of Soviet authors like Ilya Ehrenburg, it was a belief in Marxism and in revolutionary action that "crystallized scattered elements and created the possibility of a work of art." [48] The West would have to seek some such belief of its own to perform this function.

A commitment on the part of the West was equally necessary from a psychological point of view. In his "European Youth" essay, Malraux suggested that an intellectual knowledge of the elements of reality was an essentially lifeless knowledge. For him, a thing could not be "known" until it had undergone a deep emotional participation on the part of the knower. In a passage reminiscent of Proust, he wrote: "Facts are linked to an intensity, to a particular possibility of moving us, which constitutes their reality." Without this intensity, this emotional participation, "they present themselves . . . to us only as names; they are dead." [49] This is also true on an interpersonal level, he notes. Just as we hear the voices of other people with our ears but listen to our own with our throats, so do we *know* other people in a rather dead intellectual way that is quite different from the passionate knowledge we have of ourselves.[50]

This gives literature—particularly the novel—very great power. The simple biographical facts of a man's existence may "evoke a man of whom we accept nothing." We are free to reject him precisely because the facts of his life are not an experience for us and their reality may therefore be denied. We hear his life with our ears, as it were. However, when this individual is made the hero of a novel, "we become aware of him as we would become aware of ourselves," [51] i.e., with our throats. During our reading, we must accept his reality and the terms in which that reality is formulated. Obviously, for Malraux the impact of a purely journalistic account of any given situation would always be limited because the reader could accept or reject it as he chose. Essentially, he would not be involved because he would not *know*. This is not at all the case when the same situation is presented in a novel. Then the reader becomes involved—at least while he is reading—whether he wishes to be or not. The novelist strikes him inside, so to speak, and he truly knows the facts presented because of his emotional participation in them.

Furthermore, in Malraux's opinion, the novel offered still another important advantage over factual reporting. In his Viollis introduction, he observes that "Balzac created the modern novel by giving each one of his principal characters an epic dimension, by giving Grandet, Birotteau, Popinot the intensity that would have been theirs if Destiny had harnessed some Bonaparte to their lowly profession." [52] Although the novel should be rooted in reality, the novelist could present his characters and situations in such a way that they were distillations of the real. As such, they could meaningfully participate in struggles—social and otherwise—which far transcended them. Their actions and attitudes would in a certain sense constitute a concrete presentation of a philosophical position.

Why, then, didn't Malraux write a *novel* to plead the Annamite cause, utilizing the materials of his experiences in Saigon? As he saw it, the problem in Indochina was acute, but it was only a specific manifestation of a much greater problem: the conflict between nineteenth-century Western bourgeois conservatism, exaggerated in colonialism, and the youthful movements that had arisen against it. To state the matter in the restricted terms of the Indochinese situation would weaken its presentation. It was more important to attack the basic human attitude that would permit the existence of such an oppressive regime than it was to make a detailed protest about specific abuses. It was necessary to find a broader canvas upon which to paint the conflict between bourgeois fascism and the forces opposing it in the Far East: Asian nationalism and world Communism.

Although the government overthrown in Russia had been essentially feudal, not bourgeois, the Marxist revolution in that country represented the first concerted and successful attack against nineteenth-century individualism.[53] In 1925 the movement had not yet seriously threatened any other European nation, but it was agitating fiercely against what Malraux considered to be the bourgeois society par excellence: China. He regarded the events convulsing China as a prelude to what would inevitably take place in

Europe. Consequently, a novel about the situation in China would be an ideal way to present the worldwide problem he had come to know specifically in Indochina.

The Conquerors first appeared in installments in the spring numbers of the 1928 NRF. Shortly afterward, the book was issued as one of the volumes in Grasset's *Cahiers Verts* series.[54] The story centers around the historical incidents connected with the great Canton–Hong Kong strike of August, 1925. Although Malraux was not present in Canton at the precise historical moment he describes, he had, as we have seen, visited the city a very short time afterward during his trip to Hong Kong. Moreover, his close connection with the Kuomintang party (through Young Annam) had assured him of a day-to-day, virtually firsthand account of what was happening on the Chinese mainland. This extensive knowledge of the facts of the situation was probably further augmented by his personal contacts and conversations during the January, 1926, Kuomintang Congress in Hong Kong.

On one level, *The Conquerors* was an attempt to present as accurately as possible the characters and incidents of a critical moment in modern Chinese history. Indeed, many conservative French readers saw the book as little more than an overt apologia for a specific incident of anti-Western rebellion. However, on the highest level, it seems clear that Malraux was using these historical facts to present the reality of the modern world as he saw it, a world in the throes of revolution, a world whose essence was change and metamorphosis, not tradition and stability. Halfway between these two levels lay his plea for Indochina. The story was couched in Chinese terms, but the problem presented was the very one he had faced in Indochina.

Malraux himself revealed the full dimensions of his book in a remarkable speech he made on June 8, 1929, just a year after its publication. The first novel of this rather controversial young man had been an event of considerable importance, both literary and political. However, much of the discussion it provoked among French intellectuals was not at all to the point, and when the Union for Truth organized a debate on it, the young author accepted its invitation to participate.[55]

Malraux began by briefly pointing out the special role of Creator that had been thrust upon the modern novelist: "Ever since Christianity disappeared as the armature of the world, the novelist—after the philosopher—has become a man who proposes,

whether he wishes to or not, a certain number of modes of existence." Thus the reactions—favorable and otherwise—provoked
by contemporary literary creations often have more to do with the
"mode of existence" they predicate than with their merits as works
of art. For example, many of those who attacked *The Conquerors*
on literary grounds were really reacting against the world it presented, a world from which the Christian God and the Christian
"armature" were absent. Their efforts to show that the novel was
historically inaccurate were motivated, perhaps unconsciously, by a
desire to invalidate everything it stood for. In any case, noted Malraux, such attacks on historical grounds were completely un-
founded. As a novelist he had taken great pains to see that his hero
always acted "with a psychological veracity . . . in close touch
with real historical events." Although Garine was of course a fictional character and in a sense moved in a fictitious world, no one
could cite a single historical fact that would make him *impossible*.
This accuracy was important because it guaranteed "his value as a
mythical creation."

The central historical fact of *The Conquerors* was the Canton
uprising, but Malraux did not want his book to be viewed as an
argument for revolution. In his eyes, it was rather an effort to de-
fine the character of a particular collective movement, typical of
the forces working for change everywhere in the twentieth-century
world. At its heart was an alliance of two groups or mentalities. On
the one hand were the authentic Bolsheviks, represented by Borodin. These were men who had a clear revolutionary ideal derived
from the precepts of Marxism and who acted as organized elements of the political party which this philosophy had produced.
On the other hand was a very differently motivated group of reformers, represented by Garine and others. Malraux had learned
from his experiences in Indochina that the fundamental element
common to both these groups—and their principal point of
alliance—was their anti-individualism. Both were vehemently opposed to that "cult of the self" that was the distinguishing feature
of nineteenth-century Europe and one of the timeless characteristics of the bourgeois mentality. For both these reformers, Bolshevism offered an entirely different "way of living," a new metaphysic. Both of them hoped to "destroy individuality in favor of
these collective values and . . . to create a collectivity conscious
of itself." Although Garine—as the hero of the book—sometimes appeared to be a rather strong individualist in the tra-

ditional sense of the term, Malraux points out in his discourse that in the final analysis his individuality is placed at the service of an anti-individualist cause: revolutionary Communism.

Garine and Borodin are allied against the bourgeoisie and the individualism it represents, but they see this enemy in rather different lights. For the Marxist, it is merely one phase in the historical development of the class struggle. Garine, on the other hand, envisages it more as an eternal human attitude, which Malraux defines succinctly: "Any man who puts values of consideration first is thinking as a bourgeois." Since China was, as he put it, "the only empire that was ever established on the values of the bourgeoisie . . . which had a bourgeois esthetic, a bourgeois metaphysic," the revolution on Chinese soil represented the essence of the struggle for reform that was going on, however feebly, everywhere in the world, including Indochina.

Turning to an examination of the leaders of such revolutionary movements, Malraux states his belief that there is usually some evidence of "a fundamental opposition between the revolutionary leader and society before the period of his revolutionary activity." However, it may require a specific historical event—a trial, in the case of Garine—before it blossoms forth and becomes a directed, concerted action. Obviously, such an observation is also most applicable to Malraux's own case, and he further illuminates both Garine and himself with the following remarkable statement:

> In my view, the revolutionary is born of a resistance. Though a man may become aware of certain injustices and of certain inequalities, though he may become aware of intense suffering, that will never suffice to make a revolutionary of him. In the face of suffering, he may become Christian, he may aspire to saintliness, discover charity; he will not become a revolutionary. For that, it is necessary that at the moment when he seeks to intervene on behalf of that suffering, *he encounters a resistance.*

If this resistance is viewed in the terms of the Marxist dialectic, one becomes a fighter in the class war against the obstructive bourgeoisie. If it is seen in a more human, personal light, one becomes a revolutionary fighter against injustice itself, and thus against the bourgeois mentality that commits it. To be a revolutionary leader against the bourgeois class does not necessarily imply that one is a devoted Communist, à la Borodin. On the contrary, notes Malraux, when the full records of much of the movement in Russia become known, "it will be seen that a large number of Bolshevik commissars . . . had no doctrinal orthodoxy." A revolutionary can simply be someone like Garine—and Malraux himself—who fights against social wrongs, not in the name of any political doctrine, but in the name of humanity itself.

The author of *The Conquerors* is the first to admit that Garine is somewhat of a contradiction, and that this revolutionary hero does not really have a systematic philosophy of revolution as such. Rather he is caught up in

> an intrinsically revolutionary movement. He knows that the brotherhood of arms that links him with the proletariat will force him to decide in a given way, when the tragic dilemma poses itself. The essential value that he sets against what I just referred to as values of consideration, which we could also call values of order or values of prudence, is a value of metamorphosis. The Revolution that arises permits him to incorporate into it his will, which is at the service of his brothers-at-arms. He doesn't know what the Revolution will be, but he knows where he will go when he has made such and such a decision. . . . He doesn't have to define the Revolution, but to carry it out.

For men like Garine—and Malarux—a fluid situation like the one in China was essential because it permitted them to *act*. Indochina, hopelessly paralyzed, was a frustration for even the strongest of wills.

Malraux closed the discussion by insisting on what he termed the essentially metaphysical character of his novel. For Garine, his hero, the over-all question of action for revolution remained secondary to his personal need for action to escape from what he felt to be the absurdity and helplessness of the human condition:

> The whole of *The Conquerors* is a constant protest, and I have elsewhere stressed this phrase: to escape from this idea of the absurd by fleeing into the human. Certainly, one may say that one could flee elsewhere. I make no claim at all to reply to this objection. I simply say that Garine is a man who—insofar as he fled from that absurdity which is the most tragic thing a man may find himself facing—has given a certain example.

All of Malraux's subsequent novels represent in varying degrees a similar effort to redeem Man from the absurdity of his condition and give him a meaning in the revolutionary world of the twentieth century. However, *The Royal Way*, his second work, is rather unusual because it is not played out in the context of an important historical event. Essentially it is the story of two men, isolated in the jungles of Cambodia, who are struggling to find some kind of value for their lives. Malraux evidently intended to broaden the range of the story, for at its conclusion he noted that it constituted "the first volume of *Powers of the Desert*, to which this tragic introduction is only the prologue." [56] Unfortunately this project was never completed.

In *Man's Fate*, the third and greatest of his novels, he returned to the broad subject he had initiated in *The Conquerors*: the anatomy of the worldwide, anti-bourgeois revolt. Again, the scene was China. Again, an effort was made to delineate the forces involved in the struggle between conservative hangovers from the nineteenth century and the revolutionaries of the twentieth. In this story, it is Chiang Kai-shek and Ferral who are the villains. These archbourgeois are enlargements of their Indochinese counterparts, Dr. Trinh and Cognacq-Pommeraye. Although this rich and complex book is meaningful on a number of levels, one of its fundamental purposes—as with *The Conquerors*—was again to denounce the evil and inhumanity of the bourgeois mentality and the authoritarian political system it fostered.

Unfortunately the disease was spreading. The early 1930's saw the emergence of totalitarian national states on the European continent itself. Accordingly, Malraux's next two novels were directed against this new menace so close at hand. The trumped-up charges leveled by Hitler's Nazi Party against the Communist Dimitrov (and his subsequent grotesque trial, so reminiscent of colonial legal proceedings) outraged Malraux. Not only did he vigorously agitate for Dimitrov in France, but in January, 1934, he actually went to Germany to plead with government officials on his behalf. After his return from this mission he wrote a passionate indictment of the Hitlerian state and the evils it was committing. *Days of Wrath* is set in Czechoslovakia but the atmosphere of stupidity, frustration, oppression, and terror is precisely the one he had come to know during the year he lived in Saigon under Cognacq's regime.

In 1936 General Francisco Franco landed from North Africa for the avowed purpose of destroying the Spanish Republic and imposing his authoritarian bourgeois government on the people of Spain by force. Malraux rushed to join the conflict. His novel, *Man's Hope*, presents the men and ideologies that suddenly found themselves allied in this struggle to preserve human liberty and dignity. It was an alliance similar to the one he had come to know more than a decade earlier in Indochina. His final novel, *The Walnut Trees of Altenburg*, would almost certainly have continued this theme by attacking German authoritarianism. Unfortunately, the Gestapo succeeded in destroying all but the first third of the manuscript, and the anti-fascist dimension of the work is only suggested in the part that remains. It would have been especially interesting to see how he would have dealt with Stalinist Marxism which—by 1940—had obviously become as totalitarian as fascism.

Looking back over Malraux's achievements, one can see that his experience in Indochina was crucial. In a sense, the author of *Man's Fate* and *Man's Hope* was *created* by the Pnom Penh trial and the subsequent injustices he witnessed in Cochinchina. Both in style and content, the moving editorials he wrote against the Cognacq regime bridge the chasm that separated *Paper Moons* from *The Conquerors*. We have seen how, under the impact of a series of personal experiences, the young archaeologist and art historian was abruptly transformed into a deeply committed anti-authoritarian agitator. His subsequent novels as well as his numerous speeches and political activities repeat one all-important message he brought back from Indochina: that the selfish, oppressive policies of the fascist state so violently deny the deepest needs of men everywhere that they must inevitably engender revolt. This revolt initially encompasses all colors of the political spectrum and is rather disorganized. However, the more brutally it is opposed and suppressed, the more aggressive it becomes, until finally its nationalist and liberal elements are swallowed up by the more disciplined Communists. Then a new tyranny comes to take the place of the old.

The writings of Malraux are, like his mind and his personality, incredibly complex. Many who read him fail to see the great-hearted humanitarian hidden behind the brilliant intellectual façade. For him, fascism was not just the stupid, selfish, and corrupt political system he saw in Annam. It was not just the triumph of the bourgeois as a class and a mentality over everything that was young, alive, and forward-looking. It was not only a negation of the modern world, of the needs and aspirations of modern men. Fascism was a denial of human liberty, both personal and intellectual, and as such, it debased the essentially elevated dignity of mankind. Although Man's human condition might condemn him to physical misery, suffering, and death, Malraux felt that it was intolerable for *governments* to further demean him by depriving him of the one element that could redeem his life—that was indeed the very source of his worth as a human being: his freedom.

Seen in this light, the life and works of André Malraux are a passionate continuation of the youthful struggle he began in Indochina to help the helpless regain a measure of their dignity. He could not do otherwise. He has always firmly believed that the highest purpose of all art is to try "to make men aware of the greatness that they ignore in themselves." [57] For nearly forty years, as an artist and a man, he has never swerved from this commitment.

Notes

NOTES TO CHAPTER I

[1] *The New York Times*, September 21, 1924, Sec. IX, p. 6.

[2] *Ibid.*, August 3, 1924, p. 18.

[3] Pascal Pia, "Dans 'Les Voix du silence,' Malraux affirme la victoire de l'artiste," *Carrefour*, March 26, 1952, p. 5.

[4] Probably the most comprehensive and revealing compilation of contemporary articles and comments on this subject is *Les Appels de l'Orient*, the title given to the double number (9/10, February–March, 1925) of the review *Les Cahiers du mois*. It was prepared by François and André Berge, and Maurice Betz (Paris, 1925).

[5] The founding decree, together with a number of other administrative texts, was published in the first issue of the *Bulletin de l'Ecole Française d'Extrême-Orient* (hereafter referred to as the *Bulletin*), I (January, 1901), 67. For details about the organization of the School, see pp. 67–79. (In references to the *Bulletin*, the number of the fascicule will not be given unless essential.)

[6] *Bulletin*, XIX (1919), 1–98. The citation is taken from p. 3.

[7] The details concerning Lieutenant Marek and his discovery of the temple are taken from *ibid.*, p. 66, n. 1, and from *Mémoires archéologiques publiés par l'Ecole Française d'Extrême-Orient*, I: *Le Temple d'Içvarapura (Bantây Srei, Cambodge)* (Paris, 1926), viii–ix. This minute examination of the temple was written by Henri Parmentier, Victor Goloubew, and Louis Finot. The site was not listed either in Etienne Aymonier's three-volume work, *Le Cambodge* (Paris, 1901–3), or in the detailed *Inventaire descriptif des monuments du Cambodge* of E. Lunet de Lajonquière (Paris, 1902–11). After its discovery, the School gave it a tentative listing of 546 bis. Claude Vannec, the hero of Malraux's novel *La Voie royale* (*The Royal Way*) (Paris, 1930), consults this *Inventaire* and even cites from it. See the Livre de Poche edition of the novel, pp. 31–32, 39. (Subsequent citations from *La Voie royale* refer to this edition.)

[8] Essentially self-taught, he was never officially enrolled in any of the various museum or art schools in Paris. This fact was brought out by the prosecution at his trial in Pnom Penh. See below, Chapter 2. See also André Vandegans,

"Malraux a-t-il frequenté les grandes écoles?," *Revue des langues vivantes,* XXVI (1960), 336–40. Pascal Pia affirms (*loc. cit.*) that Malraux has been fascinated with art "dès l'âge le plus tendre."

⁹ *Max Jacob—Correspondance,* II: *Saint-Benoît-sur-Loire, 1921–1924,* ed. François Garnier (Paris, 1955), 215, letter to Daniel-Henry Kahnweiler dated October 12, 1923.

¹⁰ Gaëtan Picon, *Malraux par lui-même* (Paris, 1961), p. 12, n. 3.

¹¹ This information was given in the articles that appeared in French papers at the time of his trial. See below, Chapter 2. Regarding Malraux's art-collecting activities in the early 1920's, consult André Vandegans, "Le Premier Malraux: Autour de la publication des *Lunes en papier [Paper Moons],*" *Publications de l'Université de l'État à Elisabethville,* V (April, 1963), 82.

¹² In interviews with the author during the summer of 1962, two of Malraux's close friends—Louis Chevasson and Georges Gabory—suggested that this might have been the case.

¹³ Claude Vannec is quite specific in discussing this rise in the market for Asian antiques (*Voie,* p. 33). There are frequent references to it in the pages of the *Bulletin,* notably in XX (fas. 4, 1920), 205, and XXIII (1923), 544.

¹⁴ *Bulletin,* XXIII (1923), 580–81.

¹⁵ André Rousseaux, "Un Quart d'heure avec M. André Malraux," *Candide,* November 13, 1930, p. 3.

¹⁶ On Damrong, see *Bulletin,* XXIII (1923), 546–48, 579, and the yearly indexes. He is mentioned in *Voie,* p. 29. Malraux himself revealed this aspect of his Indochina mission in an interview with the Saigon paper *L'Impartial,* published on the front page of the issue of September 16, 1924.

¹⁷ He evidently succeeded in contacting some Thai collectors before he returned to France in 1926, because he revealed that the illustrations for one of his 1927 Aux Aldes volumes, Paul Morand's *Siam,* were taken from original Siamese miniatures of the eighteenth century, "conservées à la Bibliothèque Vajinara de Bangkok et dans quelques collections particulières de la même ville." See the final page of the volume.

¹⁸ *Exposition D. Galanis: Catalogue précédé d'une préface par André Malraux. Du 3 au 18 mars, 1922. Galerie La Licorne* (Paris, 1922), p. 4. This preface was subsequently reprinted almost verbatim as the article for "Galanis," in Edouard-Joseph's *Dictionnaire biographique des artistes contemporains,* II (Paris, 1931). Malraux's original handwritten text, in the possession of the present writer, was entitled "La Peinture de Galanis."

¹⁹ *La Tentation de l'Occident (The Temptation of the West)* (Paris, 1926). We shall quote from the more easily accessible 1956 edition. The present citation is from p. 77.

²⁰ See the interview with him published in *L'Impartial,* September 16, 1924. (When no specific page is given for an article cited from an Indochinese newspaper, the item appeared on the front page.)

²¹ Malraux develops this idea in the conversation between Claude Vannec and Ramèges in his *Voie,* pp. 42–43.

²² Rousseaux, *op. cit.*

²³ *Tentation,* p. 44.

²⁴ *Voie,* p. 38.

²⁵ *Ibid.,* p. 40.

²⁶ This epigram, a South Indian proverb, is also used on the title page of

La Voie royale. The original edition of *Tentation* abounds in typographical errors, including one in this proverb where the word *singes* is substituted for *songes.* Malraux did not correct this misprint in the 1956 edition. The epigram does not appear in the recently published English-language edition, *The Temptation of the West,* translated and with a preface by Robert Hollander (New York, 1961).

[27] *Accords,* No. 3–4 (October–November, 1924), p. 55.

[28] Rousseaux, *op. cit.,* p. 3.

[29] Janet Flanner, *Men and Monuments* (New York, 1957), p. 9.

[30] Malraux himself cited this section of his official "brevet." See *Indochine,* July 17, 1925, VL. (The pages of this newspaper are not numbered, and the following system based on page headings will be used: page 2—DMESP; page 3—DME; page 6—VL; page 7—PE. For further information, see below, Chap. III, n. 49.) Claude Vannec notes that his authorization is of just this type. See *Voie,* p. 32.

[31] Rousseaux, *op. cit.*

[32] Clara Malraux gives a vivid description of certain aspects of life aboard ship and of the types of people who sailed to and from Asia in her *Portrait de Grisélidis* (Paris, 1945), pp. 139–202. Léon Werth adds a number of pertinent facts in his *Cochinchine* (Paris, 1926), which first appeared as a series of articles in the review *Europe* (issues 33, 34, and 35, dated September 15, October 15, and November 15, 1925) under the title "Notes d'Indochine." See particularly issue 33, pp. 5–10. The two most extensive and vivid descriptions are to be found in Andrée Viollis' book—for which Malraux wrote the preface—*Indochine S.O.S.* (Paris, 1935), pp. 1–8, and Luc Durtain's *Dieux blancs, hommes jaunes* (Paris, 1930), pp. 8–44 and 95–108.

[33] *Tentation,* pp. 36, 46, 65.

[34] See Viollis' comments, *op. cit.,* pp. 3 ff.

[35] These citations are taken from *Tentation,* pp. 15, 59, 16, and 22, respectively. This same atmosphere is evoked in certain parts of Malraux's exotic fantasy *Royaume farfelu* (*The Fabulous Realm*) (Paris, 1928) and in the opening scenes of *La Voie royale.*

[36] Viollis, *op. cit.,* p. 4.

[37] *Tentation,* pp. 19–20; *Voie,* pp. 7–10.

[38] Descriptions of these types are to be found in the books by Viollis and and Werth cited above, but the most detailed portraits are presented in Durtain, *op. cit.,* pp. 169–216, and in Roland Dorgelès, *Sur La Route mandarine* (Paris, 1925), especially pp. 78–94, and 180–211.

[39] Probably the best succinct history of the area is Joseph Buttinger, *The Smaller Dragon: A Political History of Vietnam* (New York, 1958). A chronology of events during 1900–30 is given on pages 423–36, and there is a very comprehensive bibliography on pp. 470–520. Georges Maspéro, *Un Empire colonial français, l'Indochine* (2 vols.; Paris-Brussels, 1929–30) is a traditional general survey. The more modern period is discussed in Philippe Devillers, *Histoire du Viêt-Nam de 1940 à 1952* (3rd ed.; Paris, 1952). The books by Dorgelès, Durtain, Werth, and Viollis cited above contain a great deal of information about the economic and agricultural life of the area, as well as descriptions of its physical appearance.

[40] See *Le Temple d'Içvarapura,* p. vii. According to the 1923 *Bulletin* (XXIII, 503–4), Finot left Saigon on November 11. Concerning Aurousseau,

see the *Bulletin*, XX (1920), 238, and XXIV (1924), 308–9. A similar meeting took place between Vannec and Ramèges in Malraux's novel *La Voie royale*, pp. 41–47.

⁴¹ A preliminary decree to protect monuments in Cambodia had been issued by the King on October 18, 1923 (*Bulletin*, XXIV [1924], 649–50). However, an edict for all Indochina was not promulgated until December 23, 1924. It was published, together with a number of other pertinent documents, in the *Bulletin*, XXVI (1926), 525–688. Also included there is the letter in which Edouard Daladier, the Minister for Colonies, had asked the Chamber to enact new legislation because the previous code *"ne répond pas d'une manière satisfaisante au but recherché et . . . est, au demeurant, entaché d'une illégalité flagrante"* (p. 526). Malraux's trial had revealed the illegality to which Daladier referred. See below, Chapter 2

⁴² *L'Impartial*, October 9, 1924.

⁴³ *Ibid.*, September 16, 1924.

⁴⁴ *Voie*, p. 47.

⁴⁵ *L'Echo du Cambodge*, January 5, 1924.

⁴⁶ Parmentier was in charge of this work. See *L'Impartial*, February 16, 1924, and *L'Echo du Cambodge*, July 12, 1924, p. 2.

⁴⁷ The fundamental work on the Khmers is Lawrence Palmer Briggs' detailed study, *The Ancient Khmer Empire* (Philadelphia, 1951), which includes an exhaustive bibliography of books and articles.

⁴⁸ The best guidebook to the archaeological sites of the Angkor area is Maurice Glaize, *Les Monuments du groupe d'Angkor* (2d ed., Saigon, 1948). It includes a long introductory section giving the historical and cultural background of the civilization that built the great temples, photographs of the sites, and instructions on how to visit them.

⁴⁹ This minor monument is listed in the *Bulletin*, XXVI (1926), 628, as No. 467 of the official archaeological inventory. It is described as a "temple en grès à deux enceintes."

⁵⁰ *L'Echo du Cambodge*, July 19, 1924.

⁵¹ *Voie*, pp. 65–70. See also Rousseaux, *op. cit.*

⁵² Glaize, *op. cit.*, p. 235.

⁵³ *Voie*, pp. 76–85. This was confirmed by testimony at the trial. See Chapter II below.

⁵⁴ Glaize, *op. cit.*, p. 236.

⁵⁵ *L'Echo du Cambodge*, January 5, 1924.

⁵⁶ *L'Impartial*, July 21, 1924.

NOTES TO CHAPTER II

¹ *L'Echo du Cambodge*, January 5, 1924.

² This inflammatory article was printed again virtually in its entirety by *L'Impartial* at the time of Malraux's appeal hearing in Saigon the following July.

³ *L'Impartial*, July 21, 1924.

⁴ *Indochine Enchaînée*, No. 11, p. 1.

⁵ *Le Temple d'Içvarapura* (see above, chapter I, n. 7), p. ix.

⁶ *Bulletin*, XXIV (1924), 307–8. Cf. also *Temple, loc. cit.*

[7] See the article entitled "L'Homme à la Rose," *Le Matin* (Paris), August 3, 1924.

[8] *L'Impartial*, October 11, 1924.

[9] *Indochine*, June 29 and July 8, 1925.

[10] René-Louis Doyon, *Mémoire d'homme* (Paris, 1953), pp. 76–77, and *L'Impartial*, October 10, 1924, p. 2

[11] Marcel Arland, in *Accords*, No. 3–4 (October–November, 1924), p. 55.

[12] Doyon, *op. cit.*, pp. 78–79.

[13] See Langlois, "The Debut of André Malraux, Editor (Kra, 1920–22)," *PMLA*, LXXX, No. 1 (March, 1965), 111–22.

[14] This information is taken primarily from articles that appeared in the Paris newspapers *Le Matin*, *Le Journal*, and *L'Eclair* on August 3, 1924. See also the closing pages of the first volume (*Apprendre à vivre*) of Clara Malraux's autobiography *Le Bruit de nos pas* (Paris, 1963); Florent Fels, *Voilà* (Paris, 1957); Daniel-Henry Kahnweiler, *Entretiens avec Francis Crémieux: Mes galeries et mes peintres* (Paris, 1961).

[15] See Albert Skira, *Vingt Ans d'activité* (Paris, 1948), p. 20, where Kahnweiler recalls his association with Malraux. On *Lunes en papier*, consult Jean Hugues, *50 Ans d'édition de D.-H. Kahnweiler* (Paris, 1959), p. 7, and André Vandegans' recent and noteworthy study, *La Jeunesse littéraire d'André Malraux* (Paris, 1964), pp. 95–140.

[16] Langlois, *op cit.*, gives details on this little-known work of Malraux, as does Vandegans, *La Jeunesse littéraire d'André Malraux*, pp. 143–211.

[17] *Mercure de France*, CXXXIX (April 15, 1920), 819.

[18] Several articles in Paris newspapers at the time of Malraux's trial link him with Gabory. See below, p. 38. In an article entitled "Jeux" (*Action*, No. 6 [December, 1920], pp. 37–45), Gabory refers to "*mon ami André M. que j'ai nommé exécuteur de mes hautes oeuvres littéraires*" and notes that he sometimes passed the day "*dans les grands bars avec André M. [où] on boit la vie avec des pailles.*" Regarding the seizure of the magazine, see Florent Fels, *Voilà*, p. 77. Gabory has confirmed Fels's account.

[19] *Action*, No. 1 (February, 1920). Most of these advertisements were grouped together on a few pages at the end of the magazine.

[20] Following are Malraux's writings published before he went to Indochina in late 1923:

"Des Origines de la poésie cubiste," *La Connaissance*, I, No. 1 (January, 1920), 38–43.

"Trois Livres de Laurent Tailhade," *La Connaissance*, I, No. 2 (February, 1920), 196–97 (book review).

"La Genèse des *Chants de Maldoror*," *Action*, No. 3 (April, 1920), pp. 33–35. Reprinted in a special issue of the Franco-Belgian review *Le Disque vert* devoted to "Le Cas Lautréamont" (1925), pp. 119–23.

"Mobilités," *Action*, No. 4 (July, 1920), pp. 13–14.

"Prologue," *Action*, No. 5 (October, 1920), pp. 18–20.

"Les Champs magnétiques (Breton-Soupault); La Négresse du Sacré Coeur (Salmon)," *Action*, No. 5 (October, 1920), pp. 69–70 (book reviews).

Lunes en papier (Paris, 1921). The "*achevé*" is dated April 12.

"Les Hérissons apprivoisés: Journal d'un pompier du jeu de massacre," *Signaux de France et de Belgique*, No. 4 (August, 1921), pp. 171–77.

"Journal d'un pompier du jeu de massacre," *Action*, No. 8 (August, 1921), pp. 16–18.

"L'Entrepreneur d'illuminations," *Action*, No. 9 (October, 1921), p. 33 (book review).

Exposition D. Galanis . . . (see above, Chapter I, n. 18).

"Aspects d'André Gide," *Action*, unnumbered (March–April, 1922), pp. 17–21. A note at the end indicates that another part was to follow. It never appeared, because the review ceased publication.

"L'Abbaye de Typhaines (le Comte de Gobineau)," N.R.F. (July, 1922), pp. 97–98 (book review).

"L'Art poétique (Max Jacob)," N.R.F. (August, 1922), pp. 227–28 (book review).

"Ménalque," *Le Disque vert*, Nos. 4, 5, 6, II series (February, March, April, 1923), pp. 19–21 (on Gide).

"Malice (Pierre MacOrlan)," N.R.F. (May, 1923), pp. 836–37 (book review).

Preface to Charles Maurras, *Mademoiselle Monk* (Paris, 1923).

W. M. Frohock notes (in *André Malraux and the Tragic Imagination* [Stanford, 1952], p. 6) that Malraux is supposed to have contributed to several other reviews, including *Université de Paris*, *Dés*, and *Aventure*, during this period. This does not seem to be entirely correct. I have gone through the issues of *Université* from June, 1920, to December, 1925, and found Malraux's name nowhere. *Aventure*, organized by Marcel Arland late in 1921 with two wartime friends, Roger Vitrac and René Crevel, was, according to Arland, a *"revue d'avant-garde . . . qui flirta plus ou moins consciemment avec les dadaïstes"* (*Les Nouvelles Littéraires*, April 3, 1926, pp. 1–2). It appeared for only three issues—November, 1921; December, 1921; and January, 1922. Shortly afterward, Arland founded another review, *Dés*, which lasted for only two issues (*Les Nouvelles Littéraires*, loc. cit.); in the table of contents of the first, dated April, 1922, and given in *Mercure de France*, CLVI (June 1, 1922), 488, Malraux is not mentioned. It is possible, however, that an excerpt of *Ecrit pour une idole à trompe* appeared in the second issue. Arland apparently had a copy of the work because later he published a portion of it in his review *Accords* (October–November, 1924).

[21] The above facts and considerable additional information about the legal aspects of the case and the people involved in it were generously furnished me by a retired member of the colonial bar, a native of Pnom Penh, M. Raymond Roche. In answer to my queries, he prepared a lengthy report—subsequently confirmed by one of his colleagues—that was most useful in helping me to understand the *"dessous des cartes,"* as he put it. I am very grateful to him for his help.

[22] Perhaps the two most forceful indictments of legal practices in the French colonies are to be found in Andrée Viollis, *Indochine S.O.S.* (Paris, 1935), and Georges Garros, *Forceries humaines: L'Indochine litigieuse* (Paris, 1926). Garros had practiced law in Saigon for thirty-five years and was the father of the war hero Roland Garros (*op. cit.*, p. 186). See also chapters 5 and 8 of Ho Chi Minh's early book written under the name Nguyen Aï Quoc, *Le Procès de la colonisation française* (Paris, 1926); it has been translated into English in *Ho Chi Minh: Selected Works*, II (Hanoi, 1961), 15–144.

[23] *Indochine Enchaînée*, No. 12, p. 7.

[24] *L'Echo du Cambodge,* July 19, 1924.
[25] Most of this information on Jodin was furnished the author by M. Roche.
[26] *L'Impartial,* July 22, 1924.
[27] Chevasson emphatically confirmed this in an interview with the author, August, 1962.
[28] *L'Impartial, loc. cit.*
[29] Malraux revealed this incident in a letter he wrote to *L'Impartial,* published on the front page on September 16, 1924.
[30] *L'Echo du Cambodge, loc. cit.*
[31] *L'Impartial,* July 21, 1924. A few additional details may be found in *L'Echo du Cambodge,* July 19. The July 22 *Impartial* reported the interesting information that Crémazy had recently been made *"chef du 2e bureau à la Résidence Supérieure,"* the office in charge of internal security for the colony. The promotion was probably a reward for his "services"—including perjury—in connection with the Malraux affair. For more details on how the colonial administration used police harassment against liberals in the colony, see Léon Werth's "Notes d'Indochine," *Europe,* No. 35 (November 15, 1925), pp. 262–66.
[32] *Indochine,* June 29, 1925. He later mentioned this in a number of articles rebutting Chavigny's attacks.
[33] *L'Impartial,* July 21 and 22, 1924.
[34] *L'Echo du Cambodge,* July 19, 1924.
[35] *Indochine Enchaînée,* No. 11, p. 1.
[36] *Loc. cit.*
[37] *Ibid.,* No. 13, p. 6.
[38] *L'Echo du Cambodge,* July 26, 1924, and *L'Impartial,* October 10, 1924. According to Roche, Jodin's harsh verdict shocked a number of his professional colleagues. Evidently, however, it pleased the Administration, because shortly afterward Jodin was appointed to a higher court.
[39] *L'Echo du Cambodge,* September 20, 1924, states that the original date was September 22, but *L'Impartial* for that day indicates September 23.
[40] "Dans les Fouilles," *Comoedia,* July 17, 1925, p. 2.
[41] "Le Poète aux statuettes," *Comoedia,* August 3, 1924, p. 3.
[42] Subsequently reprinted almost verbatim as "Le Pèlerin d'Angkor," *L'Intransigeant,* August 5, 1924, p. 2.
[43] See his angry letter to Chavigny, published in *L'Impartial,* September 17, 1924.
[44] Doyon included the letter in *Mémoire,* pp. 82–84.
[45] Doyon, *op. cit.,* pp. 85–86.
[46] Doyon cited this letter, which Mme. Malraux showed him, *op. cit,* p. 86.
[47] "L'Affaire André Malraux," *L'Eclair,* August 15, 1924, p. 2.
[48] Malraux reprinted the document on the back page of the July 11, 1925, issue of *Indochine.* The body of the text there differed slightly from the version that appeared in *Les Nouvelles Littéraires.*
[49] Only the *Indochine* version contains Anatole France's comment. It was Malraux who revealed that forty-eight literary figures eventually signed the petition.
[50] Doyon gave some information (*op. cit.,* pp. 84–85), but Janet Flanner offered the most detailed recital of the tales that were making the rounds in Parisian literary circles at the time (*Men and Monuments* [New York, 1957],

pp. 8–11). She obviously got many of her facts from conversations with knowledgeable people; much of what she recounts does not appear in any other printed source I have seen.

[51] Flanner, *op. cit.*, p. 9.

[52] Alain Laubreau, "André Malraux et le prix Goncourt," *Dépêche de Toulouse*, December 12, 1933, p. 4.

[53] Flanner, *op. cit.*, pp. 9–10.

[54] "Courrier des lettres: Pour André Malraux," *L'Eclair*, August 25, 1924, p. 2. This was apparently one of the documents read during his appeal hearing. See below, p. 50.

[55] *Accords*, No. 3–4 (October–November, 1924), p. 55.

[56] From his letter to Chavigny, published in *L'Impartial*, September 17, 1924.

[57] On Chavigny, see chap. iv, pp. 83 ff.

[58] Chavigny revealed this in his comments on Malraux's letter in *L'Impartial*, September 18, 1924. He published the photograph of Malraux, a very unflattering one, on the front page of his newspaper on September 22, together with pictures of the sculpture taken from Banteay Srei. He also used the picture several times during his subsequent verbal exchanges with Malraux during the summer of 1925.

[59] *Indochine*, August 6, 1925, DME.

[60] See *L'Impartial*, September 26, 1925. Vandegans utilizes some of the texts indicated above in *La Jeunesse littéraire d'André Malraux*, pp. 215–39.

[61] Malraux indicated in 1930 that he was prepared to pursue the matter indefinitely, in order to recover the sculptures. He erroneously believed they were still in the Pnom Penh museum. See André Rousseaux, "Un Quart d'heure avec M. André Malraux," *Candide*, November 13, 1930.

NOTES TO CHAPTER III

[1] *L'Impartial*, November 3, 1924.

[2] *Ibid.*, May 10, 1924.

[3] *Ibid.*, October 17, 1924, and September 26, 1925.

[4] *Indochine*, July 18, 1925, back page.

[5] René-Louis Doyon, *Mémoire d'homme* (Paris, 1953), p. 87.

[6] It was evidently in the offices of Grasset that he also saw François Mauriac. See Mauriac's *Journal: 1932–1939* (Paris, 1947), pp. 206, 210.

[7] Daniel Halévy, in a preface to the final volume of the first *Cahiers verts* series, *Ecrits* (Paris, 1927), pp. vii–viii. Malraux's essay "D'Une Jeunesse européenne" was published in this volume. For further information on Halévy, see Frédéric Lefèvre, *Une Heure avec . . .* , Series I (Paris, 1924), pp. 161–67.

[8] See his letter in *L'Impartial*, September 16, 1924. A contract must have been signed at this time, because on October 4, 1925, Malraux wrote Grasset that the promised book was finally ready: "*Ce n'est pas sans retard que je vous apporterai le manuscrit d'un livre auquel vous avez bien voulu vous intéresser. . . . Le titre définitif de l'ouvrage étant 'La Tentation de l'Occident,' il y aurait peut-être avantage à l'annoncer dès maintenant.*" (This letter, written on stationery of the Continental Palace Hotel, Saigon, and addressed to one of the Grasset editors, is at present in the author's possession.) The

money Malraux received as an advance on royalties was probably used to pay his share of the expenses connected with the Monin newspaper project.

⁹ Max Jacob, *Lettres aux Salacrou: août, 1923–janvier, 1926* (Paris, 1957), p. 84, letter of January 5, 1925.

¹⁰ Jacob, *op. cit.*, p. 87, letter of January 7, 1925.

¹¹ The text of the agreement was printed by Malraux on the back page of the July 18, 1925, issue of *Indochine.* On July 22, a photograph of the document was published in the same newspaper.

¹² See *Indochine*, July 18 and July 22. The supplements were eventually issued in both French and Annamite, but they are not present in the Bibliothèque Nationale collection.

¹³ The exact date of their departure is not known, but in a letter of January 7, Jacob notes that "the Malrauxs were here the day before yesterday. They're on their way back to Cambodia" (*op. cit.*, p. 87).

¹⁴ *L'Impartial*, July 20, 1925.

¹⁵ *Indochine*, June 22 and 24, 1925.

¹⁶ The title of his speech was "L'Idéal de la jeunesse annamite." Extracts from it were reprinted in *La Cloche Fêlée*, which Léon Werth cited in the first installment of "Notes d'Indochine," *Europe*, No. 33 (September 15, 1925), pp. 22–23. It was Monin who had brought Werth to see Ninh, and Werth describes the interview in some detail (pp. 23–24). Chavigny names the various liberal Annamite reformers and attacks their program in *L'Impartial*, May 8, 1924. The spelling of Vietnamese and Chinese names here—and subsequently—follows that used by the editors of *Indochine*.

¹⁷ "La France et l'Indochine," *Europe*, No. 31 (July 15, 1925), pp. 257–77.

¹⁸ *Ibid.*, pp. 276–77.

¹⁹ Letter of October 4, 1925, in the author's possession.

²⁰ Letter to Edmund Wilson of October 2, 1933, in Edmund Wilson, *The Shores of Light* (New York, 1952), pp. 573–74.

²¹ Nguyen-Pho contributed a number of political articles to *Indochine* and *Indochine Enchaînée*, finally became a *rédacteur* of the latter when Malraux returned to France. He signed—"*au nom d'un groupe Jeune Annam*"—an indignant letter protesting the treatment of an Annamite patriot. He also joined Monin as a speaker at the public meeting against the arrest of Truong-cao-Dong. See *Indochine Enchaînée*, No. 16, p. 6; No. 20, p. 4; and No. 22, p. 4.

²² This pamphlet was discussed in *L'Impartial*, July 9, 1925, in connection with an article from another conservative Saigon paper, *L'Opinion.*

²³ *Indochine*, June 18 (the second issue), DME. All subsequent references to this paper are to 1925 issues.

²⁴ See the third installment of Werth, *op. cit.*, *Europe*, No. 35 (November 15, 1925), p. 265. Dejean's background and character are reflected in the signed articles he wrote for *Indochine* and for the Annamite paper *L'Echo Annamite*, which he later edited.

²⁵ *Indochine*, June 29, DMESP.

²⁶ *Ibid.*, June 23, VL. The figure of Sainte-Lise in Clara Malraux's novel *Portrait de Grisélidis* is probably to a certain extent patterned after Dejean.

²⁷ *Ibid.*, June 23, VL.

²⁸ He was not only manager (*gérant*) but reporter and columnist as well.

He urged many of the Annamite intellectuals among his friends to contribute to *Indochine*. When the paper reappeared as *Indochine Enchâinée*, he continued as manager until the eighth number. Then he went to *La Cloche Fêlée*, and Malraux took over his function. He was a close personal friend of Monin's and appeared at his side at a number of political rallies and demonstrations, notably the protest meeting organized after the arrest of the Annamite patriot Truong-cao-Dong. (For details on this meeting, led by Monin and several liberal Annamites, see *Indochine Enchâinée*, No. 20, pp. 5–7.) Dejean was also one of those who arranged the moving farewell party in honor of Monin and his family when they returned to France early in 1926.

[29] *Indochine*, June 23, VL. See also the "Local Events" page of the third issue, June 19.

[30] The physical description that Malraux gives of Garine in *Les Conquérants* (*The Conquerors*) fits Monin perfectly. Of course, there is considerable information on the man in *Indochine*, but Chavigny also reveals many facts about him in his attacks published in *L'Impartial*. See in particular the following issues: July 28, August 10, October 8, November 19 and 21, 1923; April 28 through 30, May 3 through 13, October 2 and 17, 1924; April 9, 22, 25, and almost daily between July 6 and August 25, 1925.

[31] See *L'Impartial*, July 8, 1922; October 8 and November 19, 1923; and April 22, 1924.

[32] See *ibid.*, July 6 and November 26, 1923; and April 28, 1924.

[33] *Ibid.*, May 5, 6, and 8, 1924.

[34] *Ibid.*, May 8, 1924. A full and factual account of the loan from the Chinese bank is given in *Indochine Enchâinée* at the time of Monin's final acquittal of any blame in the matter. See the article "De la Faillite politique en Cochinchine," in the issues numbered 9 (pp. 3–4) and 10 (pp. 5–6). The value of the piaster varied during this period. For purposes of comparison, I have figured it at the rate established in 1928, i.e. 10 francs, or about $2.00.

[35] Werth dedicated *Cochinchine* (or "Notes d'Indochine," as it was called when published in the review *Europe*) to his friend Monin; Malraux and Monin published excerpts serially in *Indochine Enchâinée*, Nos. 2 (pp. 8–9); No. 3 (pp. 3–4); No. 4 (pp. 3–4); No. 5 (pp. 9–10); and No. 6 (p. 3).

[36] *L'Impartial*, May 8, 1924.

[37] *Ibid.*, May 12, 1924.

[38] *Ibid.*, May 13 and May 24, 1924.

[39] See articles on this incident *ibid.*, June 20–24, 1924.

[40] A complete listing of the periodicals published in Indochina during this period may be found in Paul Boudet and Remy Bourgeois, *Bibliographie de l'Indochine française, 1913–1926* (Hanoi, 1929), pp. 190–94.

[41] See *Indochine*, July 20, VL, and July 22, DMESP.

[42] *L'Impartial*, July 8 and 20, 1925.

[43] *Ibid.*, July 24, 1925.

[44] *Ibid.*, April 22, 1925. *Indochine* published the letter of reply that Monin received from the League on the front page of its July 9 issue.

[45] *L'Impartial*, July 17, 1925.

[46] *Ibid.*, July 30, 1925.

[47] *Indochine*, July 10.

[48] *L'Impartial*, July 20, 1925; *Indochine*, June 18.

⁴⁹ The first three issues are not dated but simply numbered 1, 2, and 3, with the indication that each is a *"numéro gratuit."* They appeared on Wednesday, Thursday, and Friday. The first dated issue, Number 4, appeared on Saturday, June 20, 1925. With the exception of the first two issues—which have six pages—the paper was always eight pages long. Unfortunately, the pages are not numbered. For purposes of reference, the following system of abbreviations has been adopted, based on the heading that is found at the top of each of the pages:

> Page 2: DMESP (*Du Monde Entier—Service Particulier*).
> Page 3: DME (*Du Monde Entier*).
> Page 6: VL (*Vie Locale*).
> Page 7: PE (*Page de l'Elite*).

The back page is specifically indicated where necessary. If only the date of the issue is given, without any specific page reference, the front page is meant. This system seemed most practical, especially since the pages in the unbound Bibliothèque Nationale collection are sometimes microfilmed out of order.

⁵⁰ Under the rubric "Notre Roman sportif" was published "La Tour de la Souffrance," a "roman inédit en quinze étapes d'André Reuze," while the episodes of Pierre MacOrlan's "Les Pirates de l'avenue Rhum," were listed as "Fantaisie." Late in July began appearing Claude Farrère's adventure novel *Cent Millions d'or.* A new translation of Robert Louis Stevenson's *Le Cas étrange du Dr. Jekyll et de Mr. Hyde* was run to help arouse interest in the motion picture, which *Indochine's* editors planned to show gratis to subscribers.

⁵¹ Lefèvre's interviews were issued in a series of volumes entitled *Une Heure avec . . . .* The interview with Lévi is in the third series (Paris, 1925), pp. 105–16

⁵² *Indochine*, Nos. 9–16, June 26 through July 4. The citations here are taken from the June 26 and 30 numbers. See Lefèvre, *op. cit.*, pp. 149–67, for the same texts.

⁵³ See *Indochine*, issues dated July 15, 16, and 17; July 20 and 27; July 21; and July 24.

⁵⁴ *Ibid.*, June 25, DMESP. See below, chap. vi, for a more detailed discussion of the problem of the Emperor of Annam.

⁵⁵ *Ibid.*, issues dated June 26, July 2, July 18, August 3, July 7, and July 16.

⁵⁶ See *ibid.*, issues of June 30, July 21, July 9 and 11, July 23, and July 29.

⁵⁷ Following are Malraux's editorials in *Indochine*:

"Première Lettre de Jacques Tournebroche à Jérôme Coignard," No. 2, June 18.

"A Monsieur Je-Menotte," No. 8, June 25.

"Sur Quelles Réalités appuyer un effort annamite," No. 16, July 4.

"Première Lettre à Monsieur Henry Chavigny d'En-Avant pour-l'Arrière," No. 19, July 8.

"Sur le Rôle de l'Administration," No. 24, July 16.

"Seconde Lettre à M. Henry Chavigny d'En-Avant pour-l'Arrière," No. 26, July 18 (back page).

"Troisième Lettre à M. Henry Chavigny d'En-Avant pour-l'Arrière, professeur de délicatesse," No. 29, July 22.

"Liberté de la presse," No. 31, July 24.

"Camau—Les Trente Plaintes," No. 32, July 25.

"Camau—Lettre de Jérôme Coignard à Monsieur Maurice Cognacq, Lieutenant-Gouverneur," No. 35, July 29.

"Lettre ouverte à Monsieur Colonna, procureur général," No. 39, August 3.

"Au très pur, très noble, très loyal gentilhomme, Henry Chavigny d'En-Avant pour-l'Arrière, ancien indicateur de la Sûreté," No. 46, August 11.

"Sélection d'énergies," No. 49, August 14.

In addition to these signed editorials, internal evidence indicates that Malraux was responsible for three other long pieces: "Lettre ouverte à M. de la Pommeraye," No. 4, June 20; "Seconde Lettre à M. de la Pommeraye," No. 6, June 23; and "L'Expédition d'Isphahan," No. 42, August 6 (back page). This latter highly imaginary piece is signed with the improbable name Maurice Sainte-Rose, but the author was evidently Malraux because several passages subsequently appear, virtually verbatim, in *Royaume farfelu*. In addition, there are shorter items from his pen scattered through about two-thirds of the issues of the newspaper, usually either on the front page or in the "Revue de la presse locale" column of the "Local Events" page. As will become evident in the following chapter, they are particularly revealing of his gift for biting sarcasm. Vandegans refers to a few of Malraux's contributions to *Indochine* in his *La Jeunesse littéraire d'André Malraux*, but he does not examine them in detail nor does he deal with those that appeared in *Indochine Enchaînée*. See below, chap. viii.

NOTES TO CHAPTER IV

[1] Reprinted in *Indochine*, June 19, VL.

[2] Reprinted in *ibid.*, June 18, DME.

[3] Reprinted in *ibid.*, June 23, VL.

[4] *Ibid.*, June 19, VL. For the *Courrier's* position during the trial, see the issues of September 25 and 27, and Malraux's letter on October 6, 1924.

[5] *Ibid.*, June 19, and June 23, VL. Malraux's italics.

[6] *Ibid.*, June 20.

[7] The two citations relating to de la Pommeraye are from *Indochine Enchaînée*, No. 5, p. 3. Regarding the film, see *Indochine*, June 20. The Calendrier scandal is mentioned in *ibid.*, June 20, VL, and July 9. See also Virginia Thompson, *French Indo-China* (New York, 1937), p. 314.

[8] De la Pommeraye's article was cited by Malraux in his June 23 reply, from which the following quotations are also taken.

[9] Malraux and Monin reprinted excerpts from the chapters of *Vie orageuse* that had appeared in *Progrès Annamite*. See *Indochine*, June 18, VL, and June 25, VL. There are numerous passing references to Trinh in *Indochine*, but see particularly July 9, and *Indochine Enchaînée*, No. 6, p. 2.

[10] *Indochine*, July 10, DMESP. See also Léon Werth, "Notes d'Indochine" *Europe*, No. 34 (October 15, 1925), pp. 169 ff., for further information on how the French Colonial Administration made effective use of these subservient Annamites.

[11] On Gandhi and his influence in Annam, see below, chap. vii, and the lengthy article, "Gandhi et les intellectuels annamites," by Pham-Quynh on the "Local Events" page of *Indochine*, July 15, 16, and 17, reprinted from the Tonkin paper *France-Indochine*.

[12] *Indochine*, June 29, VL.
[13] Cited in *ibid.*, July 6.
[14] Cited in *loc. cit.* For further details, see the issues of July 7, 9, and 15.
[15] *Ibid.*, July 20, DMESP. Monin was particularly incensed at this betrayal because, as he saw it, this political group was the only organized opposition to Cognacq in the colony.
[16] See the rebuttals in *ibid.*, July 9 ("Petite Ephéméride") and 10, DME.
[17] *Ibid.*, July 10, DME.
[18] *Ibid.*, July 11, VL.
[19] *Loc. cit.*
[20] *Ibid.*, July 15, VL, and July 17.
[21] See Malraux's comments in *ibid.*, July 20, VL.
[22] *Ibid.*, July 15, VL.
[23] *Ibid.*, July 20, VL.
[24] *Ibid.*, July 15, VL.
[25] *Ibid.*, July 20, VL.
[26] *L'Impartial*, June 23. Malraux's assertion had appeared on the first page of the June 22 issue of *Indochine*.
[27] *L'Impartial*, July 6, 1925.
[28] There are almost constant references to Chavigny in the Malraux-Monin paper from this time on. However, most of the "hard" facts about him are to be found in the numerous documents cited by Malraux in his four open letters to "Henry Forward-to-the-Rear." See also Thompson, *op. cit.*, pp. 310–11.
[29] *Indochine Enchaînée*, No. 1, p. 7. The military-court records are cited in his August 11 front-page letter to Chavigny, "onetime informer for the Sûreté."
[30] The documents concerning this part of Chavigny's career are cited on the back page of the July 9 issue of *Indochine*.
[31] *Ibid.*, July 11, VL.
[32] *L'Impartial*, July 9.
[33] *Indochine*, July 23, back page. See also *Indochine Enchaînée*, No. 5, p. 6.
[34] *Indochine*, July 24. The citation below is taken from this front-page editorial.

NOTES TO CHAPTER V

[1] On Darles, see *Indochine*, July 23, and *Indochine Enchaînée*, No. 5, p. 5. See also Virginia Thompson, *French Indo-China* (New York, 1937), p. 479. Nguyen An Ninh speaks of Darles in his article "La France et l'Indochine," *Europe*, No. 31 (July 15, 1925), pp. 264, 274–75, and also describes an "interview" to which he—like Malraux—was subjected by Cognacq (pp. 270–71). Léon Werth gives further details of Ninh's meeting, in "Notes d'Indochine," *Europe*, No. 34 (October 15, 1925), pp. 185–86, from which the closing threat of the Governor, cited below, is taken. Ho Chi Minh devotes several pages to the horrors committed by Darles in *French Colonization on Trial*, reprinted in *Selected Works*, II (Hanoi, 1961), 46–49, 162.
[2] On Cognacq, see Werth, *op. cit.*, pp. 166–67, and Thompson, *op. cit.*, pp. 314–15, 479.
[3] Nguyen An Ninh, *op. cit.*, p. 270. See also Werth, *op. cit.*, p. 186.
[4] *Indochine*, June 24, 25, 30, and July 6, VL, prints details of the swindle.

Rouelle's report was published on the "Local Events" page of the June 25 and 26 issues of the paper.

⁵ *Ibid.,* July 6, VL.

⁶ Malraux's editorial "A Monsieur Je-Menotte," *ibid.,* June 25.

⁷ *Ibid.,* August 11, DMESP.

⁸ Cited from Monin's front-page editorial in *ibid.,* June 26. Further information is to be found as follows: *ibid.,* June 24, VL; June 25; June 29; July 2; July 3, DMESP; July 7; July 10, DME; and August 11, DMESP.

⁹ *L'Impartial,* July 9, 1925.

¹⁰ *Indochine,* June 23. Werth gives a vivid description of the area and writes about the frauds perpetrated against the hapless Annamite farmers ("Notes d'Indochine," *Europe,* No. 35, pp. 269–79).

¹¹ Cited in *Indochine,* July 30.

¹² Monin wrote this initial editorial and two subsequent ones (July 17 and 20) with additional information on the legal aspects of Cognacq's scheme.

¹³ *Ibid.,* July 15, DMESP. Similar swindles were revealed in *Indochine Enchaînée,* No. 6, pp. 1–2, and No. 13, p. 9.

¹⁴ *Indochine,* August 13, prints this letter in connection with a subsequent land fraud.

¹⁵ *Ibid.,* July 25.

¹⁶ *Ibid.,* July 30.

¹⁷ Ironically, Cognacq could never have obtained the land he wanted—not even under the original terms for the sale. A very wealthy and patriotic mandarin had read *Indochine's* account of the projected fraud and had been deeply moved by the letters of protest from the poor farmers of the area. After making preliminary arrangements and contacting members of his family, he went to Camau. Just before the sale was to begin, he approached Eutrope with a certificate of solvency for well over 1 million piasters. He told the auctioneer that he intended to purchase the entire tract so that he might then restore it to the rightful owners, the Annamite peasants who had cleared it. Only then did he learn that the sale conditions had been modified and his generous gesture was no longer required. See *ibid.,* July 31.

NOTES TO CHAPTER VI

¹ *Indochine,* July 15.

² *Ibid.,* June 24.

³ *Ibid.,* July 1.

⁴ *Ibid.,* August 5.

⁵ *Ibid.,* June 24.

⁶ The Rouelle interview appeared in *ibid.,* June 30. The Gallois-Montbrun article, from which the following citations are taken, appeared in *ibid.,* July 6 (on the first and second pages).

⁷ Roland Dorgelès gives details of the fiscal injustices practiced in the colony in his book *Sur la Route mandarine* (Paris, 1925), pp. 93, 204–11. A number of writers and newspapermen who had been in Indochina had written about the unhappy results of the unjust exchange laws. This agitation eventually brought the whole matter before the French legislature, and in 1928 the piaster was stabilized at 10 French francs. The first article in *Indochine's* series appeared on the front page of the June 20 issue.

[8] The interviews appeared on the front page of *ibid.*, June 27, July 3, July 10, July 21, and July 31.

[9] The title of this column varied slightly. The abuses revealed by the letters and articles published in it were essentially the same ones revealed by Dorgelès, Werth, Viollis, and Ho Chi Minh in their various books and articles. At this time, the elimination of such abusive practices—rather than obtaining Annamite independence—was the fundamental purpose of the Nationalist movement.

[10] Dejean's article in *Indochine*, June 20, DME, cites this statement.

[11] See the letter of Nguyen-van-Dang in *ibid.*, July 2, DMESP.

[12] *Ibid.*, June 20, DME. See also *ibid.*, July 27, DMESP.

[13] Translated and reprinted from an Annamite-language paper, *ibid.*, June 20, VL.

[14] *Ibid.*, June 27, DMESP.

[15] Ho Chi Minh is particularly vehement in his comments on this situation. See chap. ii, "Poisoning of the Natives," in *Selected Works*, II (Hanoi, 1961), 30–35.

[16] Léon Werth, "Notes d'Indochine," *Europe*, No. 35 (November 15, 1925), pp. 267–68; *Indochine*, July 16, DMESP.

[17] *Indochine*, June 29, DMESP.

[18] *Ibid.*, June 25, DMESP. The article was signed Ng.-Ph. (for Nguyen-Phong). The following citations are taken from it. Further discussion of the problem appeared in substantial articles in *ibid.*, July 8, DMESP; July 11, DMESP; and July 16, VL.

[19] See also Ninh, "La France et l'Indochine," *Europe*, No. 31 (July 15, 1925), pp. 257–8, and *Indochine Enchaînée*, No. 10, p. 7.

[20] *Indochine*, July 7, DMESP.

[21] *Ibid.*, July 11, DMESP. The Annamite ruler was sometimes called Emperor, sometimes King.

[22] *Ibid.*, August 5, DMESP. Nguyen-van-Pho's account of his interview with the chief of the Sûreté appeared in *ibid.*, August 7, DMESP.

[23] *Ibid.*, June 29, DMESP.

[24] *Ibid.*, July 16, DMESP, from which the citations are taken.

NOTES TO CHAPTER VII

[1] *Indochine*, June 29, DMESP. See also Nguyen An Ninh, "La France et l'Indochine," *Europe*, No. 31 (July 15, 1925), p. 262. Even generally sympathetic outsiders like Roland Dorgelès considered the Annamites a subservient, uncreative race. See *Sur la Route mandarine* (Paris, 1925), pp. 52–53.

[2] *Indochine*, June 19, VL.

[3] See, for example, *ibid.*, July 24, 28, 30, and 31.

[4] *Ibid.*, July 18, DMESP.

[5] *Loc. cit.*

[6] *Ibid.*, June 30.

[7] *Ibid.*, June 27, DMESP.

[8] *Ibid.*, July 18.

[9] *L'Impartial*, July 15, 1925. See also *Indochine*, July 18.

[10] Cited in *Indochine*, July 15, DME.

[11] Cited in *ibid.*, June 29, VL.

[12] *Ibid.*; July 11, DME; and Monin's editorial "Au Service d'Albion," *ibid.*, July 18, from which the citation is taken.

[13] *Ibid.*, June 30, DMESP.

[14] Truong specifically assails Cognacq for his suppression of Chinese news. See *ibid.*, July 3, DMESP.

[15] In *André Malraux and the Tragic Imagination* (Stanford, 1952), Professor Frohock succinctly presents the historical facts connected with the 1925 Canton-Shanghai situation (pp. 13–14, 19). For a more extended treatment, there is a most informative account by someone who was in China at the time, H. Owen Chapman, *The Chinese Revolution* (London, 1928). Although Chapman deals primarily with the revolutionary agitation during 1926–27, he makes a careful presentation of the various incidents—including the 1925 strike—that were a prelude to it. *The Tragedy of the Chinese Revolution*, by Harold R. Isaacs (rev. ed.; Stanford, 1951), is a broader and more academic treatment of the "defeat of the Chinese revolution of 1925–27" (p. vii). The value of this fundamental and still most authoritative political history of the period is increased by an extensive bibliography (pp. 365–72).

[16] *Indochine*, June 24.

[17] See *Les Conquérants* (Paris: Livre de poche), pp. 11, 13, 14, 24–25, 30, and 39.

[18] Most of these items appeared on the front page, and some were continued on the inner VL page.

[19] *Indochine*, August 3.

[20] Monin's editorial "Au Service d'Albion," *ibid.*, July 18.

[21] *Ibid.*, July 2. Sun Yat-sen had taken refuge in Cholon in 1908, and the active Indochinese interest in the Chinese nationalist movement dates from this visit. See Dorgelès, *op. cit.*, p. 163. For a very illuminating study of Sun's program, consult Shao Chuan Leng and Norman D. Palmer, *Sun Yat-sen and Communism* (New York, 1960).

[22] *Indochine*, August 8, 1925.

[23] *Ibid.*, June 19. Monin's editorial, entitled "Politique de la Chine," was published in three parts, the remainder of the text appearing on June 22 and 23.

[24] *Ibid.*, June 30, DMESP.

[25] *Ibid.*, July 16, DMESP. The article, entitled "L'Opinion des écrivains annamites," was signed by Nguyen-Tinh.

[26] *Indochine* published a "Remerciement au *China News*" on the front page of its July 10 issue, noting that Monin had been honored by the Cholon section of the Kuomintang. A photograph of the original *China News* article was published on the back page of the July 17 issue and reprinted there the following day as part of Malraux's long "Second Letter" to Chavigny.

[27] *Ibid.*, July 18, back page.

[28] *L'Impartial*, July 18, 1925.

[29] *Ibid.*, July 20, 1925. Chavigny had first suggested this in his initial article on July 17.

[30] *Indochine*, July 18, back page

[31] *L'Impartial*, July 20, 1925. The citations in the following paragraph are taken from this editorial and from those in the July 22 and July 21 issues respectively.

[32] *Ibid.*, July 24, August 5, and August 6, 1925. *Indochine* printed a letter

from the head of the union involved that completely disproved this allegation by Chavigny. See *Indochine,* August 6, DMESP.

[33] *L'Impartial,* July 29 and 30, 1925.

[34] See his "A Chavigny, vièrge et martyr," in *Indochine,* July 31, VL.

[35] *Ibid.,* August 3.

NOTES TO CHAPTER VIII

[1] See, notably, Malraux's editorial "Liberté de la presse," *Indochine,* July 24, from which the document cited below is taken, and his comments in *Indochine Enchaînée,* No. 1, pp. 1–2.

[2] *Indochine,* July 11. The italics are *Indochine's.* Letters and the incriminating memo are published in the July 1 and 2 issues.

[3] Cited in *ibid.,* July 24. Two other letters with similar information, dated June 27 and July 8, were reprinted in the same article.

[4] *Ibid.,* July 18, DMESP.

[5] *Ibid.,* August 1.

[6] *Ibid.,* July 24. Similar methods were used against all the opposition papers. See Nguyen An Ninh, "La France et l'Indochine," in *Europe,* No. 31 (July 15, 1925), pp. 266–68.

[7] *Indochine Enchaînée,* No. 12, p. 2.

[8] See below, chap. x and Epilogue. *Indochine Enchaînée,* No. 7, p. 2, revealed that Monin's servant had been beaten by the police for the simple crime of working for an "anti-français."

[9] There are articles on Varenne in *Indochine* on August 1 and 3 (DME), and in *Indochine Enchaînée,* No. 6, pp. 4–5. Although his appointment was approved by a majority of his colleagues, a few leading figures in his own socialist party protested that they had not been consulted about the move. They even talked of expelling him from the movement to which he had given faithful service for more than twenty-five years unless he could give a satisfactory justification for accepting the post.

[10] For details, see *L'Impartial,* June 20–24, 1924.

[11] *Indochine Enchaînée,* No. 5, p. 5 quotes an Annamite who gleefully points this out to Cognacq.

[12] Reprinted in part in *Indochine,* August 1, DME.

[13] *L'Impartial,* July 30, 1925.

[14] Cited in *Indochine, loc. cit.*

[15] Cited in *Indochine Enchaînée,* No. 6, pp. 4–5. Another article from a French newspaper is summarized in *ibid.,* No. 7, p. 3.

[16] These remarks appeared in *Indochine,* August 10, DME, and in *Indochine Enchaînée,* No. 8, p. 2.

[17] See *Indochine Enchaînée,* No. 1, p. 2, and No. 5, p. 3.

[18] *Ibid.,* No. 5, p. 3, and No. 1, p. 6.

[19] For a vivid description of one such meeting, see *ibid.,* No. 20, pp. 5–7.

[20] This letter was cited from the *Courrier* in the September 25, 1925, issue of *L'Impartial.*

[21] *Indochine Enchaînée,* No. 1, p. 6, and No. 5, p. 3.

[22] *Ibid.,* No. 1, p. 6. For further information about government intimidation of printers, etc., see Ninh, *op. cit.,* pp. 268–70.

[23] *Indochine,* July 3, and Harold R. Isaacs, *The Tragedy of the Chinese Revolution* (Stanford, rev. ed., 1951), pp. 70–71.

[24] *Indochine,* July 29. Although Malraux never indicated just when he was in Hong Kong and Canton, one of his friends, the author and world-traveler Paul Morand, wrote that in August of 1925 he (Morand) arrived in Hong Kong from the North of China; "exactement à la même date, Malraux arrivait à Canton, venant de Saigon" (*Les Nouvelles Littéraires,* November 10, 1928, p. 1).

[25] *Indochine Enchaînée,* No. 1, p. 6.

[26] *Ibid.,* No. 2, p. 6.

[27] Preface by Malraux to Andrée Viollis, *Indochine S.O.S.* (Paris, 1935), pp. x–xi.

[28] This deduction can be fully verified by comparing the dates of various incidents as mentioned in *L'Impartial* with the issues of *Indochine Enchaînée* in which they were also mentioned.

[29] The dates for the numbered issues are as follows:

1, Wednesday, November 4, 1925.
2, Saturday, November 7.
3, Wednesday, November 11.
4, Saturday, November 14.
5, Wednesday, November 18.
6, Saturday, November 21.
7, Wednesday, November 25.
8, Saturday, November 28.
9, Wednesday, December 2.
10, Saturday, December 5.
11, Wednesday, December 9.
12, Saturday, December 12.
13, Wednesday, December 16.
14, Saturday, December 19.
15, Wednesday, December 23.
16, Saturday, December 26. Malraux's last editorial appeared in this issue.
17, Wednesday, December 30.
18, Saturday, January 2, 1926. After this issue, the presses broke down. It took a month to repair them.
19, Tuesday, February 2.
20, Saturday, February 6.
21, Wednesday, February 10.
22, Saturday, February, 20.
23, Wednesday, February 24.

[30] *Indochine Enchaînée,* No. 1, p. 7. The announcement also noted that the paper was destined to be a "rareté bibliographique."

[31] For more on this book, see above, chap. i, n. 32, and chap iii, n. 35.

[32] Lê-the-Vinh, an occasional contributor to *Indochine,* also became printer of *Indochine Enchaînée* after Malraux resigned to return to France. See No. 16, p. 1.

[33] A list of Malraux's contributions to *Indochine Enchaînée* follows:
"Réouverture" (editorial), No. 1, pp. 1–2.
"Le Gouvernement par les traîtres" ("Questions annamites"), No. 1, pp. 10–11.

"Eloge de la torture" ("Questions annamites"), No. 2, p. 5.
"Considérations sur le Livre Vert" (editorial), No. 3, pp. 1–2.
"Pour Quelques Français Pauvres," No. 4, p. 2.
"Lettre ouverte à Monsieur Alexandre Varenne, Gouverneur Général" (editorial, with Monin), No. 5, pp. 1–4.
"Au Conseil Colonial" (editorial, with Monin), No. 6, pp. 1–2.
"Français et Annamites" (review of Paul Monet's book in "Revue de la Press Locale"), No. 6, pp. 7–8.
"L'Appel à l'opinion française" (editorial), No. 6, pp. 1–2.
"Les Notables et les impôts," No. 7, p. 8.
"La Mortalité infantile et la repartition des impôts" ("Questions annamites"), No. 7, p. 9.
"Une Protestation de plus de mille notables" (editorial), No. 8, pp. 1–2.
"La Liberté de la presse indigène" (editorial), No. 9, pp. 1–2.
"Mytho—Toujours les coutumes de guerre" ("Chronique des Provinces"), No. 9, pp. 7–8.
"De L'Indifférence aux grandeurs humaines" ("Chronique de Saigon"), No. 10, p. 6.
"Encore?" (editorial), No. 11, pp. 1–2.
"Excès de confiance," No. 11, p. 2.
"Le Retour de M. Outrey" (editorial), No. 12, pp. 1–2.
"Bardez" ("Chronique de Saigon"), No. 12, pp. 6–7.
"Bardez" ("Chronique de Saigon"), No. 13, p. 6.
"Bardez" ("Chronique de Saigon"), No. 14, pp. 4–5.
"Considérations sur la domination française de l'Indochine" (editorial), No. 15, pp. 1–2.
"Ce que nous pouvons faire" (editorial), No. 16, pp. 1–2.
"Nos Interviews: Interview du gouverneur de la Chynoiserie," No. 19, p. 2.
"Nos Interviews: Les Bonnes Institutions et la manière de s'en servir. Interview de M., Président de la Chambre de commerce," No. 21, pp. 1–2.
    In addition to these signed or initialed articles, Malraux also contributed parts of "Chronique de Saigon" in the issues numbered 1, 2, 3, and 7.
    None of these issues is paginated; our page references are counted from the first printed sheet.
    ³⁴ *Indochine Enchaînée*, No. 7, p. 5.

NOTES TO CHAPTER IX

¹ *Indochine Enchaînée*, No. 6, p. 2.
² *Ibid.*, No. 5, pp. 1–4 for the citations below.
³ Information on the fraudulent election for the Chamber of Agriculture is scattered through various issues of *Indochine Enchaînée*; see particularly No. 2, pp. 1–2, and No. 5, p. 2.
⁴ *Ibid.*, pp. 7–10. Nguyen An Ninh gives information on similar frauds in "La France et l'Indochine," *Europe*, No. 31 (July 15, 1925), pp. 275–76.
Ibid., No. 5, p. 9.
⁶ *Ibid.*, No. 1, p. 5; also No. 3, p. 1; No. 9, pp. 3–4; and No. 12, p. 2.
⁷ This was one of the two articles published in *ibid.*, after Malraux had left Saigon. Issue No. 21, pp. 1–2 (February 10).
Ibid., No. 19, p. 2 (February 2).

[9] *Ibid.*, No. 7, p. 6.

[10] On the election of Chavigny, see *ibid.*, No. 1, p. 7. The Governor's report is discussed in No. 3, pp. 1–2, and No. 5, pp. 1–6

[11] *Ibid.*, No. 3, p. 1.

[12] *Ibid.*, No. 7, pp. 1–2. Duoc's speech is reprinted in issues No. 9, pp. 9–11, and No. 10, pp. 11–13, from which the citations in the following paragraphs are taken.

[13] *Ibid.*, No. 7, p. 6, and No. 10, p. 13. Chavigny mentions the expulsion of Malraux in his brief tendentious account in *L'Impartial*, November 25, 1925.

[14] *L'Impartial*, November 25, 1925.

[15] *Indochine Enchaînée*, No. 7, pp. 1–2, from which the citations below are taken.

[16] *Ibid.*, No. 7, p. 6, and No. 9, p. 8.

[17] *Ibid.*, No. 9, p. 8. See also Monin's bitter comments in No. 10, pp. 1–2.

[18] *Ibid.*, No. 9, pp. 1–2, and 8. The citations below are taken from the editorial comments on page 2.

[19] *Ibid.*, No. 9, pp. 1–2.

[20] *Ibid.*, No. 9, p. 8.

[21] For a succinct account of Varenne's efforts and the reasons for his downfall, see Philippe Devillers, *Histoire du Viêt-Nam de 1940 à 1952* (3d ed.; Paris, 1952), pp. 43–45, and Thomas E. Ennis, *French Policy and Developments in Indochina* (Chicago, 1936), pp. 104–6. The latter book quotes a lengthy portion of the interesting speech Varenne made in Hanoi on December 21, 1925, which—because of its liberal sentiments—aroused certain figures in France and eventually brought about his recall. Devillers is also valuable because he provides an indication of the activities of Chavigny and others as late as 1945.

NOTES TO CHAPTER X

[1] Notably in his *Indochine Enchaînée* editorials, "Considérations sur le Livre Vert" (No. 3, pp. 1–2), and "Lettre ouverte" (No. 5, pp. 1–4). See also "Réouverture," in No. 1, pp. 1–2.

[2] See—among others—his remarks in "Chronique de Saigon," *ibid.*, No. 1, p. 7, and No. 10, p. 6.

[3] *Ibid.*, No. 10, p. 7.

[4] *Ibid.*, No. 12, p. 1. He ridicules Chavigny's desire to become a deputy on page 2 of that issue.

[5] *Ibid.*, No. 1, pp. 10–11. The concluding remark of the editorial is cited below.

[6] *Ibid.*, No. 4, p. 2.

[7] *Ibid.*, No. 7, p. 9, from which the citation below is taken.

[8] *Ibid.*, No. 8, pp. 1–2. The quotation is from page 2. See also "Les Notables et les impôts," in No. 7, p. 8.

[9] See "Mytho—Toujours les coutumes de guerre," in *ibid.*, No. 9, pp. 7–8. The quotation below is from p. 8.

[10] *Indochine*, August 4, VL. See also July 22, pp. 1, 6.

[11] *Indochine Enchaînée*, No. 2, p. 5. See also Werth, "Notes d'Indochine," *Europe*, No. 33 (September 15, 1925), pp. 31–32, and No. 34 (October 15,

1925), pp. 172 ff. Malraux later wrote a bitter article against such brutal police methods for the Parisian paper *Marianne*. See "S.O.S.," *Marianne*, October 11, 1933, p. 3.

[12] These appeared in *Indochine Enchaînée*, No. 11, pp. 1–2; No. 12, pp. 6–7; No. 13, p. 6; and No. 14, pp. 4–5. Monin also wrote an editorial on the subject in No. 10, pp. 1–2. Facts given below are taken from these articles and from the long summation of the defense lawyer, Gallet, which was printed in *Indochine Enchaînée*, No. 16, pp. 6–7; No. 17, pp. 5–8; and No. 18, pp. 5–8.

[13] *Ibid.*, No 11, p. 2.

[14] *Ibid.*, No. 11, p. 1.

[15] *Ibid.*, No. 12, p. 7.

[16] *Ibid., loc. cit.*

[17] *Ibid.*, No. 13, p. 6.

[18] The vivid description of these courtroom scenes is given in *ibid.*, No. 17, pp. 5–8. The quotation is from p. 5.

[19] *Ibid.*, No. 12, p. 7.

[20] *Ibid.*, No. 18, p. 7.

[21] *Ibid.*, No. 13, p. 6. The information on Maurel is given in No. 17, p. 5.

[22] *Ibid.*, No. 13, p. 6. Monin, a fellow lawyer, comments upon this development in his editorial, p. 2.

[23] *Ibid.*, No. 14, p. 4.

[24] *Ibid., loc. cit.*

[25] Information on these actions and the text of the telegram may be found in *ibid.*, No. 15, p. 4.

[26] *Ibid.*, No. 13, p. 6.

[27] *Ibid.*, No. 12, p. 6.

[28] *Ibid.*, No. 16, p. 2. Malraux apparently did not return directly to France. A convention of Kuomintang leaders was held in Hong Kong in January, and he almost certainly attended some of the meetings. It was here that he probably obtained additional information (later used in his novel *Les Conquérants*) about the problems of the Nationalist-Communist split in the ranks of the Nationalist movement. He also went to Japan. A letter he wrote immediately after landing in France is on Japanese stationery, and his wife later lent a photograph she had taken in Japan to the editors of *La Revolution Surréaliste*, an avant-garde review (ca. 1927). See Marcel Jean, *Il Surrealismo* (Milan, 1959), p. 132.

NOTES TO EPILOGUE

[1] M. Saint-Clair, *Galerie privée* (Paris, 1947), pp. 133–34; 138.

[2] Part of a June 8, 1929 discussion was reprinted in "La Question des Conquérants," *Variétés* [a Belgian review], October 15, 1929, pp. 429–37.

[3] See the description of the autumn meetings in *Les Nouvelles Littéraires*, September 18 (p. 3), and October 2 (p. 3), 1926.

[4] See *Les Noyers de l'Altenburg* (Paris: Gallimard, 1948), pp. 111–50. Gide, having just returned from his eye-opening trip to Africa, doubtless gave Malraux warm support on the colonial question. There are occasional indirect references to Malraux's participation in anticolonial meetings in leftist publications of the late 1920's and early 1930's.

⁵ These were, respectively, "S.O.S.," *Marianne*, October 11, 1933 (p. 3), and the Preface to Andrée Viollis, *Indochine S.O.S.* (Paris, 1935), pp. vii–xi.

⁶ Among the most important and detailed books on the subject published in France at the time were Luc Durtain, *Dieux blancs, hommes jaunes* (1930); Louis Roubaud, *Viet Nam* (1931); and Yvonne Schulz, *Dans la Griffe des jauniers* (1931). The Colonial Administration made frantic efforts to justify itself by issuing a series of White Papers in Hanoi and Hué. Between 1930 and 1934, some seven volumes of "Documents" were prepared by the Direction des Affaires Politiques et de la Sûreté; they were published under the general title *Contributions à l'histoire des mouvements politiques de l'Indochine française.*

⁷ Viollis, *op cit.*, p. ix

⁸ *Ibid.* The document is cited in full in the Appendix; the portion quoted here is on pages 235–36.

⁹ All these facts are amply substantiated by Durtain, Roubaud, and Schulz and by documents presented in the Appendix, *ibid.*, pp. 131–249.

¹⁰ Malraux, "S.O.S."

¹¹ Cited in Viollis, *op cit.* (pp. 158–59), from an article in the Indochinese newspaper *Petit Populaire du Tonkin*, April 1, 1932.

¹² *Ibid.*, pp. xiii, 1.

¹³ On the Viollis family, see *Les Nouvelles Littéraires*, July 10, 1926 (pp. 1–2), and December 1, 1928 (p. 10). Also Frédéric Lefèvre, *Une Heure avec . . .* (Paris, 1927), pp. 227–44.

¹⁴ *Esprit*, December, 1933. A dispute about them continued in the pages of the review for over a year.

¹⁵ The original printing was dated September, 1935. The book was reissued late in 1949, at a time when history was repeating itself in Indochina. In this later edition, a preface by Francis Jourdain was substituted for the earlier one by Malraux, perhaps out of consideration for the latter's important political role in the Gaullist party.

¹⁶ Viollis, *op. cit.*, p. xi.

¹⁷ *Ibid.*, p. ix.

¹⁸ *Loc. cit.*

¹⁹ *Ibid.*, pp. ix–x.

²⁰ *Ibid.*, p. x.

²¹ *Loc. cit.*

²² "S.O.S." For further details, see the trial records in Viollis, *op cit.*, pp. 131–59.

²³ "S.O.S." See Viollis, *op. cit.*, pp. 150–52, for his testimony in full.

²⁴ For documents on this affair, see Viollis, *op cit.*, pp. 160–90.

²⁵ *Ibid.*, p. xvi.

²⁶ Saint-Clair, *op cit.*, p. 138.

²⁷ *Ibid.*, p. 136.

²⁸ See his interview in *L'Impartial*, September 16, 1924, p. 1.

²⁹ These dates appear at the end of the book, p. 205.

³⁰ The article appeared under the heading "André Malraux et l'Orient," on the second page of the July 31, 1926, issue of the paper.

³¹ The essay was one of a collection published in Grasset's *Cahiers Verts* under the title *Ecrits* (Paris, 1927). See "D'une Jeunesse européenne," pp. 129–53.

[32] See the list of Malraux's works on page ii of the original edition of *La Tentation de l'Occident.*

[33] "Jeunesse," pp. 138–39.

[34] *Ibid.*, pp. 133–34.

[35] *Ibid.*, pp. 151–53.

[36] Letter of October 4, 1925, in the author's possession.

[37] Issue of June 1, 1927. See pp. 813–18.

[38] *Ibid.*, pp. 815–16.

[39] *Ibid.*, p. 815.

[40] *Loc. cit.*

[41] *Ibid.*, p. 817.

[42] *Ibid.*, p. 818.

[43] *Loc. cit.*

[44] *Ibid.*, pp. 817–18.

[45] "Jeunesse," p. 137.

[46] Viollis, *op. cit.*, p. vii.

[47] *Ibid.*, p. vii.

[48] *Ibid.*, pp. viii–ix.

[49] "Jeunesse," p. 141.

[50] "La Question des *Conquérants*," p. 430. Malraux amplified this idea in *La Condition humaine.*

[51] *Loc. cit.*

[52] Viollis, *op. cit.*, p. viii. Malraux subsequently expanded many of these ideas on the novel.

[53] "La Question des *Conquérants*," pp. 432 ff

[54] The date of printing was September 10, 1928

[55] "La Question des *Conquérants*," pp. 429–37. The quotations in the following discussion are taken from this article unless otherwise indicated.

[56] See p. 270.

[57] *Le Temps du mépris* (Paris, 1935), p. 9.

Index